SNAKE OIL

HOW
XI JINPING
SHUT DOWN
THE
WORLD

MICHAEL P SENGER

Snake Oil: How Xi Jinping Shut Down the World

Copyright © 2021 Michael P Senger

ISBN 978-1-957083-77-3 (Hardcover)
ISBN 978-1-957083-78-0 (Paperback)
ISBN 978-1-957083-79-7 (EPUB)

First printing, 2021

CONTENTS

PROLOGUE

When Chairman Mao passed away in 1976, China underwent a period of rapid reform under the new leadership of paramount leader Deng Xiaoping. Having seen little growth for half a century, China soon became one of the world's most dynamic economies. Mao's policies had kept China stagnant, but with Deng's reforms, China achieved practically unheard-of economic growth of nearly 10% per year from 1980 to 1989.[1] For China's workers, wages in Deng's international investment zones seemed fantastically high. Rural factories fueled the surge, letting peasants earn money they'd never dreamed of.[2]

It was the 1980s, and business was China's business. China's entrepreneurs, shut out of the economy under Mao, got rich as they led the country's transformation into a manufacturing powerhouse. Western investors got rich, seeing record profits as they flocked in to make use of China's previously destitute labor force. Chinese Communist Party bosses got rich facilitating lucrative contracts and business deals. Even workers began to feel rich as wages across China more than doubled. Everyone was getting rich. You just had to be there.

Amid all this progress, China's brightest students were exposed to liberal ideas for the first time. Though the economy grew quickly, corruption was rampant, and the best opportunities were reserved for Party elites. Hardly any Chinese had a meaningful say in government.

A democracy movement began to develop with the support of reformist General Secretary Hu Yaobang. Hu was well-known for his liberalism and his frank, honest opinions. After visiting Tibet in 1980, Hu explicitly apologized for China's misrule during Mao's reign.[3] Hu encouraged students and intellectuals to raise controversial subjects, including democracy, human rights, and legal limits on power, and began targeting corruption among high-ranking CCP officials. Everything Hu did irked the CCP's hardliners.

In 1986, students and intellectual leaders launched pro-democracy protests in dozens of cities. Deng Xiaoping disliked the protests and wanted their leaders dismissed from the Party, but Hu refused. For this, Deng forced Hu's resignation.[4]

Hu was replaced as General Secretary by his equally reform-minded colleague Zhao Ziyang. The year Zhao served as General Secretary is still widely viewed as the most open in the history of modern China. The CCP had officially banned pro-democracy demonstrations, but Hu was now a symbol—a man who wouldn't sacrifice his convictions—and the protests continued. When Hu suddenly died in April 1989, students flocked to Beijing's Tiananmen Square, sparking a protest movement of unprecedented scale.[5]

Deng ordered the protesters to stop, but for the first time in over 40 years, the people refused. The next day, a line of students four miles long marched on Tiananmen Square. Soviet leader Mikhail Gorbachev arrived to greet them. Deng was humiliated.

All of China seemed to support the students, and over the course of May 1989, millions joined in the Tiananmen Square protests. Factory workers, teachers, doctors, even soldiers and staff of the Party's propaganda outlets joined in. They had the tacit support of General Secretary Zhao, who pushed for dialogue, believing the Party should appeal to the protesters' feelings of optimism and patriotism. The end of authoritarianism in China now felt inevitable. Many CCP leaders began to think nothing could stop the blossoming of democracy in Tiananmen Square—not with the whole world watching, the cameras rolling, capturing the hope and enthusiasm of millions of Chinese for viewers around the world.[6]

But in late May, Deng convened the CCP's highest governing body, who sharply criticized Zhao's strategy. They urged Zhao to declare martial law, but Zhao refused. In his last recorded appearance, Zhao pleaded with the protesters to end their hunger strike and promised that dialogue would remain open. Zhao was ousted as General Secretary and was never heard from again.[7]

Deng convened a meeting of Party elders and martial law was declared the next day. Deng met with military leaders and finalized orders for units to converge at 1:00 AM on June 4, 1989, using any means necessary to clear the square.[8]

That night, hundreds of tanks and tens of thousands of soldiers descended on Tiananmen Square. By morning, the protesters were surrounded. They were in disbelief. Former soldiers, believing the People's Liberation Army served the people, insisted the troops wouldn't fire. Initially, protesters thought the troops were using rubber bullets. But as screams filled the air, the reality set in.

Soldiers charged at the protesters using assault rifles, bayonets, and expanding bullets. The PLA erected machine guns directly in front of Heroes Monument, and the air erupted with deafening bursts as the gunners fired indiscriminately on the defenseless crowd. Tanks ripped through the throngs of fleeing protesters, crushing many more.[9]

In the span of a day, the PLA had killed thousands of innocent Chinese citizens, and thousands more were gravely wounded—mostly ordinary residents of Beijing. The protest leaders, China's best and brightest students among them, were imprisoned and tortured. Deng Xiaoping congratulated the PLA on a job well done.[10]

Above all, the Tiananmen Square Massacre had been the result of a misunderstanding of who Deng Xiaoping really was and what his reforms really meant. A longtime member of Mao's inner circle, Deng had never been as moderate as his admirers liked to pretend. Following Mao's re-engagement with the west after meeting with Henry Kissinger and Richard Nixon, Deng had supported market reforms because they made China rich, but he had no taste for western democracy, human rights, or liberalism. Western media fawned over Deng the reformer, but that was largely because he'd made them so much money. Even economic growth under Deng's regime was exaggerated; it was largely catch-up to the rest of the world following Mao's long, tyrannical rule.

As China had reopened economically, the world believed Deng's regime would be open to democratic reforms, even if that meant relinquishing its hold on power. Deng believed no such thing. His vision had never included political tolerance. Much of what the world thought they knew about Deng Xiaoping was simply a lie.

Under Deng's rule, punishments for minorities and those who stepped out of line were arbitrary and cruel. Chinese citizens were frequently executed for petty crimes, either real or imagined.[11] After the Tiananmen Square Massacre, many of Hu and Zhao's liberal reforms were rolled back.

The Chinese government drew widespread condemnation for Tiananmen Square, and China was briefly isolated. But President George H.W. Bush, former head of the U.S.-China Liaison Office, privately resolved to resume commercial relations, and sanctions were quickly lifted.[12] By the end of the Bush presidency, it was business as usual, and the rest of the world soon followed.

For anyone who cared to see, Tiananmen Square is where the principles of the postwar international order died. Beginning at

Tiananmen Square, the CCP sought to prove that even the newest information technology could be subverted to tyrannical ends, and that ideas really could be killed with the right amount of violence. They gambled that the free world's commitment to human rights could be worn down with enough patience.

Over the coming decades, information did not liberalize the authoritarian world. Instead, the world became more like China. And 30 years later, the free world would be forced to confront the true cost of the devil's bargain it had struck with the Chinese Communist Party in the aftermath of Tiananmen Square.

SNAKE OIL

HOW
XI JINPING
SHUT DOWN
THE
WORLD

MICHAEL P SENGER

INTRODUCTION

In March 2020, liberal democracy ground to a sudden stop.

Like the Reichstag Fire of 1933, historians may never know how SARS-CoV-2 came about. For scientists, exploring its origins would be a rewarding endeavor if it weren't precluded by an immovable force—the jackboot of Xi Jinping's Chinese Communist Party. "President Xi's persistent refusal to allow an independent international investigation into the origins of the virus is more than a lack of responsibility," wrote one leading epidemiologist, "it is a declaration of contempt for human life. It is a crime, a crime that cost lives for a nation to say, 'We own the right to refuse to be investigated, to have the evidence examined.' Most every other country in the world would have called for the investigation themselves."[13]

"A declaration of contempt for human life" might shock those less familiar with the career of Xi Jinping, the princeling wunderkind who soared through the ranks of the Party after spending a terrifying youth in Mao's Cultural Revolution. But to the dissidents, reporters, and exiles who know him more intimately, Xi's callousness is unsurprising. Since Xi came to power just ten years ago, Chinese media has been censored; international websites have been blocked; activists, journalists, lawyers, and intellectuals have been silenced; over one million officials have been punished for "corruption;" Marxism-Leninism and Maoist symbolism have been revived; thousands of churches and mosques have been demolished; Hong Kong was forcefully crushed; millions of Uyghur Muslims and other Turkic minorities have been detained in concentration camps; and, in a two-sentence bulletin released one afternoon in 2018, term limits were eliminated from China's constitution, effectively crowning Xi paramount leader for life.[14]

The CCP's initial cover-up of the virus and the complicity of the World Health Organization are widely remembered.[15] This cover-up cost lives and engendered lurid theories about the virus' origins. But while intelligence agencies spent months investigating these theories, the world employed an unprecedented response that proved far more devastating than the virus itself, leading to the greatest economic collapse since the Great Depression, widespread hunger, and the disappearance of countless lives and livelihoods.[16] Across the world, governments implemented measures modeled on the mass quarantines imposed in China, commonly referred to as "lockdowns."

What, if anything, individual citizens knew about the virus was of little relevance; in no instance were they consulted. No votes were held. In the span of a month, the long-cherished rights of nearly half the world's population were upended. Schools were shut, "inessential" businesses were closed, and families isolated where they could. Unemployment in the United States reached as high as 14.7% and highways jammed with vehicles awaiting their turn at food banks.[17] In India, millions of migrants were tossed out of work and forced to march in exodus to far-off villages.[18] In Africa, food lines stretched for miles.[19] Quarantined migrants in Saudi Arabia were left to die. "The guards just throw the bodies out back as if it was trash."[20] The chief of the United Nations World Food Program forewarned of a "famine of biblical proportions" with 265 million people "literally marching to the brink of starvation."[21] Around the world, suicides and deaths from treatable ailments spiked.[22]

No other country could recreate China's "success" against the virus. Having stampeded into lockdowns with no clear goal in mind, governments bumbled from one justification to another—

"flattening the curve," preventing a "second wave," getting the outbreak "under control," "waiting for a vaccine," or even "eliminating COVID-19" entirely—importing an ever-darker swathe of illiberal mandates along the way, all in the supposed interest of "public health."

It was the greatest geopolitical catastrophe since the Second World War, and the largest man-made famine since the Great Leap Forward. And it was all for nothing. Lockdowns had never been about science. Rather, they'd sprung into global policy on the order of the CCP princeling who would become the most influential member of the Baby Boom generation; an aberration thrust upon the world through an unprecedented, international influence operation.

By corrupting global institutions, promoting forged data, publishing fraudulent science, and deploying propaganda on an unprecedented scale, the CCP under Xi Jinping transformed the snake oil of lockdowns into "science," the greatest crime of the 21st century to date. The story of how he did it, and why, begins at turn of the last century, in the yellow loess of Yan'an.

CHAPTER I

REDDER THAN RED

The achievement and maintenance of the dictatorship of the proletariat is impossible without a party that is strong by virtue of its solidarity and its iron discipline. But iron discipline is not possible without unity of will—without complete and absolute unity of action on the part of all party members. Least of all can iron discipline be 'blind.' On the contrary, iron discipline demands conscious and voluntary submission, for only conscious discipline can be true iron discipline. – Joseph Vissarionovich Stalin, The Foundations of Leninism, 1924

The Chinese Communist Party was founded in 1921. Thousands joined in the early '20s as the CCP fought alongside the nationalist Kuomintang against China's warlords. When the Kuomintang turned against the communists in 1927, the CCP's original leaders were killed. This leadership vacuum was filled by an ambitious land-reform advocate named Mao Zedong.[23]

Mao could never compete with the Party's urbane founders, but their elimination gave him an opening. Mao fought against the Kuomintang from the Jiangxi Soviet, the largest of the CCP's areas of control.[24] In 1933, the Kuomintang sieged Jiangxi, forcing Mao to retreat in the Long March. Mao's forces fought their way north to arrive in Yan'an in 1935. Mao freed several local leaders including Xi Jinping's father, Xi Zhongxun, who had been sentenced to death by a rival faction. As Xi Jinping later recalled, "Without Mao my father would have been no more; without Mao there would be no Xi Jinping today."[25]

In Yan'an, Mao neutralized his remaining rivals and molded the Party in his own image. The invasion of the Japanese forced an alliance between the CCP and the Kuomintang, but by the end of World War II the Chinese Civil War had already resumed. The CCP's path to victory remains shrouded in mystery. Historians still cannot reconstruct important episodes or even who the leaders were. At the end of World War II, the CCP controlled one town, Yan'an, and its members accounted for less than 0.01% of China's population. But through their mastery of propaganda they mobilized millions to fight for them, masking their communist movement as the true incarnation of the nation's will. Four years later, China was theirs.

Even more remarkably, the CCP was horribly unpopular wherever they ruled. They introduced communist reforms during the Chinese Civil War and, as the great sinologist László Ladány recalled, "All suspected enemies were treated brutally; one could walk about in the North Chinese plains and see hands sticking out from the ground, the hands of people buried alive... Luckily for the communists, government propaganda was so poorly organized that people living in regions not occupied by the communists knew nothing of these atrocities."[26]

Once the country was theirs, the CCP extended these practices to all of China. By 1952, 80% of all Chinese had been forced to take part in mass accusation meetings or public executions. During these proceedings, the crowd was forced to roar their approval in unison, ensuring collective participation in the murder of innocents. The victims were not selected for what they had done, but for who they were or sometimes simply to meet the Party's quota of executions. This was repeated every two to three years.[27]

Millions of Chinese fought against the western coalition in the Korean War, which proved extremely costly. In 1957, Mao invited open debate about his policies during his Hundred Flowers Campaign, but he was shocked by the criticism and purged thousands of intellectuals as a result. Instead of implementing these reforms, Mao announced his new economic plan—better known as the Great Leap Forward.

During this period, nearly all of China's villagers were transported to communes with strict production quotas. The Great Leap Forward involved massive investment but produced little to show for it, resulting in the largest man-made famine in human history (though at the time, experts around the world agreed no famine was occurring). The total number of deaths remains unknown, but official estimates range from 15 to 50 million. As Ladány wrote:

> All spoke of food shortage and hunger; swollen bellies, lack of protein and liver diseases were common. Many babies were stillborn because of their mothers' deficient nutrition... Peasants lacked the strength to work, and some collapsed in the fields and died. City government organizations and schools sent people to the villages by night to buy food, bartering clothes and furniture for it. In Shenyang the newspaper reported cannibalism. Desperate mothers strangled children who cried for food.[28]

For this, Mao was briefly sidelined. But fearing his decline, Mao began a campaign to return to power, and in 1966 officially launched the Great Proletarian Cultural Revolution. It was during this period that Xi Jinping would experience his coming of age.

Xi Jinping was born in Beijing in 1953. His father, Xi Zhongxun, was notable among Party leaders for his relative moderation. In

1952, Xi Zhongxun reversed hardline land reform policies in Xinjiang and freed hundreds of Uyghur herders.[29] When the Tibetans fought back against the CCP, he tried to push for a peaceful solution. The Dalai Lama later gifted him a watch that he kept for the rest of his life.[30]

At home, however, it was another story. Xi Zhongxun was a brutal disciplinarian who would scream, lash out at his wife, and beat Xi Jinping and his siblings. In public, the model statesman; in private, the tyrant.[31]

In 1962, Xi Zhongxun was stripped of his titles for defending the honor of a purged comrade.[32] In 1966, Mao launched his Cultural Revolution, setting radical youths, called Red Guards, against the Party hierarchy. The stated goal was to purge all vestiges of capitalism and traditional Chinese society, imposing Mao Zedong Thought as China's dominant ideology. Red Guards attacked anyone they perceived as Mao's enemies and destroyed China's cultural relics *en masse*. Books were burned, intellectuals were persecuted, and countless officials were purged.

Xi Jinping and his confidants rarely speak of his experience in the early Cultural Revolution.[33] Xi's parents were tortured and his father was exiled to central China. A bookish boy, Xi's boarding school was shut and he was sent to School No. 25, where he and his friends were bullied and beaten relentlessly as children of a "black gang." Xi's home was ransacked and his elder sister was coerced into suicide.

In one incident, Xi was paraded onto a stage wearing a heavy metal dunce cap. His mother was forced to attend and shout "Shame on Xi Jinping!" along with the crowd. But Xi never lost faith in the Party, later recalling how he "recited the thoughts of Chairman Mao every day late into the night."[34]

Xi's father was imprisoned in 1968 and Xi was sentenced to juvenile detention, but he avoided this fate when Mao launched the "down to the countryside" movement, sending over 16 million youth to work on farms and learn about rural life. Age 15, Xi was sent to live in a cave house in Yan'an. As he later recalled, "It was January 1969. Everyone was crying, there wasn't anyone on the train who didn't cry. But I was the only one laughing. The only one laughing..."[35]

Xi couldn't stand farm work and ran away to Beijing, but he was caught and sentenced to a forced labor camp for reeducation. Xi later returned to Yan'an and this time threw himself into his work, impressing the locals. He joined the Communist Youth League in 1971 after being rejected seven times, and officially joined the CCP in 1974 after being rejected nine times. In the words of a friend, after the Cultural Revolution, most youth "made up for lost time by having fun," but Xi "chose to survive by becoming Redder than Red."[36]

Xi earned a spot at Tsinghua University, China's most prestigious school. His father regained his freedom and was fully rehabilitated after Mao's death. Xi's father used his connections to land Xi a prime job at the Central Military Commission. Xi began a journey through China, working his way up the ranks of the Party.

The clever young Xi was the model Party man. He effortlessly mastered debts and derivatives and became proficient in the trendy buzzwords of the business elite. With soldiers he spoke in military idiom, and among Party members shifted easily to the coded jargon of Marxism.[37] To the common people, he exemplified the ideals of patriotic service and family life, while he charmed wide-eyed foreigners with relatable tales of trying to find time for his exercise routine.[38] Unlike other members his age, he didn't drink much or womanize, dressing plainly and riding a bicycle even when his rank permitted him an official car.[39]

Meanwhile, Xi Zhongxun was elected to the Politburo in 1982. In 1987, when the Politburo forced Hu Yaobang to resign, Xi Zhongxun was the only member who stood up to defend him.[40] He retired the following year.

Xi Jinping became an alternate member of the Party Central Committee in 1997 and governor of Fujian three years later. In a party notorious for corruption, Xi had a reputation for thinking ahead and staying clean; of these traits, coupled with his lineage, the Party elite took notice. In 2006, when Shanghai's Party chief was fired, Xi was picked to replace him. Just seven months into his appointment, Xi leapt directly onto the Politburo Standing Committee, China's highest governing body. Six months later, Xi was named Vice President, unexpectedly becoming successor to the General Secretary.

Insiders agree that Xi was chosen at least in part because of his father, with General Secretary Jiang Zemin believing Xi would share his father's moderation. The Xi family had suffered in the Cultural Revolution, fostering admiration among the commoners. Xi was also picked in part for his obscurity, Jiang believing the elders could control Xi as they had his predecessors. By contrast, Xi's rival Bo Xilai was passed over due to his charisma, the elders believing—ironically—that Bo might develop a personality cult like Mao.

Xi's ascent represented a soft coup by China's "princelings," direct descendants of Mao's revolutionaries. For many years, Beijing's highest ranks had been occupied by technocrats, but the princelings saw themselves as inheritors to an empire their parents had won. In private, some referred to the current leaders as "hired hands." "The feeling among us is: 'Hu Jintao, Wen Jiabao, your fathers were selling shoelaces while our fathers were dying for this revolution.'"[41]

Since Deng Xiaoping's ascent in 1978, most Chinese had experienced a period of moderation, economic success, and global interconnection. The most dystopian excesses of Mao's Cultural Revolution had been reversed. Though never condoned, religious practice became increasingly common. Young activists and bloggers could often flout censorship rules, knowing punishments would be modest.

But that progress had always conflicted with the CCP's darker pathologies and insecurities. The Party lived in chronic fear of China's dissidents and minority communities, knowing any independent organization could pose a threat to its rule. Privately, CCP leaders worried that their governing institutions wouldn't be strong enough to prevent the rise of another absolute leader like Mao.

In November 2012, Xi Jinping was elected General Secretary of the Chinese Communist Party. In light of his steady career, his struggles in the Cultural Revolution, and his father's reputation, Xi was widely expected to be a moderate reformer who would continue leading his country toward openness and global cooperation.

Xi Jinping had other plans.

CHAPTER II

CHAIRMAN OF EVERYTHING

Why did the Soviet Union disintegrate? Why did the Soviet Communist Party collapse? An important reason was that their ideals and beliefs had been shaken. In the end, the ruler's flag over the city tower changed overnight. It's a profound lesson for us! To dismiss the history of the Soviet Union and the Soviet Communist Party, to dismiss Lenin and Stalin, and to dismiss everything else is to engage in historic nihilism, and it confuses our thoughts and undermines the Party's organization at all levels. – Xi Jinping, New Southern Tour Speech, 2012

Xi Jinping assumed his role as General Secretary understanding his country to be in danger. Among friends, Xi confided his disgust with the commercialization of China—debased by the perversions of wealth, drugs, corruption, and pornography, threatening the CCP's foundational values.[42]

Xi had long studied the collapse of the Soviet Union and required his comrades do the same, including a six-part documentary about the subversion of communism through western values. In this telling, the downfall of the Soviet Union began the day Khrushchev denounced Stalin, and Gorbachev's decision to expose his people to western ideas was suicide. In his speeches, Xi repeatedly identified the Soviet Union as the most prominent victim of American subversion. He would never let this fate befall his Party.[43]

In 2013, Xi's General Office issued a secret directive known as Document No. 9, describing an "intense, ideological struggle" for survival, with "the very real threat of western anti-China forces and their attempts at carrying out westernization." According to Xi's directive, the ideas that threatened China included "independent judiciaries," "human rights," "western freedom," "civil society," "freedom of the press," and the "free flow of information on the internet."[44] To let the Chinese people contemplate these concepts would "dismantle our Party's social foundation" and jeopardize the world's socialist future.

The CCP's nationalists are painfully aware that China used to be the center of the world and refer to China's exploitation by imperial powers as the "century of humiliation," which ended only when they took control. In Xi's words, "Only socialism can save China, and only socialism can develop China."[45] Circumstance forces cooperation with the decadent capitalists, but the two systems cannot long co-exist. In this view, democracy and human rights are nothing but propaganda to delegitimize communism and inspire its enemies, and America's allies and international institutions are mere tools for imposing its will.[46] The Party values the liberal international order, but abhors its liberal values.

In Xi's words, as China became most nations' largest trading partner, "the world also deepened its dependence on China." China was now positioned to "transform the global governance system."[47] Xi aimed to re-center the world economy through his international Belt and Road Initiative, encouraging the export of the "China model." In Xi's vision, this party-state model would mark a new chapter in the history of human society. Democracy and human rights would fall away, reduced to parochial traditions in a smattering of barbary nations.[48]

Xi Jinping revered Xi Zhongxun, as did many Chinese. As a child, Xi's father had regaled him with war stories, their band of revolutionaries overcoming insurmountable odds to vanquish the imperialists and the Japanese invaders. Xi fretted that this generation wasn't prepared to make these types of sacrifices. He believed his comrades lacked faith in the "eventual demise of capitalism and the ultimate victory of socialism," and believed Party members must be prepared to sacrifice everything for the Party's "ideals that reach higher than heaven."[49]

In Xi's words, "Since the end of the Cold War, countries affected by western values have been torn apart by war or afflicted with chaos. If we tailor our practices to western values ... the consequences will be devastating."[50] To counter this threat, Xi embedded the Party into every layer of Chinese society. "From east, west, south, north to center, the government, the military, the people to academics, the Party leads all."[51]

Xi became "Chairman of Everything."[52] He acquired ten titles, assuming control of the Party, state, and military hierarchies, and the committees on foreign policy, the internet, the courts, and the secret police. Previous presidents led through Deng Xiaoping's "collective Presidency," but Xi fired the entire Politburo Standing Committee and stacked it with close friends. The only members with any real authority were Xi, propaganda chief Liu Yunshan, and Secretary of Discipline Wang Qishan, who implemented Xi's vast anticorruption campaign.[53]

Through his anticorruption campaign, Xi rooted out "tigers and flies"—both high- and low-ranking officials.[54] Xi empowered Wang's investigators to detain and interrogate at will, and they pursued anyone who might pose a threat.[55] By 2020, over one million officials had been sentenced.[56] Xi dispensed with the norm that retired leaders were safe once they left office, prosecuting former Politburo Standing Committee member Zhou Yongkang and taking control of Zhou's modern surveillance empire.[57] Xi faced countless assassination attempts, but through his bodyguard Wang Shaojun, Xi controlled the Central Security Bureau, closely monitoring Party leaders and their physical space.[58]

Xi takes history seriously and considers himself personal caretaker of China's mythos. His speeches brim with allusions to ancient Chinese scholars.[59] He delights in touring laboratories and centers of scientific innovation, and dabbles in complexity science in his spare time. Chinese state media juxtapose Xi's days governing Shanghai's glittering towers with his years in the caves of Yan'an, which he describes as "seven years of rural life that gave me something mysterious and sacred."[60] Xi flouted the Party's post-Mao ban on personality cults; official media fawn over "Uncle Xi."

Xi revived Maoist symbolism and Maoist demands for conformity, explaining that the media must serve as the Party's "throat and tongue" and warning academics and officials against "irresponsible talk."[61] Marxism-Leninism is once again taught in every school as "Xi Jinping thought."[62] Thousands of churches and mosques across China have been demolished, and images of Christ replaced by images of Xi.[63] The government once tacitly permitted VPNs, letting users reach websites blocked in China; but in 2015 most VPNs were blocked. China's internet is sterilized and flooded with propaganda and disinformation.[64]

Xi's war on western values includes surveillance and coercion of dissidents, students, and media outside China. In Xi's view, culture and ideology spill across borders; to fight this war, so must the hand of the communist state.[65] The Chinese state threatens foreign companies with cyber-attacks and holds their employees hostage. The Party cuts celebrities, industries, and even entire countries off from Chinese markets. The CCP bribes foreign officials, buys foreign media companies, sponsors foreign protests, and intimidates foreign researchers, activists, and media personalities. Surveillance, blackmail, harassment, bribery, and threats to family members have silenced the Party's critics and brought one western-based publication after another into line. If the Party can win by silencing ideas at their source, it does so.[66]

Beginning in July 2015, Chinese police rounded up hundreds of human rights lawyers and activists in the "709 crackdown."[67] More reporters have been jailed in China than in any other country, rendering investigative journalism all but extinct.[68] In 2017, Chinese reformer Liu Xiaobo became the second Nobel laureate to ever die in prison, the first being Carl von Ossietzky, who perished in a concentration camp in 1938 after exposing Germany's clandestine rearmament under then-Chancellor Adolf Hitler.[69]

CHAPTER III

FANGKONG

For if crime and disease are to be regarded as the same thing, it follows that any state of mind which our masters choose to call 'disease' can be treated as crime; and compulsorily cured. It will be vain to plead that states of mind which displease government need not always involve moral turpitude and do not therefore always deserve forfeiture of liberty. For our masters will not be using the concepts of Desert and Punishment but those of disease and cure... The new Nero will approach us with the silky manners of a doctor, and though all will be in fact as compulsory as the tunica molesta or Smithfield or Tyburn, all will go on within the unemotional therapeutic sphere where words like "right" and "wrong" or "freedom" and "slavery" are never heard... Even if the treatment is painful, even if it is life-long, even if it is fatal, that will be only a regrettable accident; the intention was purely therapeutic... But because they are 'treatment,' not punishment, they can be criticized only by fellow experts and on technical grounds, never by men as men and on grounds of justice. – CS Lewis, The Humanitarian Theory of Punishment, 1949

By the early 20th century, no living European had set eyes on Tibet. Ruled by the monastic Lamas, approximately 80% of Tibet's national budget went to education, and every family sent their youngest son to a monastery to study mathematics, medicine, philosophy and the arts. Buddhism was central to life, with 68 days per year marked by religious festivals that included the entire population.[70]

Tibet had been independent for centuries, but in 1949, Chairman Mao vowed to liberate Tibet from theocracy and the influence of Anglo-American imperialists. This puzzled Tibetans, as virtually none knew what an Anglo-American imperialist was.[71] In 1950, Chinese troops overran Tibet's small defense force and marched on Tibet's capital, Lhasa. The Dalai Lama was forced to accept the Seventeen Point Agreement for the Peaceful Liberation of Tibet.[72]

In 1954, the Dalai Lama visited Beijing to negotiate, expressing enthusiasm for communism's stated egalitarian principles. Deeply uninterested, Mao turned to the Dalai Lama and spat out his true feelings for Tibet's future: "Religion is poison."[73]

By 1959, massacres had begun in Eastern Tibet, and refugees poured into Lhasa. No famines had ever previously been recorded, but now there were widespread food shortages. The PLA fitted guns on rooftops and troops patrolled the streets. A popular uprising was met with overwhelming brutality, and the Dalai Lama was forced into exile.[74] Following the 1959 uprising, 15% of the Tibetan population was imprisoned, half of whom died.[75] Over the next four years, during Mao's Great Leap Forward, 20% of all Tibetans starved.[76]

During Mao's Cultural Revolution, Tibet's culture was systematically destroyed.[77] Monks and nuns were forced to denounce their faith and attend struggle sessions. The thousands of monasteries that were repositories of Tibetan civilization were shelled and dynamited, their treasures and scriptures looted and burned.[78]

When Hu Yaobang visited Tibet, he saw ruins that looked a thousand years old pocking every valley—but they had only just been destroyed.[79] Hu tried to humanize the CCP's policy toward

Tibet, but his reforms were reversed. Today, Tibetans undergo near-constant surveillance and monitoring.[80] Little reliable information reaches the outside world, but what is known is that at least half a million Tibetans have been detained in a massive system of concentration camps constructed across China's western provinces, pursuant to the CCP's unique hybrid of public health and security policy: *Fangkong*.[81]

The venomous embrace between western elites and China began half a century ago when Henry Kissinger argued that relations with the CCP could drive a wedge between China and the USSR.[82] Glasses clinked as China opened for business and the Soviet Union collapsed. It was a masterstroke, even for a wunderkind like Kissinger, and China became the cornerstone of his legacy. Surely, Kissinger felt, such a feat entitled him to a bit of the spoils. Just a nibble—after all, China was still a poor country, far from a geopolitical rival.

What started as a nibble became an addiction, and Kissinger grew rich as he greased access to Chinese officials, paving the way for more influence peddlers to follow. Before long, western elites were gorging themselves, gobbling up Chinese money like bears in a honey shop, and with each dip of their paw their greed only swelled. Big tech was the greatest beneficiary, and CCP money powered Silicon Valley's startups—a romance kindled by a longtime friendship between future California Senator Dianne Feinstein and future General Secretary Jiang Zemin.[83]

For decades, western policymakers insisted they saw China as a rival. But once China became their source of wealth and prestige, they came to see the CCP as a friend and a model. The western China class was born.[84]

Nearly every western industry had a stake in China, and they all learned to play by CCP rules. Employees could be fired for so much as liking one tweet about Tibet. The film industry was the first to complain about China, but Hollywood soon came to appease Beijing, happily passing all their scripts through CCP censors to tap into China's enormous market.[85]

Think tanks and research institutions like the Atlantic Council, the Center for American Progress, and the world-famous Brookings Institution all gorged themselves on Chinese money.[86] Elite universities developed an entire business model around the CCP. Chinese money came in through donations and full-freight tuition, and in exchange professors signed lucrative side deals selling federally-funded research to the CCP.[87] Whole academic careers could be made or broken by one's views on China.

The number of American industries and companies that lobbied against measures to decouple Chinese technology is a staggering measure of how closely the two systems have been integrated. Companies including Nike and Coca-Cola went so far as to lobby against forced labor prevention. Stories that Beijing was stealing scientific and military secrets, running spy networks in Silicon Valley, compromising legislators, and paying huge retainers to professors were downplayed. Signs that the CCP posed a threat in any way were muted and dismissed.

For the few good guys who understood what was going on, partisanship was beside the point. The CCP's behavior was downright terrifying—as was the seeming inability of core institutions to take it seriously. "Through the 1980s, people who advanced the interests of foreign powers whose ideas were inimical to republican form of government were ostracized," said one former intelligence official in the Obama administration, "but with the advent of globalism, they made excuses for China, even bending the intelligence to fit their preferences." Ret. Brig. Gen. Robert Spalding, a former Trump administration official, agreed: "It's so pervasive, it's better to ask who's not tied to China."[88]

Human rights organizations have helped bring many of the CCP's crimes to light. But in truth, the CCP's atrocities have long been enabled by an international system that downplays them, controls the conversation around them, and actively discourages meaningful action to mitigate them.

In China, over a million members of one religious group have been detained in labor camps, tortured and reeducated. Their biometric data is catalogued and their movements tracked. An independent tribunal found their organs being harvested on an industrial scale. The Chinese press has described them as a "poisonous tumor" that must be "eradicated."[89]

This description could pertain to several of China's minority groups, but it most accurately applies to the practitioners of Falun Gong, a Buddhist discipline that grew dramatically after the end of Mao's rule. By 1998, China had over 50 million Falun Gong adherents. Their subsequent persecution established the CCP's playbook for mass repression, internet censorship and surveillance.

Yet major news outlets have gone decades without mentioning Falun Gong. The New York Times ran 17 articles with Chinese datelines about Falun Gong in the first half of 2001; in the 18 years since, just five—a collapse that began just after the Times's senior staff met with CCP officials to negotiate unblocking their website in China.[90] In 2010, the Washington Post killed an article about Falun Gong after a phone call from the Chinese embassy.[91] Canada's national broadcaster canceled a Falun Gong documentary after the CCP threatened its rights to the 2008 Beijing Olympics.[92] This collective amnesia is a case study in how western media constructs reality to treat engagement with the CCP as palatable, while professing solidarity with its victims.

Even human rights organizations have been reluctant to discuss Falun Gong. In 2005, Human Rights Watch issued a report that included this brief, chilling reference:

> Several petitioners reported that the longest sentences and worst treatment were meted out to members of the banned meditation group, Falungong... even long-time Chinese activists are afraid to say the group's name aloud. One Beijing petitioner said: 'Petitioners are usually locked up directly. But the worst is [she whispers] Falungong. They have terrible treatment, not like the others...'[93]

In the years since, Human Rights Watch never discussed Falun Gong again.

Abandoned by the western elite, Falun Gong took their fate into their own hands, launching media networks that have become focal points for international resistance to the CCP. But as their resistance threatened the elite narrative, Falun Gong, ironically, came under attack from mainstream publications. As one sociologist described their predicament: "Woe be to any people who dare to both reject the hegemonic vision of the CCP and the liberal west's progressive alternative, for that group faces the relentless defamation and violence of the first and the cruel apathy of the second."[94]

An entire generation of academics, journalists, policymakers, and MBAs had learned to tell the story of a modernizing China. Trade with China would lead to democratization, they insisted, even as tech giants sold Orwellian technology to Chinese security agencies and forced labor gave the CCP a virtual monopoly in global manufacturing.[95] The tendrils of the CCP's totalitarian system gradually extended into western institutions. By the early 21st century, virtually everything the most educated westerners thought they knew about China was wrong.

Xi Jinping had seen the west accept the atrocities at Tibet and Tiananmen Square. He'd watched the western media memory hole the Falun Gong. He'd seen disinformation campaigns by rogue states tip the political scales in one free nation after another.

And he smiled. For a collective dedication to a narrative grounded in truth and the rule of law, the only thing Xi had to fear, had broken down.

Over decades in power, the CCP had constructed a multilayered system for stifling dissent in China based on the Soviet psychological warfare technique of *Zersetzung*, which translates roughly to "psychological decomposition."[96] The regime's threats instill fear of open discourse about reality, resulting in self-censorship. To avoid the cognitive dissonance of this silence, individuals willfully play down the evidence before their own eyes. The collective psychological effects are deceptively enormous.

After consolidating his power at the 19th Party Congress in 2017, Xi pushed the CCP's foreign influence into overdrive. He unleashed the CCP's sophisticated apparatus of censorship and propaganda on the world in an unprecedented campaign to shape global narratives, using covert activities to isolate independent media, subvert democratic norms, and nullify national sovereignty.[97] The lightning speed with which the CCP spread its tentacles allowed it to gain considerable ground without drawing attention. Even as Beijing achieved unprecedented levels of influence, international approval of both China and Xi rose sharply.

The CCP presented its style of governance as a model for other countries to follow. Meanwhile, Beijing's representatives exploited the 21st-century information environment to gain leverage over international politics and global media.[98] China's state media has accounts all over websites blocked in China—including some of the most-followed media accounts on Facebook.[99] Media channels built over time with fluff about Chinese culture and pandas can be activated at key moments to deliver propaganda to enormous audiences.

Some CCP disinformation bots have been found to have over 10,000 followers and to have tweeted in 55 different languages.[100] In the hours and days after Houston Rockets manager Daryl Morey tweeted about Hong Kong in 2019, nearly 170,000 tweets were directed at him by users in China.[101] Social media companies have generally shirked the problem. When the U.S. State Department provided a sample of 250,000 accounts likely involved in COVID-19 disinformation, Twitter refused to take action.[102] A study identified thousands of fake accounts still promoting Serbian-Chinese cooperation even after Twitter deleted thousands of others.[103]

The CCP's social media army uses artificial intelligence to generate accounts with pictures of seemingly real, but fictitious people.[104] What Xi's flunkies may lack for brains, they more than make up for with their raw legal impunity; this was demonstrated in 2021 when a brand new Twitter account was caught having been instantly verified despite falsely representing itself as a medical doctor. One of the account's followers was China Daily Chief Chen Weihua—confirming the CCP's ability to generate fake, verified Twitter "doctors" without consequence.[105]

CCP officials have gone to great lengths to develop "friendly" relations with private media and reporters, encouraging them to create content promoting Beijing's favored narratives. Those whose coverage pleases the CCP are rewarded with contracts and political appointments. Beijing sponsors well-funded "trainings" in China to cultivate foreign journalists, and visitors understand they're expected to reciprocate.[106]

The CCP cultivates foreign outlets to produce favorable content and manipulates international search results on platforms like Google.[107] CCP-friendly tech giants provide censorship and surveillance assistance; as gatekeepers of information transmission, they open the door to whole new levels of influence.[108]

The CCP spends billions of dollars to spread its messages across the world, and rarely are connections to China disclosed. These economic ties give Beijing crucial leverage to suppress critical coverage, silencing negative commentary and independent media with ever-greater frequency. Media owners and executives enforce censorship by killing stories and dismissing journalists.[109] The CCP uses intermediaries—advertisers, tech companies, governments, and international organizations—to prevent or punish the publication of unfavorable content.[110]

The CCP has begun taking steps to influence democratic elections directly. In 2018, a newspaper in Iowa—a state with unique influence in U.S. elections—included a four-page supplement on how the U.S.-China trade war would hurt farmers, fondly recalling Xi's time in Iowa as a young man.[111]

Commentators, journalists, and media outlets who criticize the CCP face cyberattacks and assaults; denial-of-service attacks have penetrated international sites including the Wall Street Journal and GitHub.[112] Censorship in China can threaten major outlets financially. Within 24 hours after China temporarily blocked the New York Times's website, the company's stock fell 20%.[113]

Within China, local officials and their plainclothes enforcers obstruct foreign correspondents and security forces detain journalists' family members.[114] The 2018 annual survey of the Foreign Correspondents' Club of China yielded "the darkest picture of reporting conditions inside China in recent memory."[115]

The CCP has shown itself especially adept at silencing China's minority populations. The way to keep unrest from going viral, the CCP had learned, was to quarantine it.

The Muslim Uyghurs are concentrated in Xinjiang, or East Turkestan, a region rich in resources. In 1944, Uyghur leaders led a successful rebellion to establish the Second East Turkestan Republic.[116] Shortly after the CCP came to power, the Republic's leaders began negotiations with Beijing and the Soviet Union. The Soviets urged them to cooperate with the CCP.[117]

President Ehmetjan Qasimi had fought a long time for Uyghur independence, and he refused to allow the newly-formed Republic to be absorbed by China.[118] Impressed, Comrade Stalin invited the Republic's leaders to Moscow to continue negotiations in person—but they were all killed when the plane crashed on the way there.[119] Terribly saddened, Soviet Deputy Vyacheslav Molotov telegrammed longtime communist Saifuddin Azizi—future Chairman of the CCP's Xinjiang Uyghur Autonomous Region—with instructions to keep the news secret so as not to upset the bereaved population.[120] By the time Azizi released news of the accident long after, the country was under the control of the PLA. That was end of Second East Turkestan Republic.

Ever since the CCP's takeover of Xinjiang, the Party has debated how best to manage the disputed territory. Moderate leaders included Xi Jinping's father, who stopped uprisings in northern Xinjiang by reversing hardline communist policies—even Mao couldn't take issue with the results.[121]

Terrorist attacks in Xinjiang grew worse in the early 2000s. A deadly attack in 2009 killed nearly 200 people in Urumqi, Xinjiang's capital.[122] China's moderate leaders, including General Secretary Hu Jintao, continued to emphasize economic development as the answer—a longstanding policy dating back to the '80s.

Xi Jinping saw things differently. Xinjiang was a critical terminus point in his Belt and Road Initiative, and disruptions would pose a threat to the CCP's interests.[123] Xi pointed to the Soviet example: "In recent years, Xinjiang has grown quickly and the standard of living has risen, but even so, ethnic separatism and terrorist violence have been on the rise."[124] Xi warned that violence spilling over from Xinjiang could taint the Party's image. Ultimately, as happened in the Soviet Union, this type of separatism could even lead to the downfall of the Party itself.

In 2014, after Uyghur militants killed 31 people, Xi traveled to Xinjiang to oversee the situation. During his trip, two Uyghur militants staged a suicide bombing that injured nearly 80 people.[125]

Xi was not impressed. Later that day, he told officials in Urumqi, "People who are captured by religious extremism—male or female, old or young—have their consciences destroyed, lose their humanity and murder without blinking an eye." "The methods that our comrades have at hand are too primitive."[126]

Following his trip, Xi laid the groundwork for what would become his signature policy: The detainment, reeducation, and "quarantine" of over one million Uyghur Muslims and other minorities "infected with extremism" in a massive system of concentration camps across Xinjiang and Tibet.

"There must be effective reeducation and transformation of criminals," he told officials.[127] Xi likened Islamic extremism to both a virus and an addictive drug, and declared that addressing it could be done only through "a period of painful interventionary treatment."[128]

Xi called for an all-out "people's war" using the "organs of dictatorship" to address this "crucial national security issue." "The weapons of the people's democratic dictatorship must be wielded without hesitation or wavering." Xi urged officials to ignore international criticism. "Don't be afraid if hostile forces whine or malign the image of Xinjiang." "We must be as harsh as them, and show absolutely no mercy."[129]

A directive on how to handle minority students returning to Xinjiang in 2017 offers the most detailed discussion of the camps—and how the Party whitewashes the public narrative while implementing a much darker reality. The script instructs officials to tell the students that their relatives had been "infected" by the "virus" of Islamic radicalism and must be "quarantined" and "cured":

> Question 4: 'Since it's just training, why can't my family come home?'
>
> Answer: 'It seems that you're still misunderstanding how concentrated education works. Usually, you would return home for winter or summer vacation without problem. But if you were careless and caught a virus like SARS, you'd have to undergo enclosed, isolated treatment, because it's an infectious illness. If you weren't thoroughly cured, as soon as you returned home you would infect your family with this virus, and your whole family would fall ill. The Party and government would not be so irresponsible that they would let a family member go home before their illness was cured and their thinking thoroughly transformed—a situation in which they would do harm to others...'

Question 5: 'Did they commit a crime? Will they be convicted?'

Answer: 'They haven't committed a crime and they won't be convicted, it's just that their thinking has been infected by unhealthy thoughts, and if they don't immediately receive education and correction, they'll become a major threat to society and your family. It's very hard to totally eradicate viruses in thinking in a short time.'[130]

Having laid the groundwork for the reeducation of the Uyghur people, Xi turned his gaze south to China's wealthiest and most troublesome region: Hong Kong.

In 1898, the United Kingdom had obtained a 99-year lease for Hong Kong. Diplomatic negotiations later led to the Sino-British Joint Declaration, pursuant to which the CCP guaranteed Hong Kong's liberal system for at least 50 years following its return to China—a principle called "one country, two systems." On July 1, 1997, British soldiers lowered the Union flag and Hong Kong was returned to China. The world was optimistic that Hong Kong represented China's future, and the people of Hong Kong were hopeful that China would come to emulate its most prosperous city.[131]

Xi Jinping was equally optimistic that there would soon be little to distinguish Hong Kong from China. He'd personally see to that.

Xi's State Council issued a white paper claiming "comprehensive jurisdiction" over the Hong Kong territory—completely redefining "one country, two systems."[132] The white paper sparked a backlash, and in July 2014 over half a million Hong Kongers participated in the annual march for human rights. In response, Xi's Congress passed the "31 August Decision," rejecting open nominations for the city's chief executive.[133]

Their rights flagrantly violated, in September 2014 students launched a series of demonstrations throughout Hong Kong. When police used tear gas, the protesters brought umbrellas to defend themselves; their movement would thereafter be known as the "Umbrella Revolution."[134]

By December 2014, the protests had dwindled. But a powerful message had been sent. "The movement has been an awakening process for Hong Kong. People who weren't interested in politics before are now and aren't afraid to get arrested, especially the young people," said one leader.[135]

The 31 August Decision had its intended effect, and in 2017 Xi installed his personal stooge Carrie Lam as Hong Kong's Chief Executive. In March 2019, Lam's government introduced an Extradition Bill to deport alleged fugitives to Mainland China.[136] On June 9, 2019, over a million Hong Kongers marched against the extradition laws—the beginning of Hong Kong's broadest expression of public anger in decades. A second march drew nearly two million—roughly a quarter of Hong Kong's population.[137]

Over the subsequent months, protesters stormed Hong Kong's legislature and staged sit-ins at the airport. They targeted symbols of Party authority, developing secret codes and risking arrest on a daily basis. After a teen died in a fall from a parking garage during a police operation, students turned university campuses into fiery battlegrounds.[138]

In late November, the protesters earned a stunning victory. Led by a surge from young Hong Kongers, pro-democracy candidates won most of the local council seats.[139] It was a vivid expression of the city's anger with the CCP and promised to further embolden the pro-democracy movement. "Unless the Council is doing something concrete to address the concerns of the Hong Kong people," said one pro-democracy leader, "I think this movement cannot end."[140]

In Hong Kong, democracy activists persist, knowing their lives will be ruined. Teenagers have been jailed for years for speaking up for the freedom so many discount. Young people have sacrificed their futures, and rich men their fortunes, because they refused to accommodate tyranny. They keep fighting, even if they cannot "win." Forget what freedom is worth, and a Hong Kong democracy activist will be happy to remind you.

On January 1, 2020, protesters returned to the streets of Hong Kong in full force, beginning the new year the way they'd spent much of the old.[141] But as the protests continued in the coming weeks, something changed. The Umbrella Revolution's unstoppable momentum suddenly dwindled. Increasing numbers stayed home as the world's attention turned to events taking place in another part of China, as the first reports emerged of a virus that would give people everywhere a firsthand experience of life under the new leadership of General Secretary Xi Jinping.

CHAPTER IV

UNRESTRICTED WARFARE

What must be made clear is that the new concept of weapons is in the process of creating weapons that are closely linked to the lives of the common people. Let us be clear that the first thing we say is: The appearance of new concept weapons will elevate future warfare to a level which is hard for the common people—or even military men—to imagine. Then the second thing we say is: The new concept of weapons will cause ordinary people and military men alike to be greatly astonished at the fact that commonplace things that are close to them can also become weapons with which to engage in war. We believe that some morning people will awake to discover with surprise that quite a few gentle and kind things have begun to have offensive and lethal characteristics. – Qiao Liang and Wang Xiangsui, Unrestricted Warfare, 1999

In early 2020, anyone who logged onto social media was greeted with a barrage of videos that alleged to depict scenes of a novel virus plaguing the residents of Wuhan, China.[142] These sensations captured Wuhan residents in various pantomimes of pandemic horror, terrifying millions of viewers around the world. Some showed their victims foaming at the mouth and collapsing in the streets. Others featured officials in hazmat suits hovering over lifeless bodies, apparently struck down by the virus before they could get to a hospital. It was a virtual buffet of terror.

Imagine logging onto Facebook and seeing your friend's post of a man foaming at the mouth, captioned "sure, just the flu..." You continue scrolling and see many similar videos shared by friends, family, and coworkers. It was a powerful message and it impacted the global psyche for two months straight, before the world had any other information about this "novel" virus.

For the naturally skeptical, the videos tended to look hysterical and fake. In one, a team of police with the word "SWAT" on their uniforms—in English—caught a man with a butterfly net for removing his mask.[143] Official Chinese accounts widely shared an image of a hospital wing supposedly constructed in one day, but which actually showed an apartment 600 miles away.[144] In one of the biggest viral sensations, videos showed Chinese people spontaneously keeling over and dying from the virus in scenes likened to *Zombieland* and *The Walking Dead*.[145] In hindsight, many were downright comical; in one notorious clip, the spontaneously dying man throws his arms out to catch himself.[146]

Many dismissed the videos, claiming there's always fake or sensational news online. But this was different. This campaign was organized, sophisticated, and used expert messaging sprinkled with clever psychological suggestions. The videos had been hand-picked, edited, and manipulated to tell the world a specific story. They played night and day into the darkest, most personal fears of anyone who watched them. The comments from those sharing the clips ranged from the sarcastic: "Just the flu"—shaming those who downplayed the virus—to wild theories that the virus caused brain hemorrhages and sudden death. And they engendered a specific narrative: "A deadly virus is coming to get you, and your government will downplay it and tell you it's 'just the flu.' But it's not. It's a clear and present danger to you and your family."

At the time these videos appeared, no one outside China knew whether COVID-19 caused sudden death. When fear, confusion, and distrust were rampant, cool-headed citizens found it difficult to speak sensibly about a virus for which there was little information. And even for those who didn't buy in outright, there was always that nagging voice in their mind: "What if..." That little "what if," embedded into the unconscious mind, was perhaps the most powerful effect of all.

Another viral sensation claimed to show dead COVID-19 victims lining the streets and waiting to be picked up like trash. As one user tweeted about the video: "Wuhan China. Dead Bodies waiting 4 pickup. Coronavirus NO ordinary Virus. Is it intentionally released BIO WEAPON?"[147]

Imagine watching this video and picturing your hometown's streets lined with bodies, struck down by some "BIO WEAPON." That's terrifying. And it was also a lie. The video actually showed people sleeping on the streets in Shenzhen, over 600 miles from Wuhan.[148] But this imagery and the idea that a "BIO WEAPON" was on the way were extremely powerful. Would you stay locked in your home to save yourself from a bioweapon? After that, you just might.

Photos of officials in hazmat suits were everywhere, playing into a narrative about people trying in vain to "escape" Wuhan. The stories were dramatized tales of victims who tried desperately to flee, but were either killed by hazmat-clad officials or collapsed and died before making it out. Vivid, relatable tales invoking the human spirit and the will to live. "These people are just like you!" Except that these stories weren't real. The man in the photo did not have COVID-19; in reality, he was a passed-out drunk.[149]

Another theme in the videos was authorities apprehending, detaining, or killing COVID-19 victims to help save the world. Imagine seeing doctors so frightened of a virus that they're forced to use weapons against innocent victims. Suddenly, COVID-19 felt like the apocalypse, with "good" and "evil" trading places. A virus so terrible that doctors had to do evil things; heroes had to act like villains!

Some of the most influential footage showed authorities welding residents into their homes, both for their own good and—even more—for the good of the world. Another video featured a woman lying dead in the street and the story was that she had been shot at the border by doctors as she attempted to flee. Powerful, emotional, themes. And that unconscious "what if..." Could it be true? A virus so awful that doctors were forced to become jailers and killers to save mankind? "Was I not taking this seriously enough? Am I ignoring the truth? What if..."

But like all the others, this video was a lie. A screenshot revealed that the actual video had nothing to do with COVID-19—it was a well-documented motor-scooter accident. But the video was artfully edited to tell a completely different story.[150] Videos that purportedly showed actual encounters were just training videos, often with actors. Yet whoever posted these videos went to great lengths to make them look like real-life takedowns.

There were hundreds of these videos floating around social media—nearly all of them went viral, and many news outlets covered them as well. They shaped the initial narrative about COVID-19. But they were all fake, and most were quietly wiped from the internet in the months to come.

The videos had painted the Chinese government's response in a terrible light. "These poor Wuhan residents were dropping dead in the streets!" But Chinese state media never mentioned them or indicated they were fake—a point one would expect they'd want to make loud and clear. And despite all that terror, no journalists or public officials ever asked who made them, who posted them, and why. The first building blocks of the mass hysteria over COVID-19 that led to the shutdown of the world had been fabricated. Surely a bombshell of that magnitude would concern everyone, or at least pique the interest of journalists and politicians? But it didn't.

Thanks to those videos, millions of people were primed to distrust coolheaded leaders and scientists. A year prior, if westerners had been told they would voluntarily shut down their cities and lock themselves in their homes, they'd have laughed. But many were bamboozled into believing a virus causing brain hemorrhages, seizures, and sudden death was coming, and if they didn't shut down, lock up, and surrender their liberties, millions would die. That message was made loud and clear for two months.

While an embattled minority of experts tried to calm the fray, a frantic public was thinking about all those Wuhan residents dying in the streets. The Wuhan fear videos were the first of several perfectly-timed events that would provide the rationale for a fearful public to trade away their rights and livelihoods for lockdowns and restrictions—they crafted a powerful narrative and pre-programmed countless minds.

While the Wuhan videos consumed social media, most mainstream viewers had their first encounter with COVID-19 fear propaganda through a story picked up by global media outlets in early February 2020 about a doctor named Li Wenliang. Li had supposedly noticed an unusual incidence of pneumonia and warned his friends that hospital staff were being quarantined. Li's message went viral on social media, so the story went, causing panic and anger among the people of Wuhan, for which Li was admonished by local authorities on January 3, 2020. Days later, in a private meeting with the Politburo Standing Committee, Xi Jinping had gravely determined that the situation in Wuhan would require their personal supervision. Li was later named a national hero.

Li Wenliang's story does not withstand scrutiny.[151]

Wuhan is the largest city in central China. It remains a mystery why 27 patients experiencing symptoms of pneumonia in a city of 19 million people might be notable. But on December 31, 2019, the Wuhan municipal government—the same government that supposedly admonished Li Wenliang for sharing this information days later—was so *not* intent on covering up those cases that it made an alarmist public announcement about them on its website: "On December 31, 2019, the Wuhan Municipal Health Commission notified the epidemic situation of pneumonia in Wuhan."[152]

The very next day, on January 1, 2020, two days before Li's supposed admonishment, People's Daily, China's *largest* newspaper, picked up the story and reported it in the most alarmist fashion: "27 Quarantined in Wuhan Due to Viral Pneumonia."[153] Even more telling was the article's target audience: It appeared only on People's Daily's English website. It was meant for westerners.

Even more puzzling is that People's Daily wanted English readers to know this: "White-clad medical workers were busy spraying sanitizer in the market with their faces masked." The article included a terrifying graphic of a coronavirus in a human lung—eight days before Chinese authorities officially disclosed that the virus was "a new type of coronavirus."[154] People's Daily even alerted the English-speaking world to some "internet rumors" about what these few dozen cases might portend: "Without responding directly to online rumors that these cases may be related to severe acute respiratory syndrome, widely known as SARS..." Ironic, given that the earliest online rumors about an outbreak of a SARS-like virus had come from People's Daily itself.[155]

Over the course of the next week, more and more global media reports of a SARS-like outbreak in Wuhan began appearing, all citing the same source: The Wuhan Municipal Health Commission's website. BBC ran what appears to be the first story citing the Wuhan Municipal Health Commission's website on January 3, headlined: "China Pneumonia Outbreak: Mystery Virus Probed in Wuhan."[156]

On January 3, 2020, the same day Li Wenliang was "admonished," the CCP was so *not* intent on covering up COVID-19 that they directly reported 44 cases of viral pneumonia to the World Health Organization (WHO).[157] Even the WHO couldn't help but note that "the symptoms reported among the patients are common to several respiratory diseases, and pneumonia is common in the winter season." A few dozen cases of viral pneumonia simply weren't worth agitating about. But agitating is exactly what the CCP did, first denying "clear evidence" of human-to-human transmission on January 11, then confirming human-to-human transmission a week later, before shutting down Wuhan days after that.[158]

In fact, the first time the world ever heard the name "Li Wenliang" was on January 27, 2020—a month *after* he had allegedly sent his viral messages—when a purported exposé of party malfeasance featuring an interview with Li was published in one of the CCP's most venerated state propaganda outlets: Beijing Youth Daily.[159]

Image searches for screenshots of Li Wenliang's famous messages "blowing the whistle" on COVID-19 turn up nothing prior to January 27, a month after they'd supposedly gone viral— but, coincidentally, the same day Beijing Youth Daily first told of Li's purported existence. Beijing Youth Daily's supposed exposé featured an interview with Li in which the story of his social media posts and subsequent reprimand was told for the first time.[160]

The New York Times first reported on Li Wenliang on February 1, 2020, five days after his debut in Beijing Youth Daily.[161] If the New York Times had done even cursory fact-checking, they'd have realized Li and his "viral" warnings had been invented just days prior by Chinese state media. In fact, the only international media outlet that had reported Li's story up to that point was Caixin Global, a Chinese state media organization.[162] Rubber-stamping state media from a totalitarian dictatorship would seem to be a serious violation of the Times's publication guidelines—though the New York Times had at least one Pulitzer-winning bureau chief who did exactly that for decades: Walter Duranty, who'd spent years in Moscow whitewashing Stalin's atrocities for a global audience.[163]

Each article about Li Wenliang contains a unique interview; Li's portion of the original interview in Beijing Youth Daily and the second interview in Caixin Global both total over 1,200 words.[164] It's unclear how Li provided these responses, given Beijing Youth Daily reported he had been hooked up to a ventilator and receiving "high-flow oxygen therapy" on January 27.[165] Though perhaps the ubiquitous images of Li first released by China's largest international propaganda outlet, Global Times, give a clue. Though they claim to show Li near death's door, upon closer inspection what they really show is a man in perfectly good health wearing a non-intrusive breathing mask that can be taken off in seconds—sometimes holding his identification card.[166] Like the rest of the Li Wenliang story, these images were shared with top news outlets and splashed onto front pages across the world, searing them into the consciousness of everyone who saw them. Just days later, media outlets everywhere were carrying sensational front-page articles about the death of Li Wenliang—a name Beijing Youth Daily had unveiled less than two weeks prior.[167]

Media outlets around the world published hagiographic obituaries of Li Wenliang, but it's highly unlikely that any of these events ever took place. Rather, from the very beginning, the CCP had done everything in its power to stoke panic around COVID-19, and the sensational tale of Li blowing the whistle on a cover-up of this "SARS-like" virus added a veneer of legitimacy to the Party's own alarmism. Li Wenliang's story is, quite simply, propaganda—an intentional distraction from the fact that a "cover-up" of a deadly virus contradicted the CCP's own well-documented communications.

The story of COVID-19 had begun with a panoply of absurd events and outright lies. This is the story of how lockdowns, having sprung into human consciousness on the order of Xi Jinping, were propagated into global policy with a total absence of precedent, analysis, or logic—one of the most audacious psychological operations in all recorded history.

Lockdown proponents frequently justified their policies by comparing them to actions taken during the Spanish flu a century prior.[168] But a cursory examination of those measures reveals that nothing remotely approximating lockdowns was ever imposed. In the words of federal Judge William Stickman in *Cnty. of Butler v. Wolf*, citing the work of preeminent historians:

> Although this nation has faced many epidemics and pandemics and state and local governments have employed a variety of interventions in response, there have never previously been lockdowns of entire populations—much less for lengthy and indefinite periods of time...[169] While, unquestionably, states and local governments restricted certain activities for a limited period of time to mitigate the Spanish Flu, there is no record of any imposition of a population lockdown in response to that disease or any other in our history.[170]

Not only are lockdowns historically unprecedented in response to any previous epidemic or pandemic in American history, but they were not even mentioned in recent guidance offered by the U.S. Centers for Disease Control and Prevention (CDC). Judge Stickman continues:

> Indeed, even for a 'Very High Severity' pandemic (defined as one comparable to the Spanish Flu), the guidelines provide only that 'CDC recommends *voluntary* home isolation of ill persons,' and 'CDC might recommend *voluntary* home quarantine of exposed household members in areas where novel influenza circulates.' This is a far, far cry from a statewide lockdown...[171]

> The fact is that the lockdowns imposed across the United States in early 2020 in response to the COVID-19 pandemic are unprecedented in the history of our Commonwealth and our Country. They have never been used in response to any other disease in our history. They were not recommendations made by the CDC. They were unheard of by the people of this nation until just this year. *It appears as though the imposition of lockdowns in Wuhan and other areas of China—a nation unconstrained by concern for civil liberties and constitutional norms—started a domino effect where one country, and state, after another imposed draconian and hitherto untried measures on their citizens.*

Judge Stickman's intuition regarding the history of lockdowns was in line with the opinion of the foremost infectious disease scholars. As Dr. D.A. Henderson, the man widely credited with eradicating smallpox, wrote in 2006, "Experience has shown that communities faced with epidemics or other adverse events respond best and with the least anxiety when the normal social functioning of the community is least disrupted."[172] In fact, no western scientist had ever publicly supported lockdowns until Xi Jinping personally authorized the "unprecedented lockdown of Wuhan and other cities beginning on January 23."[173]

Xi's lockdown of Wuhan had been inspired by the CCP's pet hybrid of public health and security policy: *Fangkong,* the same policy that inspired the reeducation and "quarantine" of over one million Uyghur Muslims and other minorities "infected with extremism" throughout Xinjiang and Tibet.[174] Xi later affirmed that he had issued these instructions to the Politburo Standing Committee on January 7, 2020—but his instructions have never been revealed.[175] Chinese business leader Ren Zhiqiang penned an open letter in which he requested Xi's instructions be made public:

> So, what happened in December? Why wasn't information made available promptly? Why did CCTV on January 1 investigate news about eight rumormongers? And how could we have the January 3 admonishment? Why was the United States notified of the outbreak on January 3? Why not mention the various crises that happened before January 7? Why haven't the January 7 instruction been made public, not yet even today?! How were various national-level meetings able to gather after January 7? Why are you still traveling abroad? Why did you celebrate Spring Festival in Yunnan?[176]

For this letter, Ren Zhiqiang was sentenced to 18 years in prison.[177]

When the Wuhan lockdown began, the WHO's representative in China noted that "trying to contain a city of 11 million people is new to science... The lockdown of 11 million people is unprecedented in public health history..."[178] Human rights observers expressed concerns.[179] As one told the New York Times, "The shutdown would almost certainly lead to human rights violations and would be patently unconstitutional in the United States."[180]

But those concerns didn't stop the WHO from effusively praising the CCP's "unprecedented" response just days after the lockdown began: "The measures China has taken are good not only for that country but also for the rest of the world."[181] Having met with Xi in Beijing days prior, WHO Director Tedros Adhanom added that he was personally "very impressed and encouraged by the president [Xi]'s detailed knowledge of the outbreak" and the next day praised China for "setting a new standard for outbreak response."[182] Tedros continued:

> The level of commitment (of the leadership) in China is incredible; I will praise China again and again, because its actions actually helped in reducing the spread of the novel coronavirus to other countries...[183]

But six days in, the lockdown—being "unprecedented in public health history"—had produced no results, so Tedros was actually praising human rights abuses with nothing to show for them.

On January 23, 2020, the Chinese government forced 57 million residents of Hubei province into their homes—horrifying western observers—and the Wuhan fear videos began flooding international social media that same day.[184] Two days later, on January 25, Eric Feigl-Ding, a nutritional epidemiologist with little background in infectious disease, tweeted, "HOLY MOTHER OF GOD, the new coronavirus is a 3.8!!! How bad is that reproductive R0 value? It is thermonuclear pandemic level bad."[185] This was the first of a years-long series of false, hysterical, and wildly-popular tweets by the previously unknown Ding, by virtue of which he gained hundreds of thousands of followers and became one of the leading proponents for strict COVID-19 mandates, despite his evident lack of qualifications.[186]

But then, amid all that terror, suddenly there was hope! Beginning in February 2020, the Chinese government began reporting an exponential decline in COVID-19 cases. In its February report, the WHO waxed rhapsodic about China's triumph:

> General Secretary Xi Jinping personally directed and deployed the prevention and control work ... China's *uncompromising* and *rigorous* use of non-pharmaceutical measures to contain transmission of the COVID-19 virus in multiple settings provides *vital lessons* for the global response.[187]

Shortly after, the WHO held a press conference during which Assistant Director-General Bruce Aylward—who later disconnected a live interview when asked to acknowledge Taiwan—told the press:

> What China has demonstrated is, *you have to do this.* If you do it, you can save lives and prevent thousands of cases of what is a very difficult disease.[188]

Two days later, in an interview for China Central Television, Aylward put it bluntly: "Copy China's response to COVID-19."[189] Months later, Canada's parliament summoned Aylward for questioning, but the WHO forbade him from testifying.[190]

There are several glaring issues with the WHO's recommendations.[191] First, the WHO's conclusion that this "rather unique and unprecedented public health response in China reversed the escalating cases" is a logical fallacy.[192] While it was possible that a more "flat" curve in Wuhan could be attributed to the CCP's lockdown, it was at least as likely that Wuhan had simply witnessed the natural course of this "novel" pathogen. With no possible comparison or control group, the mere issuance of a policy "unprecedented in public health history" should not have automatically meant it was effective—

especially given the WHO's own 2019 guidance for pandemic influenza did not advise border closures, mass contact tracing, or quarantine even of "exposed individuals" under any circumstance.[193]

Further, the WHO did not consider other countries' economic circumstances, demographics, or even their number of COVID-19 cases—which were very few in most of the world—before telling the entire world: "You have to do this." This conclusion by the world's foremost public health body was, at best, criminally negligent.

Rather than considering these absurdities, scientists quickly began drafting plans in nearly every language to imitate China's lockdowns.[194] The New York Times immediately cited the WHO's report, snapping into a pro-lockdown stance it clung to for years with shockingly little introspection: "China 'took one of the most ancient strategies and rolled out one of the most ambitious, agile and aggressive disease-containment efforts in history.'"[195]

The idea of locking down an entire state or country and forcibly shutting its businesses had never been entertained, discussed, or implemented in any pandemic literature until it was done by Xi Jinping in January 2020. Lockdowns had never been tried before 2020 or tested before 2020, even on a theoretical basis. Xi had brought the concept of "lockdown" into human history; it otherwise never would have entered the collective imagination. Anytime anyone endorsed a lockdown, they were endorsing a Xi Jinping policy.

No one was more outraged by the CCP's COVID-19 coverup than Xi Jinping. Xi personally saw to it that the local officials in Wuhan were punished for how they'd treated poor Li Wenliang during his tragically short existence.[196] January 27 to February 7, 2020. Less than two weeks old. May he rest in peace.

But now it was time to move forward. Regardless of one's opinion about the CCP, the world had to set all that aside, because they were faced with a novel pandemic unlike anything they'd seen before—and in the span of a few weeks, Xi's "public health" policy had become the world's go-to pandemic response. All the nations of the free world were exposed, lined up and vulnerable like so many dominoes. What a shame it would be if someone happened to come along and give them that one, little *tip*.

CHAPTER V

JUST STAY HOME

There are no historical observations or scientific studies that support the confinement by quarantine of groups of possibly infected people for extended periods in order to slow the spread of influenza. A WHO Writing Group, after reviewing the literature and considering contemporary international experience, concluded that 'forced isolation and quarantine are ineffective and impractical.' Despite this recommendation by experts, mandatory large-scale quarantine continues to be considered as an option by some authorities and government officials.

The interest in quarantine reflects the views and conditions prevalent more than 50 years ago, when much less was known about the epidemiology of infectious diseases and when there was far less international and domestic travel in a less densely populated world... The negative consequences of large-scale quarantine are so extreme (forced confinement of sick people with the well; complete restriction of movement of large populations; difficulty in getting critical supplies, medicines, and food to people inside the quarantine zone) that this mitigation measure should be eliminated from serious consideration. – Dr. D.A. Henderson, Disease Mitigation Measures in the Control of Pandemic Influenza, 2006

In October 2015, Xi Jinping made his only visit to the United Kingdom as General Secretary of the CCP.[197] A busy man, Xi's trip lasted just four days, and he visited just one university:

Imperial College London. At Imperial, Xi announced "a series of new UK-China education and research collaborations" including "nanotechnology, bioengineering... and public health."[198] In a speech welcoming Xi and his wife, a goodwill ambassador to the WHO, Imperial College President Alice Gast described Imperial as "China's best academic partner in the west":

> Imperial College London strives to be just that, China's best academic partner in the west... As China's top research partner in the U.K., Imperial's academics and students benefit from collaboration on a daily basis.[199]

In February 2020, Imperial proved just how valuable "China's best academic partner in the west" could be. Just as the hysteria surrounding Li Wenliang and the Wuhan fear videos began to die down, the second act of the COVID-19 terror campaign began with a bombshell report from Imperial College London, its predictions seeming to validate the visceral horror that social media users had been experiencing all month.

An Imperial team led by physicist Neil Ferguson had run a computer model predicting that, by October 2020, more than 500,000 people in the U.K. and 2.2 million in the U.S. would die of COVID-19.[200] Ferguson's team recommended months of strict social distancing to prevent this, and his work was instrumental in convincing many world leaders to adopt lockdown policies. The Imperial model predicted that the U.S. could incur up to one million deaths even with "enhanced social distancing."[201] In reality, by the end of October, according to the CDC and the U.K. National Health Service (NHS), approximately 230,000 deaths in the U.S. and 37,000 deaths in the U.K. were attributed to COVID-19.[202]

Shortly after, Ferguson's team produced another report titled *Evidence of initial success for China exiting COVID-19 social distancing policy after achieving containment*, concluding:

For the first time since the outbreak began there have been no new confirmed cases caused by local transmission in China reported for five consecutive days up to 23 March 2020. This is an indication that the social distancing measures enacted in China have led to control of COVID-19 in China.[203]

Ferguson, of course, had no way of knowing if this was in fact true, and his conclusion directly contradicted that of the western intelligence community around the same time.[204] In a December interview, Ferguson recalled how China had inspired his lockdown recommendations:

I think people's sense of what is possible in terms of control changed quite dramatically between January and March… It's a communist one party state, we said. We couldn't get away with it in Europe, we thought… And then Italy did it. And we realised we could… If China had not done it, the year would have been very different.[205]

A study by researchers at UCLA compared the accuracy of various institutions' COVID-19 models. Across all time periods, the models produced by Imperial College had far higher rates of error—*always* too high:

The Imperial model had larger errors, about 5-fold higher than other models by six weeks. This appears to be largely driven by the aforementioned tendency to overestimate mortality. At twelve weeks, MAPE (mean absolute percentage error) values were lowest for the IHME-MS-SEIR (23.7%) model, while the Imperial model had the most elevated MAPE (98.8%).[206]

Imperial's inaccuracy continued unabated. Prior to the U.K. ending its COVID-19 restrictions on July 19, 2021, dubbed "Freedom Day," Ferguson predicted that after ending restrictions, "100,000 cases a day is almost inevitable."[207] Instead, cases per day fell dramatically after the U.K. ended its restrictions, falling from over 35,000 on July 18 to around 27,000 on July 23.[208]

Just as Neil Ferguson's infamous models were giving COVID-19 hysteria a veneer of legitimacy, another piece of sophistry by thinkfluencer Tomas Pueyo began making the rounds among policymakers. Pueyo came to sudden fame for his March 10 article *Coronavirus: Why You Must Act Now*, in which he implored world leaders to implement lockdowns on China's model: "The total number of cases grew exponentially until China contained it. But then, it leaked outside, and now it's a pandemic that nobody can stop."[209]

Pueyo was an MBA with no relevant credentials or prior interest in epidemiology, and there was little to indicate where he'd gotten his ideas. When asked, Pueyo wrote: "You might have also noticed my two MSc and the several viral applications I built that gathered millions of users—with very similar dynamics"— invoking his experience with viral media applications as a qualification to discuss the spread of viruses in the biological sense.[210] As one lecturer at Sheffield University summarized:

> The experts are back in fashion. So the story went during the early stages of the Covid-19 crisis... This turned out to be an unsustainable position... Pueyo made no claims to special expertise or relevant credentials, and a glance at his Medium profile showed no previous interest in epidemiology, but rather a range of posts with titles such as *What the Rise of Skywalker Can Teach About Storytelling* and *What I Learned Building a Horoscope That Blew Up on Facebook*. This all seemed like a poor fit for the new age of expert deference that we were supposed to be experiencing, but... [*Coronavirus: Why*

You Must Act Now] received a stunning 40 million views in the first nine days since publication and has been translated into over 40 languages.[211]

Pueyo's article went viral at an astonishing pace.[212] Reactions were mixed. Many top commenters expressed shock at Pueyo's lack of qualifications, and accused him of being a "liar and a fraud."[213] As one top comment on Pueyo's Medium article stated:

> It is irresponsible of medium to publish this article by someone with no background in medicine, public health, epidemiology or statistics without a peer review by people in those fields.[214]

Others questioned how someone with no experience or previous interest in epidemiology was suddenly one of the most influential voices in a public health emergency:

> Are you kidding me? This techbro previously best known for marketing his fellow techbros, and for a book about the hidden meaning of Star Wars ... has gone viral as a pandemic expert, despite not knowing the difference between linear and exponential, or anything about the context for South Korean epidemiological successes? There's a special ring of hell for people who self-promote in times like these.[215]

Undeterred, Pueyo went on tour advising state legislators on implementing lockdowns and, within days, had posted links to high-quality translations in dozens of languages.[216] His 6,000-word article had been so popular, so the story went, that readers had produced immaculate translations in nearly every language.

Pueyo's article contained many oddities. It several times referred to the coronavirus as a "pandemic," but as of March 10, the WHO had not yet declared a pandemic, and per the article, cases accounted for less than 0.0015% of the world's population.[217] In the article, Pueyo implored leaders:

> But in 2–4 weeks, when the *entire world* is in lockdown, when the few precious days of social distancing you will have enabled will have saved lives, people won't criticize you anymore: They will thank you for making the right decision.

Not only was the coronavirus not yet a pandemic, but as of March 10 there were fewer than 200 cases in the entire developing world outside China—fewer than one case per 20 million people. There was no good reason to believe the entire world would be in lockdown in two to four weeks.

On March 19, Pueyo posted another Medium article titled *The Hammer and Dance*, explaining the strategy Pueyo described as "the Hammer"—quick, aggressive lockdowns when outbreaks occur—followed by "the Dance"—tracing, surveillance, and quarantine measures.[218] In the months to come, all the epidemiological predictions in Pueyo's articles were quickly falsified. But, like Neil Ferguson's models, Pueyo's articles had played a disproportionate role in the normalization of lockdown measures.

Around the same time Pueyo's articles began circulating, the German Ministry of the Interior (BMI) specifically commissioned models that would justify "measures of a preventive and repressive nature."[219] Scientists delivered. On March 20, 2020, the German Society of Epidemiology published a six-page paper forecasting horrifying outcomes if extraordinary actions weren't taken.[220] The model justified the BMI's subsequent publication, on March 22, of a notorious strategy paper—later dubbed "the Panic Paper." The Panic Paper was secretly distributed to

Germany's parliament and media leaders, playing an outsized role in Germany's March 2020 lockdown.[221]

The Panic Paper was leaked after BMI refused to release it under the Freedom of Information Act.[222] Despite being published just three days after Pueyo's article, the Panic Paper relied heavily on Pueyo's work, referring to intermittent lockdowns and surveillance as the "Hammer and Dance." The term "Hammer and Dance" had no history in epidemiology—Pueyo had invented it just three days prior.[223]

The Panic Paper was characterized by illiberal sentiments unparalleled in the history of postwar Germany—but this mystery quickly subsided when more was revealed about its authors. One author was Otto Kölbl.[224] Kölbl had been "researching socio-economic development in China" since 2007.[225] From 2005 to 2006 he was a language teacher at Northwestern Polytechnical University in Xi'an, China. He ran his own blog called "rainbowbuilders.org" in which he'd described Hong Kong as "parasitic" and praised the CCP's exemplary governance of Tibet.[226] Like Pueyo, Kölbl was very unqualified to be advising world leaders on epidemiology or public health, fields in which he had no background.

Maximilian Mayer was another author of the Panic Paper.[227] Mayer taught at the University of Nottingham in Ningbo China and Tongji University in Shanghai, and was a research fellow at Renmin University Beijing.[228] Mayer's research interests included China's foreign and energy policy, climate politics, and international relations, and he edited *Rethinking the Silk-Road: China's Belt and Road Initiative and Emerging Eurasian Relations*.[229] Like Pueyo and Kölbl, Mayer lacked any qualifications in epidemiology or public health, the fields on which he'd advised the German government via the Panic Paper.

Later, hundreds of pages of emails containing communications leading up to the Panic Paper were provided to Germany's independent Corona Committee.[230] In one email, Mayer wrote that he was delivering "secret" information about the Chinese response, and in another specifically recommended: "We suggest the motto 'collectively distanced.'"[231]

Toward the end of the emails, the BMI minister who'd arranged the study asked the participants to provide their personal emails and phone numbers because "we don't know how long the networks will be reliably functioning"—as if the coronavirus might somehow take down professional email networks but leave personal ones intact. Of the 210 pages of emails that led to the publication of the German strategy paper, 118 pages were blacked out entirely. The emails contained frequent discussion of China, but nearly all of these references were redacted. The stated reason: "May have adverse effects on international relations."[232]

Ferguson's models, Pueyo's articles, and national abominations like the German Panic Paper all predicted millions of deaths in countries that eschewed lockdowns, giving a veneer of academic legitimacy to the visceral terror gripping the world. These papers are well-known to have played outsized roles in world leaders' decisions to shut down their countries. But at the same time leaders were digesting these predictions, the CCP was engaging in a broad, systematic, and largely clandestine propaganda campaign to normalize and promote lockdown measures.

Within China, the CCP has long paid hundreds of thousands of full-time social media propagandists, and also pays for social media posts on an *a la carte* basis, totaling hundreds of millions of comments each year.[233] Xi had unleashed these activities globally, and they escalated dramatically along with COVID-19.[234] In general, social media companies have only been able to detect obvious automated activity, while fake, personally-managed accounts can be created with ease.[235] This worked out nicely for the CCP, who'd always preferred the human touch.[236]

On March 9, 2020, Italy became the first country outside China to implement a national lockdown. Chinese experts arrived in Italy on March 12 and two days later advised stricter measures: "There are still too many people and behaviors on the street to improve."[237] On March 19, they repeated that Italy's lockdown was "not strict enough." "Here in Milan, the hardest hit area by COVID-19, there isn't a very strict lockdown... We need every citizen to be involved in the fight of COVID-19 and follow this policy."[238]

Italy was simultaneously bombarded with Chinese propaganda and disinformation. From March 11 to 23, roughly 46% of tweets with the hashtag *#forzaCinaeItalia* (Go China, go Italy) and 37% of those with the hashtag *#grazieCina* (thank you China) came from bots.[239]

Shortly after, the entire world was bombarded with propaganda extolling the virtues of China's heavy-handed approach.[240] On March 12, Twitter user @manisha_kataki posted a video showing Chinese workers disinfecting streets, admiring China's strategy: "At this rate, China will be back in action very soon, may be much faster than the world expects." As the New York Times noted, this tweet was not shocking, funny, or newsworthy, yet it was shared hundreds of thousands of times; Israeli company Next Dim flagged the activity as state-sponsored.[241]

Hundreds of thousands of clandestine quote-tweets of @manisha_kataki's post expressed admiration for China's lockdowns and pleaded for governments to emulate them, while denigrating those who failed to follow suit. These governments included, but were not limited to: Nigeria, Ghana, South Africa, Namibia, Kenya, France, Spain, Colombia, Brazil, Canada,

Australia, India, Germany, the United Kingdom, and the United States.[242]

The quote-tweets used many languages to complain in nearly-identical terms about being told to "wash their hands," denigrating other governments' comparatively lax responses in contrast to China's full lockdown of Wuhan. Other suspicious quote-tweets explicitly implored leaders to copy China and lock down cities and countries. Twitter responded to the Times's article by deleting 170,000 accounts the next day—but most of the accounts involved in this ring remained active many months later.[243]

On March 15, social media bots began wildly sharing a YouTube video of Italian residents imploring the world to follow them into lockdown, which the bots dubbed a "message from the future."[244] According to the video's caption, "It is believed nations like the U.S., England, France, Spain and Germany are about 9-10 days behind Italy in the COVID19 progression. We asked people from all around Italy to record a message to the themselves of 10 days prior."[245] The video quickly went viral and gained over 8.3 million views.

As more countries shut down, some suspicious activity took a darker turn. South Dakota Governor Kristi Noem famously refused to issue a statewide lockdown.[246] Suspicious accounts began filling her Twitter feed with abuse to pressure her to do so. Upon closer examination, some of these accounts would hurl similar abuse at governors thousands of miles apart.[247] The online abuse of anti-lockdown leaders continued for some time. When Brian Kemp, the first U.S. governor to end his state's lockdown, paid homage to the late Representative John Lewis, his Twitter feed was stormed in conspicuous, vulgar language that attacked his anti-lockdown stance.[248]

Some CCP propagandists were identifiable by their advocacy for China's policies and abuses. In one example, a model CCP propaganda account, @AmerLiberal, showed both strong support for China's abuses—including in Xinjiang and Hong Kong—and antipathy for China's key rivals, India and the United States. The account strongly and consistently supported lockdowns all over the world.[249]

Chinese state media bought numerous Facebook ads advertising China's pandemic response—all of which ran without Facebook's required political disclaimer.[250] Simultaneously, Chinese state media began describing "herd immunity" as a strategy violating "human rights":

> Sweden will not test people with mild symptoms. UK and Germany tried to build a 'herd immunity', which will expose many people to the risk of death. These countries are unwilling to invest more resources in epidemic control. What about human rights? What about humanitarianism?"[251]

Initially, U.K. Prime Minister Boris Johnson also opted for a strategy centered on herd immunity. But on March 13, suspicious accounts began storming his Twitter feed and likening his plan to genocide. This language almost never appeared in Johnson's feed before March 12, and several of the accounts were hardly active before then. The U.K. locked down days later.[252]

Sweden, whose leaders were unique in forgoing lockdowns, became a primary target of the CCP's propaganda campaign.[253] Sweden's rift with the CCP predates COVID-19. In January 2020, Beijing had threatened Swedish trade ties over an award given to Gui Minhai, a Swedish publisher detained in China.[254] In the words of China's state-run Global Times:

Chinese analysts and netizens doubt herd immunity and called it a violation of human rights, citing high mortality in the country compared to other Northern European countries. 'So-called human rights, democracy, freedom are heading in the wrong direction in Sweden, and countries that are extremely irresponsible do not deserve to be China's friend...'[255]

That was, of course, before the WHO adopted the bold, contradictory strategy of rewriting the definition of herd immunity wholesale. Throughout most of 2020, the WHO's definition of herd immunity had properly included "immunity developed through previous infection"—but on October 15, 2020, the WHO effectively erased the eons-long history of natural immunity from its website:

'Herd immunity', also known as 'population immunity', is a concept used for vaccination, in which a population can be protected from a certain virus if a threshold of vaccination is reached. Herd immunity is achieved by protecting people from a virus, *not* by exposing them to it.[256]

While the world digested the terrible prophecies of those like Ferguson, Pueyo, and the German BMI amidst an unprecedented propaganda onslaught, the scientific foundations for lockdown policies were simultaneously being laid.

Underpinning the policy of "lockdown" was the concept of "asymptomatic spread." According to this concept, healthy individuals or "silent spreaders" might be responsible for a significant number of SARS-CoV-2 transmissions.[257] The idea of preventing asymptomatic spread was the sole basis for subjecting healthy people to lockdown restrictions—and a significant departure from prevailing public health guidance. According to the WHO, "Early data from China suggested that people without symptoms could infect others."[258] This idea of asymptomatic spread was reflected in the WHO's February report from Wuhan.[259]

Significant asymptomatic spread was believed to be a novel and unique feature of SARS-CoV-2 based on several studies performed in China.[260] Multiple studies from other countries could not find any transmission of SARS-CoV-2 from asymptomatic individuals.[261] A German study co-authored by Christian Drosten claimed to find *"Transmission of 2019-nCoV Infection from an Asymptomatic Contact in Germany,"* but the researchers didn't actually speak to the woman before they published the paper, and officials later confirmed that she did, in fact, have symptoms while in Germany.[262] A paper from McGill University concluded that "transmission in the asymptomatic period was documented in numerous studies," but every one of those studies was conducted in China; where studies outside China tried to replicate these findings, they failed.[263]

Further fanning the hysteria, the early lockdowns of several large cities were followed by large spikes in deaths of hospitalized patients. In the early stages of the crisis, the overuse of mechanical oxygen ventilators killed thousands of innocent patients before a grassroots campaign put a stop to the practice. These deadly recommendations for mechanical ventilators also came from China.[264]

In early March 2020, the WHO released COVID-19 provider guidance to healthcare workers.[265] The guidance recommended escalating quickly to mechanical ventilation to treat COVID-19 patients, a departure from past experience.[266] In doing so, they cited guidance from Chinese journal articles claiming that "Chinese expert consensus" called for "invasive mechanical ventilation" as the "first choice" for people with moderate to severe respiratory distress—in part to protect medical staff.[267] As the Wall Street Journal later reported:

> Last spring, doctors put patients on ventilators partly to limit contagion at a time when it was less clear how the virus spread, when protective masks and gowns were in short supply. Doctors could have employed other kinds of breathing support devices that don't require risky sedation, but early reports suggested patients using them could spray dangerous amounts of virus into the air, said Theodore Iwashyna, a critical-care physician ... At the time, he said, doctors and nurses feared the virus would spread through hospitals. 'We were intubating sick patients very early. Not for the patients' benefit, but in order to control the epidemic and to save other patients,' Dr. Iwashyna said, 'That felt awful.'[268]

Early and frequent use of mechanical ventilators became a common theme, and it had devastating consequences.[269] On March 31, 2020, Dr. Cameron Kyle-Sidell, who'd been working at one of the hardest-hit hospitals in New York City, acted as an early whistleblower, sounding the alarm in a widely-shared video:

> We are operating under a medical paradigm that is untrue... I fear that this misguided treatment will lead to a tremendous amount of harm to a great number of people in a very short time... This method being widely adopted at this very moment at every hospital in the country ... is actually doing more harm than good.[270]

By May 2020, it was common knowledge in the medical community that early ventilator use was hurting, rather than helping, COVID-19 patients, and that less invasive measures were in fact very effective in assisting recoveries.[271] A New York City study found a *97.2% mortality rate* among those over age 65 who received mechanical ventilation.[272] The WHO's "early action" ventilator guidance, citing Chinese journal articles, had killed countless thousands of patients across the world.

In a matter of weeks, the world had dismissed a century of epidemiological research and adopted the model of the Chinese Communist Party. The WHO's pandemic response plan, updated as recently as October 2019, and its national counterparts in every developed nation, were tossed aside.[273]

South Australia's Chief Health Officer later recalled how the WHO's Bruce Aylward—who'd instructed the world to "Copy China's response to COVID-19"—urged her into this course of action:

> While we were somewhat prepared and we thought about pandemics and we had a pandemic preparedness plan and such, nobody in the world really envisaged how huge it was going to be. But we had a very insightful video lecture from Dr Bruce Aylward leading the World Health Organization's investigation into China. And he said to us, 'Do not underestimate this virus. It is terrible. And if you can do something about stopping it getting in, do everything you possibly can.'[274]

In the U.K. Government's official Coronavirus Action Plan from March 3, 2020, discussing social distancing, school closures, and rapid COVID test and vaccine development, nearly every source the Government cited was from China.[275] All the measures outlined in New Zealand's official COVID-19 Elimination Strategy document—"physical distancing" "widespread testing" "surveillance"—were adopted from China based on the reported success of the CCP's Wuhan lockdown.[276] The New Zealand Department of Health deleted this document from its website one day after it received widespread attention on Twitter, after having been posted there for over a year.[277]

On March 24, two days after the notorious "Panic Paper" was circulated, the German government published a second strategy paper containing a "catalog of measures" to be implemented by Germany's CDC, "based on the scientific findings of expert teams from the University of Bonn / University of Nottingham Ningbo China," and other foundations. This strategy paper outlined, in detail, the steps to implement lockdowns, mass testing, home quarantine, and quarantine facilities, among other draconian measures. The catalog even included "coordination" measures including the takeover of all "central coordination of the COVID-19 crisis" by a "minister for special tasks," and public "education" measures including "appeals to the public spirit." The document specifically suggested the use of two words that would soon become a worldwide propaganda slogan during the COVID-19 crisis: "Together apart."[278]

One after another, world leaders and their national bureaucracies fell in line, halting all social and economic activity for the first time in history. In March 2020, the Dutch government commissioned a cost-benefit analysis concluding that the health damage from lockdown would be six times greater than the benefit.[279] They ignored it, claiming "society would not accept" the optics of an elderly person unable to get an ICU bed. The Dutch government knowingly took a course of action that would cause *health damage*—let alone economic damage—six times worse for the Dutch people, out of a concern for optics.

The decision had been made to adopt measures from a totalitarian country including lockdowns, terror campaigns, and flagrant violations of the Nuremberg Code, all without informing the public. The entire healthy population was locked up, elderly people were tossed out of hospital beds, and legislation was passed, without debate, removing fundamental rights to movement, association, work, education, religious worship, and access to medical care.

Authoritarian regimes often engaged in campaigns of anarchic trolling, but the real power of disinformation is that a regime with the CCP's manpower can make any message go viral at just the right time. A hodgepodge of viral communications can be released through proxies and intermediaries to give political decisions an organic feel. In this case, the decision to "copy" China's lockdown had been driven disproportionately by a few early viral communications including the Wuhan fear videos, Neil Ferguson's models, Tomas Pueyo's articles, and social media astroturf campaigns like the videos of Italian residents and the legions of posts demanding leaders shut down their countries.

The result was an abrupt philosophical shift. In less than two weeks in March, the ethical burden of COVID-19's toll shifted in such a way as to inevitably thrust the world into moral panic and a manic feedback loop.

In February 2020, COVID-19 containment was still being discussed in sensible terms of social and economic cost. As one physician wrote in The Atlantic: "Certain containment measures will be appropriate, but widely banning travel, closing down cities, and hoarding resources are not realistic solutions for an outbreak that lasts years."[280] On February 27, the New York Times considered the cost to society too great to justify even temporary school closures, noting the tendency for officials to just "do something" to give voters the impression the government is in charge, "even if it's not relevant."[281] Sensible questions were still being asked, and discussion of them could still be found in the media. Could the world really control this? What would be the cost of mitigation?

Two weeks later, everything, everywhere, was closed. In two weeks, the world had gone from "stay home if you're sick" to "stay home at all costs, all the time, sick or not."

In those two crucial weeks, the moral burden of COVID-19's outcome suddenly shifted as a global consensus emerged that China's declining case numbers had been a result of its "draconian" lockdown measures. China's success was a beacon— one to which the world should aspire! The political and public health establishment seized upon the idea that the people's fate was in their hands—just as China's had been—a feedback loop into which a terrified and propagandized public bought with little resistance.

With the sense of control firmly established, failure to stop COVID-19 was now a moral failing. If leaders could stop the virus, but chose not to, this could only be due to a lack of resolve. And no one had shown more resolve in stopping COVID-19 than Xi Jinping.

CHAPTER VI

EVERYTHING IS FAKE

It is as though mankind had divided itself between those who believe in human omnipotence (who think that everything is possible if one knows how to organize the masses for it) and those for whom powerlessness has become the major experience of their lives. – Hannah Arendt, The Origins of Totalitarianism, 1951

On January 13, 2020, six days after Xi Jinping convened the Politburo Standing Committee to discuss the supervision of Wuhan, the WHO accepted the world's first COVID-19 PCR testing protocol, created in record time by a team including Victor Corman, Christian Drosten, and Olfert Landt. They'd been provided with the gene sequences for the protocol by Chinese scientists at the Wuhan Institute of Virology.[282]

The WHO released the Corman-Drosten Protocol on January 21, the same day it was submitted to the journal Eurosurveillance for peer review.[283] Eurosurveillance finished its peer review the very next day—an extraordinarily quick turnaround.[284] Of the thousands of publications at Eurosurveillance since 2015, not one other paper was reviewed and accepted in one day; on average, the process took over 100 days.[285] But perhaps this was unsurprising, given Drosten sat on the board of Eurosurveillance, a flagrant conflict of interest.[286] Amid popular outrage, Eurosurveillance issued a statement refusing to disclose its peer review records.[287]

A team led by molecular biologist Pieter Borger submitted a retraction request for the Corman-Drosten protocol, citing multiple, fatal errors.[288] The most glaring issue was that, at the time the protocol was submitted, there was no reason to even believe widespread PCR testing would be necessary:

> The authors introduce the background for their scientific work as: 'The ongoing outbreak of the recently emerged novel coronavirus poses a challenge for public health laboratories as virus isolates are unavailable while there is growing evidence that the outbreak is more widespread than initially thought.' ... there were 6 deaths world-wide on January 21st 2020 – the day when the manuscript was submitted. Why did the authors assume a challenge for public health laboratories...?

Borger's report went on to specify ten major flaws with the Corman-Drosten protocol, the most glaring being the fact that it was based on *in silico* (theoretical) gene sequences provided by China:

> The first and major issue is that the novel Coronavirus ... is based on *in silico* sequences, supplied by a laboratory in China.

Corman and Drosten's PCR protocol, the world's original gold standard and most commonly used test for COVID-19 infection, had every indication of being fraudulent. What's more, as early as January 10, before either China or the WHO had given any indication of human-to-human transmission, Olfert Landt's company, TIB-Molbiol, had a fully functional test kit ready to ship.[289]

In just 30 days, a health crisis had been discovered, exceptional attributes had been attributed to a "novel" virus, a PCR test had been peer reviewed and released by the WHO, and test kits had been shipped all over the world. By contrast, R. E. Hope-Simpson had studied influenza for nearly 50 years, his work culminating in his magnum opus *The Transmission of Epidemic Influenza* in 1992 without being able to make specific conclusions.[290] What poor Hope-Simpson couldn't do in 50 years—hindered as he were by such inconveniences as ethics and truth—Xi Jinping, the WHO, Corman, Drosten, and Landt had done in days.

By March 2020, following WHO guidance, labs across the world had begun mass PCR testing for COVID-19—yet another departure from all previous pandemic guidance.[291] Otto Kölbl and Maximilian Mayer, the China lobbyists who authored Germany's Panic Paper, had likewise deemed PCR testing necessary in their original March 4 document, *Learning from Wuhan—there is no Alternative to the Containment of COVID-19.*[292]

Fundamental to PCR testing is the concept of "cycle thresholds." The higher the cycle threshold, the lower the viral load needed to trigger a positive test. If the PCR cycle threshold were set too high, a "positive" result would not indicate any meaningful amount of virus. As NIH Director Anthony Fauci mentioned in July 2020, a cycle threshold of 35 or more should not be considered a positive:

> If you get a cycle threshold of 35 or more ... the chances of it being replication-confident are minuscule... So, I think if somebody does come in with *37, 38, even 36, you got to say, you know, it's just dead nucleotides, period.*[293]

The WHO published its testing guidance for COVID-19 on March 19, 2020.[294] The WHO's guidance contained only three studies discussing PCR cycle thresholds. All three were from China, and all used cycle thresholds from 37 to 40.[295]

As described by the New York Times, most laboratories in the U.S. set their cutoff for PCR cycle thresholds from 37 to 40: "Most tests set the limit at 40, a few at 37."[296]

Doctors interviewed by the New York Times agreed that anything above 35 cycle thresholds was too sensitive. Dr. Michael Mina, epidemiologist at the Harvard T.H. Chan School of Public Health, said he would have set the figure at 30, or even less. Using current testing standards with 37 to 40 cycle thresholds:

> In three sets of testing data that include cycle thresholds, compiled by officials in Massachusetts, New York and Nevada, up to 90 percent of people testing positive carried barely any virus... In Massachusetts, from *85 to 90 percent* of people who tested positive in July with a cycle threshold of 40 would have been deemed negative if the threshold were 30 cycles, Dr. Mina said. 'I would say that none of those people should be contact-traced, not one,' he said.[297]

In a ruling on November 11, 2020, the Court of Appeal of Lisbon cited a study by "some of the leading European and world specialists," showing that if someone tested positive for COVID-19 at a cycle threshold of 35 or higher, "the probability of... receiving a false positive is 97% or higher."[298]

Based on guidance issued by the WHO, citing three studies from China, laboratories and manufacturers across the U.S. and many other countries were using cycle thresholds of 37 to 40 for COVID-19 PCR tests, pursuant to which positive COVID-19 case counts had been inflated as much as ten- to thirty-fold.

PCR technology had been invented in 1983 by American biochemist Kary Mullis to allow scientists to study tiny samples of DNA in detail. For this, he won the Nobel prize in chemistry. At a panel discussing PCR in 1993, Mullis stated very plainly that PCR should not be used for diagnosing illness:

> With PCR, if you do it well you can find almost anything
> in anybody... PCR is just a process that you use to make a
> whole lot of something out of something. It doesn't tell
> you that you're sick, and it doesn't tell you that the thing
> you ended up with was really gonna hurt you or anything
> like that.[299]

In 2020, "fact checkers" came out in force, arguing that Mullis
did not say PCR couldn't be used to detect viruses.[300] In typical
"fact-checker" fashion, this was a straw-man argument. What
Mullis had said is that the PCR method *can* manufacture
anything if just one molecule is present. PCR technology
"searches" for a specific gene sequence, and then doubles the
gene material when it's found. This doubling can be done any
number of times. Each doubling is called a "cycle." Again, in
Mullis' words:

> If you can amplify one single molecule to something that
> you can really measure, which is what PCR can do, then...
> there's very few molecules that you don't have one single
> one in your body... that could be thought of as a misuse of
> it, to claim that [test result] is meaningful.[301]

Whether or not one could measure the genetic material, and
thereby conclude one "had" a virus, was purely a function of the
number of doublings. At 60 cycles, 100% of people would test
positive. The more tests are done, the more people would test
"positive," with the majority having *zero* live virus.[302]

In a 1996 interview, Mullis had choice words for Anthony Fauci,
then head of the U.S. response to AIDS. Mullis was especially
critical of Fauci's use of PCR:

> These guys like Fauci get up and start talking and he
> doesn't know anything about anything and I would say
> that to his face. Nothing. The man thinks you can take a

blood sample and stick it in an electron microscope and if it's got a virus in there, you'll know it. He doesn't understand electron microscopy and he doesn't understand medicine and he should not be in a position like he's in. Most of those guys up there on the top are just total administrative people and they don't know anything about what's going on with the body... They make up their own rules as they go; they change them when they want to. And they're smug—like Tony Fauci does not mind going on television in front of the people who pay his salary and lying directly into the camera.[303]

Mullis passed away in August 2019. Albert Einstein, a lifelong pacifist, had been horrified to learn that his work was used to create nuclear weapons. Imagine how fellow Nobel laureate Kary Mullis would feel knowing his work had been used to defraud the world, despite his specific instructions that it never be used for diagnostic purposes. The PCR test could pick up any amount of viral matter any time and yield endless "cases"—a permanent pandemic. Of this feature, Xi Jinping, a longtime fan of both Mullis and Fauci's work, was well aware.

The WHO's PCR guidance was paired with new international ICD-10 codes for COVID deaths to make COVID-19 quite possibly the deadliest accounting fraud of all time.[304] According to this coding guidance, a "confirmed case," indicated by a positive PCR test, was coded U07.1.[305] Symptoms were not necessary for U07.1 to be recorded on a death certificate. A decedent known to have had contact with a SARS-CoV-2 positive person who, while neither testing positive nor having any symptoms, was to be deemed a suspected COVID-19 case and given the code U07.2.

Neither the U07.1 nor the U07.2 codes required any evidence that the decedent actually had COVID-19—the disease sometimes caused by SARS-CoV-2. The WHO clearly described this in their International Guidelines for coding of COVID-19 deaths, defining a death "due to" COVID-19 as follows:

> A death due to COVID-19 is defined for surveillance purposes as a death resulting from a clinically compatible illness, in a probable or confirmed COVID-19 case, unless there is a clear alternative cause of death that cannot be related to COVID disease (e.g. trauma).[306]

A clinically compatible illness could be any influenza-like illness. The WHO's Guidelines went on:

> COVID-19 should be recorded on the medical certificate of cause of death for *all* decedents where the disease caused, or is assumed to have caused, or contributed to death.[307]

Per this guidance, even if the individual had died of cancer, as long as they had tested positive for SARS-CoV-2, or were even suspected of having been exposed, the death would be registered as "due to" COVID-19. If a decedent had tested positive, or been in contact with anyone who had, a COVID-19 death was essentially *fait accompli*. For good measure, the WHO Guidelines made that quite clear:

> There is no provision in the classification to link COVID-19 to other causes or modify its coding in any way... Therefore, always apply these instructions, whether they can be considered medically correct or not... A manual plausibility check is recommended ... for certificates where COVID-19 was reported but *not* selected as the underlying cause of death for statistical tabulation.[308]

In the U.K., any death within 28 days of a positive PCR test was to be included in the COVID-19 fatality total, regardless of context.[309] In the U.S., the cutoff was generally 60 days.[310] When there was no positive test, but a patient had symptoms like fever or shortness of breath, attribution to COVID-19 was encouraged. The result was a terrifying number of supposed "COVID-19 deaths" that bore little relation to the number of "excess deaths" in a given year, even in states and countries that employed few lockdown measures.[311]

By August 2020, the CDC was reporting the presence of comorbidities in 94% of COVID-19 deaths.[312] For 385,067 COVID-19 deaths reported for 2020, *"cardiac arrest"*; *"ischemic heart disease"*; *"vascular and unspecified dementia"*; *"renal failure"*; *"heart failure"*; *"cardiac arrhythmia"*; *"other diseases of the circulatory system"*; *"cerebrovascular diseases"*; *"malignant neoplasms"*; *"Alzheimer disease"*; and *"intentional and unintentional injury, poisoning, and other adverse events"* are listed as comorbidities 303,710 times in total. Each of these is an extraordinarily deadly condition with no relation to respiratory infection.[313]

The CDC was apparently well aware this was happening. Once vaccines became widely available, the CDC disclosed that they would not count fully-vaccinated deceased persons who asymptomatically or incidentally tested positive as COVID-19 deaths, in sharp contrast to their counting of unvaccinated patients.[314] The U.K. NHS followed suit. After 16 months counting all who tested positive as COVID-19 patients, the NHS instructed hospitals "to identify patients actually sick from COVID-19 separately to those testing positive" allegedly "to help analyse the effect of the vaccine programme."[315] When former FDA Commissioner Scott Gottlieb was asked about this, he explained that the CDC was not testing post-vaccination breakthrough cases "for cost reasons." Apparently, after conducting over 500 million COVID-19 tests, the CDC couldn't count post-vaccination cases "for cost reasons."[316]

In May, CDC Director Rochelle Walensky stated that with regard to COVID-19 deaths among fully-vaccinated individuals:

> I also want to convey that now many, many hospitals are screening people for COVID when they come in, so not all of those 223 cases who had COVID actually died of COVID. They may have had mild disease, but died, for example, of a heart attack.[317]

The CDC had never made such a clarification for unvaccinated individuals—even when the enormous number of "COVID-19 deaths" was being cited everywhere by policymakers, courts, and the press. On the contrary, in 2021 the U.S. government began paying an unprecedented $9,000 for the funeral expenses of anyone whose death certificate showed the death "may have been caused by" "COVID-19-like symptoms"; if the death certificate did not show that, it could be amended.[318]

It remains a mystery what exactly someone who died with COVID-19 did to be more deserving of funeral funding than a person who died of any other cause. But the absurd number of "COVID-19 deaths" generated by this coding regime created a terrifying number that could be used to rationalize any manner of devastation caused by governments' totalitarian response to COVID-19—from bankruptcies and mental health crises to deaths from lockdowns themselves, relabeled "COVID-19 deaths."

Mass PCR testing and manipulative death coding guidance were the basic numerical foundations of the lockdown fraud, creating an absurd number of "COVID-19 deaths" that could be deployed relentlessly for political purposes, both to increase alarm and to shame those opposed to lockdown measures. But the CCP was aided and abetted at virtually every stage of this fraud by a global media apparatus that reliably toed its lines. They did so with regard to the origin and spread of SARS-CoV-2 and the efficacy of lockdown measures.

While much of the CCP's pro-lockdown influence was surreptitious, its overall stance in support of global lockdowns was explicit. In a video posted by China's official foreign spokesperson, a 7-year-old girl recited a script—in English—on the importance of strict social distancing and masking among children:

> I can't go to school. I can't see my friends... But I know all these sacrifices will be worth it. I have stayed at home for two months already. I wear mask. I wash my hands. I don't go to crowded areas in order to stop the virus spreading. Because I know, if I don't do so, I might be infected, and infect my dad, my mum, and my brother. If they are sick, they might die... Coronavirus is a global health emergency... It should not be a political matter to be used against other nations. I am only seven years old. I understand it, but why do some adults don't get it? To those national leaders, stop blaming each other ... The virus won't go away by winning a political argument... I have this common sense, why don't you?[319]

On July 7, FBI Director Christopher Wray disclosed that the CCP had specifically approached local politicians to endorse its pandemic response:

> We have heard from federal, state, and even local officials that Chinese diplomats are aggressively urging support for China's handling of the COVID-19 crisis. Yes, this is happening at both the federal and state levels. Not that long ago, we had a state senator who was recently even

asked to introduce a resolution supporting China's response to the pandemic.[320]

Through its institutional influence, the CCP could veil the medieval pseudoscience of lockdowns with a cloak of academic legitimacy. Speaking through official channels, the CCP would shame governments that did not adopt strict lockdowns and relentlessly advertised its pandemic response.[321] As Global Times, China's largest international propaganda outlet, wrote in March 2020: *"US political elites attempt to save economy before people's lives."*[322] The core message was always the same: China was the only country to have managed COVID-19 perfectly. Those who did otherwise were inhumane.

The overarching lie hammered by the CCP into elite discourse was that "China controlled the virus." Of course, "China controlled the virus" was a boldfaced lie. China never controlled SARS-CoV-2; its infection data was manifestly forged, as was confirmed early on by the intelligence community.[323]

In truth, for as much as the CCP attacked Sweden and others for pursuing herd immunity, China had simply forged its data and quietly adopted a herd immunity strategy in February 2020. The CCP thus exploited the fact that most westerners didn't realize the full implication of China's backslide into totalitarianism. The CCP could convince westerners that it did, indeed, "control the virus" despite all the evidence staring them in the face—because how could an entire country lie?

A 2020 New Yorker article titled *How China Controlled the Coronavirus* was a perfect example.[324] The title was, of course, a lie. But being mostly benign, the article was shared widely among both China watchers and Chinese state media—for different reasons. For western elites, the article was a detailed look inside China. But for the CCP, all that mattered was the title: *How China Controlled the Coronavirus*. Reinforcing that lie, and giving high society a reason to share it, ensured that China's fake data remained paramount in scientific discourse.[325] This fact did not escape China expert Geremie Barmé—inventor of the term "Great Firewall"—who wrote that Hessler's work reminded him of "another American journalist, a man who reported from another authoritarian country nearly a century ago... Walter Duranty."[326]

Through this method, the CCP could pull its lie, "China controlled the virus," from the mouths of elites around the world. A widely-cited poll of economists by the University of Chicago in March 2020 demonstrated this phenomenon at work. Nearly all the economists agreed with the prompt: "Abandoning severe lockdowns at a time when the likelihood of a resurgence in infections remains high will lead to greater total economic damage than sustaining the lockdowns to eliminate the resurgence risk."[327] The prompt implicitly ratified the idea that a "severe lockdown" really could "eliminate the resurgence risk"—a feat that had been "accomplished" by just one country in history: China, two weeks prior. By agreeing to this statement, the economists threw their credentials behind the lie.

In true Orwellian fashion, within China, the CCP pretended to believe its lie only on the basis of its own convenience, reserving the right to use COVID-19 as a pretext for unrelated authoritarian whims—demolishing retirement homes, detaining dissidents, expanding mass surveillance, canceling Hong Kong's Tiananmen Square vigil and postponing its elections for one year.[328] In Xinjiang, COVID lockdowns went on perpetually and involved widespread hunger, forced medication, acidic disinfectant sprays, shackled residents, screams of protest from balconies, crowded "quarantine" cells, and outright disappearances.[329]

For ordinary CCP members, when Wuhan locked down it likely went without saying that the lockdown would "eliminate" the coronavirus; if Xi willed it, then it must be so. Conveniently, it mattered little whether 99.9% of CCP members actually believed lockdowns worked. Promoting lockdowns was the Party line, and ordinary CCP members need not know whether their leaders actually believed it, only pretended to believe it, or had deliberately intended lockdowns as a kind of fraud. This was the totalitarian pathology George Orwell called "doublethink."

"China controlled the virus" was an ingenious Orwellian euphemism. By ensuring this line, "China controlled the virus," was slipped into establishment discourse the world over, the CCP bombarded elites with that lie, day in, day out, so they would know what was expected of them. In a world where nations were committed to doing everything to control COVID-19, the real meaning of "China controlled the virus," was "China controlled the virus, and no one else has. Therefore, do whatever China says."

The CCP understood the origins of totalitarianism. The fatal flaw of communism was the pathological pursuit of an unobtainable goal—the end of class. Under COVIDism, the CCP had turned elites against their own people through the pathological pursuit of another unobtainable goal—the end of COVID.

Lockdown propaganda relied on two key principles inherent to virtually all official communications on COVID-19. The first was that China's measures were the only ones ever proven "effective." The second was that fear was necessary to ensure compliance with lockdown measures. The risk of COVID-19 had to be emphasized—even exaggerated—to ensure the compliance necessary for lockdowns to succeed.

In the U.K., state scientists later admitted they'd used fear to change minds in a series of interviews: "Using fear as a means of control is not ethical. Using fear smacks of totalitarianism."[330] "The use of fear has definitely been ethically questionable. It's been like a weird experiment." "Psychologists didn't seem to notice when it stopped being altruistic." In the words of one Member of Parliament:

> If it is true that the state took the decision to terrify the public to get compliance with rules, that raises extremely serious questions about the type of society we want to become. If we're being really honest, do I fear that Government policy today is playing into the roots of totalitarianism? Yes, of course it is.[331]

Through messaging that targeted humans' innate fear of contagion, the perception of a large portion of the population would detach from any real data about the virus. According to the most widely-cited study on COVID-19's infection fatality rate (IFR) by age, the average IFR for those under 40 years old was around 0.01%.[332] But in surveys conducted regularly by the University of Southern California, on average, Americans under 40 consistently estimated their chance of dying if they contracted the virus to be around 10%, a 1,000-fold overestimation.[333]

Likewise, in October 2020, the WHO's peer-reviewed bulletin showed COVID-19's overall IFR across all age groups to be about 0.23%.[334] John Ioannidis, the world's most-cited physician, believed the IFR to be lower and published his own peer-reviewed study showing the overall IFR to be about 0.15%.[335] In 2021, Public Health England revised its official estimate for COVID-19's IFR to below 0.1%.[336] But in a poll conducted by the Menzies Research Centre, by June 2021 Australians on average estimated their chance of dying if they contracted the virus to be 38%, an overestimation of more than 200-fold.[337]

Such an egregiously misinformed populace rendered democratic accountability for lockdown measures impossible. More so because, as a study by Cardiff University demonstrated, the primary factor by which citizens judged the threat of COVID-19 was their own government's decision to employ lockdown measures.[338] "We found that people judge the severity of the

COVID-19 threat based on the fact the government imposed a lockdown—in other words, they thought 'it must be bad if government's taking such drastic measures.' We also found that the more they judged the risk in this way, the more they supported lockdown." The policies thus created a feedback loop in which the measures themselves sowed the fear that caused citizens to believe their risk of dying of COVID-19 was hundreds of times greater than it really was, in turn causing them to support more lockdown measures.

While fear rendered rational discourse about the virus impossible, the inherent flaws in PCR testing ensured that no state or country would ever "eliminate" COVID-19 as China claimed. China's lockdown measures would always be the only "effective" measures. Whether COVID-19 cases went up, down, or sideways, the solution would always be the same: "Be more like China."

Regardless of any actual danger posed by COVID-19, even if the risk was virtually zero—as it was in the case of young children— constant fear would ensure the population perceived the risk to be high and thus support more lockdown measures. To "succeed," those measures had to be more like China's. These were the two key principles of lockdown propaganda; when they were combined, the real message emerged: "Fear is necessary to ensure compliance with China's measures."

In a 2015 speech to the PLA, Xi Jinping outlined his vision for the CCP's international propaganda:

> Wherever the readers are, wherever the viewers are, that is where propaganda reports must extend their tentacles, and that is where we find the focal point and end point of propaganda and ideology work.[339]

The Chinese government has financial stakes in virtually every top global media outlet, and friends in corporations, universities, and governments.[340] It was the same pattern every time. Pre-existing financial relationships with China led to trusting information from China, endorsing the CCP's narrative, and ultimately advocating the global adoption of CCP policies. Owing to this combination of naivety, groupthink, and outright corruption, scientists and journalists generally incorporated information from China into their work as true, when in fact nearly every bit of information that had come from China with regard to COVID-19 was a lie.

Media narratives aligned almost perfectly with the political goals of the CCP at any given time. Global media outlets legitimized a ludicrous narrative in which the CCP's two-month lockdown of Wuhan had swiftly eliminated domestic cases from all of China, but not before the virus spread everywhere outside China, where governments now had no choice but to implement the CCP's lockdown measures.

Articles from March 10, 2020, illustrate how media outlets adopted China's narrative in unison. *"How China Slowed Coronavirus: Lockdowns, Surveillance, Enforcers,"* reported the Wall Street Journal.[341] *"Those containment efforts do appear to have been successful, with the number of new cases slowing to a trickle in recent weeks,"* CNN admired.[342] *"Xi asserts victory on first trip to Wuhan since outbreak... China's epidemic statistics suggest that its efforts have been effective,"* trumpeted the Washington Post.[343] *"The World Health Organization has praised Beijing's response... 'This epidemic can be pushed back,' Dr. Tedros said, 'but only with a collective, coordinated and comprehensive approach that engages the entire machinery of government,'"* the New York Times repeated.[344]

For journalists, indulging the fiction that China controlled the virus appears to have begun as a little white lie—a little something in exchange for all those goodwill seminars and ad placements. It was silly, of course, but what harm could that do?

The snowball effect of this little white lie, that China controlled the virus, was soon apparent in journalists' own writing. One after another, they fell victim to their own collective propaganda. Within months, they'd been transformed into foaming-at-the-mouth communists, their every word dripping with illiberalism as they implored the world to emulate China:

"The U.S. has absolutely no control over the coronavirus. China is on top of the tiniest risks," the Washington Post gushed.[345] *"The verdict is in,"* Politico ruled, *"China has outperformed, while the once-respected American system has disastrously faltered."*[346] *"U.S. Says Virus Can't Be Controlled. China Aims to Prove It Wrong,"* the New York Times admired.[347] *"China beat the coronavirus with science and strong public health measures, not just with authoritarianism,"* the Conversation lectured.[348] *"In a Topsy-Turvy Pandemic World, China Offers Its Version of Freedom,"* the New York Times suggested.[349] *"China eradicated Covid-19 within months. Why won't America learn from them?"* Salon whined.[350]

Western media outlets came about as close as possible to an outright merger with Chinese state media while projecting the superficial criticism necessary to maintain the illusion of independence. Inconvenient facts were suppressed, inconvenient questions silenced, and all of it was built on the collective fantasy of controlling a common respiratory pathogen—a feat the epidemiology profession had agreed was impossible and self-destructive just months prior.

The truth is that the origin of lockdown "science" could not be factually discussed without the Chinese government looking very bad—something media investors were reluctant to allow. It was even harder to explain phenomena like the fake videos of residents dropping dead during Wuhan's lockdown, which went viral all over global websites blocked in China, without implying some degree of foul play by the CCP. So instead, overcompensating for Beijing, media outlets portrayed China as not only a responsible international stakeholder, but an admirable one—one that should be followed!

The public was led to believe that lockdown measures were grounded in rigorous "science," and that by following them, they were "following science," when in fact the only analysis had been, "China claimed they eliminated the virus this way, so we can too." The world was fighting a virus from China with a public health policy from China that effectively turned the world into China, and the narrative of the day was that all this was perfectly normal.

From the outset, Chinese state media had made it explicit that the CCP's measures were a referendum on human rights. As China Daily explained: *"When it comes to human rights, China prioritizes the right to live."*[351] *"The unprecedented outbreak has tested different national systems, capabilities and different human rights dimensions,"* Global Times observed, *"The Chinese government upholds the principle that 'life is supreme.'"*[352] *"Life comes first, nothing is more important than life,"* opined China's Foreign Spokesperson.[353] *"Judging from the desperate situation in Sydney and the military reinforcement, Australia is aware that the right to life is the most important of human rights,"* Global Times concluded.[354]

In and of itself, the lie that China had eliminated COVID-19 through its two-month lockdown of Wuhan was unbelievably daft. But what made the lie so powerful was that it was repeated—frequently, consistently, and earnestly—by many of the most prestigious and influential institutions across the western world. Furthermore, because the CCP fully intended its COVID-19 measures as a referendum on human rights, moderates could be tempted into carrying the CCP's water by endorsing the lie that China's measures had succeeded, even when debating their cost:

"China's Official Covid Rates Are Down. But Has That Come at the Cost of Human Rights?" Human Rights Watch puzzled.[355] *"The CCP has and needs no better narrative instrument than a highly visible demonstration of its model's success, particularly when compared to the foundering responses of many Western democracies,"* CSIS conceded.[356] *"The Chinese Communist Party reached deep into private business and the broader population to drive a recovery, an authoritarian approach that has emboldened its top leader, Xi Jinping,"* the New York Times proffered.[357] *"I could see the negative effects on my daughters, who were desperate for interaction with other children. But it was also true that the strict Chinese shutdown, in combination with border closings and contact tracing, had eliminated the spread of the virus,"* the New Yorker weighed.[358]

Surely, many such moderates were trying to be diplomatic; but owing to the nature of the debate, such timidity was, in this instance, complicity. By endorsing the lie that China had, in fact, "controlled the virus," these moderates were reinforcing the referendum that a terrified population had to choose between liberty and safety—the same referendum that the CCP had intended from the beginning. Having been inundated with fear messaging, much of the population would emphatically choose safety.

When China's data was left out of the mix, it was clear that no country was ever able to "crush" the coronavirus. Instead, the SARS-CoV-2 virus appeared to mysteriously resurge in "waves" despite the use of these draconian, economically-suicidal measures. As Harvard epidemiologist Martin Kulldorff wrote: "Among infectious-disease epidemiology colleagues that I know, most favor focused protection of high-risk groups instead of lockdowns, but the media made it sound like there was a scientific consensus for general lockdowns."[359]

The metrics preferred by media outlets shifted constantly to best suit the narrative of a supervirus that could be crushed only through utmost submission to the collective will. A focus on mortality rates would shift suddenly to hospitalizations and then to the ephemeral metric of "cases"—whatever best rationalized the public anxiety.

With few exceptions, this failure to "crush" the virus was attributed, absurdly, to lockdowns' leniency, rather than to their evidently fraudulent scientific origins. Journalists floundered to construct reality in a way that would please both their investors and the CCP while being at least remotely plausible to their middle class readers. Journalists' downplaying and suppressing any information that contradicted this science-fiction narrative left those that trusted them confused and scared, faced with a seemingly unbeatable virus with inexplicable characteristics and a crisis that made no logical sense.

The resultant reporting was not only harmful and misleading, but inherently contradictory and just plain bad. "The science" would change constantly, sometimes overnight, each time presented by the media as a major breakthrough—though in virtually all cases the supposed "breakthrough" was a fact that had been known about coronaviruses for decades. "Immunity to the coronavirus may persist for years... possibly a lifetime," the New York Times finally reported in May 2021—that readers believed otherwise, for over a year, tells you all you need to know about the quality of scientific discourse surrounding COVID-19.[360]

In early 2021, as the vaccines upon which lockdowns were originally premised became widely available, scientists and media outlets introduced the concept of "variants" to justify ever more lockdowns. The word "variants" was hardly ever used before 2021.[361] Headlines from major media outlets can then be seen methodically walking back the purported efficacy of COVID-19 vaccines between March and October of 2021 from 100% to 50%—one percentage point at a time.[362]

After months of shaming anti-lockdown protesters, western media outlets joined Chinese state media—along with many of the previously-identified Twitter bots that had advertised China's lockdowns—in waxing rhapsodic about racial justice protests of unprecedented scale following the death of George Floyd in May 2020.[363] Once those protests died down, the media returned to shaming anti-lockdown protesters. In hindsight, the idea that those opposed to governments claiming indefinite emergency powers were "neo-Nazis," as the New York Times reported, might seem laughably Orwellian.[364] But that absurd line was astonishingly effective in chilling resistance to lockdowns, primarily because readers simply couldn't believe their own media would publish propaganda. As CNN reported in an "open letter" from health professionals about the George Floyd protests:

> As public health advocates, we do not condemn these gatherings as risky for COVID-19 transmission. We support them as vital to the national public health and to the threatened health specifically of Black people in the United States... This should not be confused with a permissive stance on all gatherings, particularly protests against stay-home orders. Those actions not only oppose public health interventions, but are also rooted in white nationalism.[365]

Throughout the summer of 2020, media outlets including the New York Times, the Washington Post, Wired, and Vanity Fair all claimed that the secret to Japan's success was widespread masking.[366] Mask use and social distancing only increased, yet the number of COVID-19 cases in Japan rose exponentially. By summer 2021, Japan was in a state of emergency and had to cancel spectators for the summer Olympics.[367] Iceland was declared by media outlets to have "beat" COVID-19 several times, but despite a 70% vaccination rate, by August 2021 COVID cases in Iceland were at an all-time high.[368] Cases were likewise at or near all-time highs in Australia, South Korea, Vietnam, Thailand, and several other Southeast Asian countries that the media had declared a "success" on numerous occasions.[369]

What might have begun as a superficially reasonable desire not to interfere with governments' emergency decisions soon evolved into its own set of twisted journalistic norms. Channeling Walter Duranty's infamous defense of Stalin's Holodomor, "You can't make an omelet without breaking a few eggs," all the unimaginable harms of lockdowns were attributed to "pandemic disruptions."[370] Even those, like global famine, which were an obvious consequence of stopping the economy, were attributed to the "pandemic"—as if a respiratory virus with an IFR under 0.2% had caused a global famine all on its own.[371]

If the attribution of lockdown harms to the "pandemic" was intended as some kind of diplomatic nicety, it's entirely unclear who was meant to benefit. If anything, misattributing the cause of people's deaths to exculpate the policies that led to them was not only insulting to the deceased but only served to perpetuate the policies that killed them. Of course, these innumerable, egregious errors were never admitted or discussed, the norms of journalistic accountability and open debate having long since been jettisoned. Lockdown harms were not discussed simply because they were not discussed, and that was that.

The media was prohibiting debate about lockdowns, implying that dissent was immoral, when the policy itself was killing people. With all discussion of collateral damage effectively suppressed to support the narrative most charitable to the CCP, the world was stampeded away from the light-touch methods that were previously acknowledged to be the only practicable means to fight a respiratory virus—hygiene, shielding the vulnerable, expanding hospital capacity, and generally letting healthy people go about their lives. Instead, the world was driven mad with the fantasy of emulating the "success" of a totalitarian dictatorship.

Scientists and journalists had used their credentials to stamp CCP propaganda as "science." For those bold enough to do so, debating this "science" was like debating how many angels could dance on the head of a pin. It quickly became clear that no number of self-explanatory charts would ever persuade these "scientists" that SARS-CoV-2 was not a supervirus and "lockdown" was not real science. But they had to cling to that lie, because once the truth was known, everyone would know they'd caused all this ruin for nothing.

Not that the journalists and scientists were alone in this regard. Far from it. The narrative that lockdowns were perfectly good "science" had been embedded into the identity of much of the public, and many of them, as much as journalists and scientists, did everything in their power to prevent the revelation that they'd supported a destructive lie. In retrospect, the components of the fraud are so glaringly obvious, and its mechanics and methods so overtly Orwellian, it's hard not to conclude that illiberalism became something of a global fad in 2020.

Every step of the way, the international synchronization of lockdown mandates gave a cosmopolitan veneer to policies that were inherently unscientific, unprecedented, ineffective, totalitarian, brutal, and dumb. Elites saw other countries doing them and thought they must be sound. For over a year, the world watched educated professionals pretend not to know the basics of how respiratory viruses and vaccines worked. But most frightening of all was not so much the rampant groupthink, gullibility, scientism, and directed reasoning; it was that despite all the horror stories and studies of the catastrophic harms caused by lockdowns, most professionals simply couldn't be bothered to consider them a very big deal.

In their defense, no regime had ever used propaganda in quite this way—at least on a global scale. Nazi and Soviet propaganda had been extremely effective in warping the world's perception for decades, but that was largely limited to hiding crimes within their own regions. Here, the CCP was using propaganda to transform the world into itself, turning elites against their own people.

Millions surely suspected the lockdown fraud but felt some subtle aversion to saying so. They didn't want to seem radical or un-woke, or they thought it was someone else's job. Many refused to speak up for fear of the backlash against science, the professional class, and China. And, among those who really did believe China's COVID-19 narrative, or merely pretended to, all the authoritarian methods that supposedly contributed to China's "success"—including censoring, canceling, and firing those who disagreed—were on the table.[372] Even esteemed journalists chose to stay anonymous in their interviews with anti-lockdown scientists.[373] The vast majority of professionals simply lacked the courage to speak up publicly against the fanatical minority armed with these illiberal powers in their crusade for "Zero Covid."

The sum of these small acts of cowardice was the vacuum of accountability on which the fraud depended. By mid-2020, when one searched for journalists, officials, celebrities, or anyone else researching the CCP's influence on the lockdown policies turning the world into China, there were none.

Xi Jinping always believed that true leadership meant leading by example. One evil deed, on its own, may not amount to much. But to be one of history's great dictators, one had to bring out the evil in others. These leaders had performed several evil miracles over long careers of tyranny. Xi had his work cut out for him if he was going to make the cut.

But he was up to the challenge, and he was well on his way. The Soviet Union had tried to beat the west; Xi Jinping had simply bought it. Politicians, scientists, journalists, and common professionals of all stripes became comfortable repeating big, deadly lies about the world's response to COVID-19. Few really believed the virus was all that dangerous. They pretended to, but it was just a pretext to kiss up to those who could benefit them and be cruel and aloof to those who couldn't. The real virus Xi had unleashed was the abyss of the human soul.

CHAPTER VII

THE WORLD ACCORDING TO XI

是故百戰百勝，非善之善者也；不戰而屈人之兵，善之善者也。– 孫子, 孫子兵法, 春秋時代

For to win one hundred victories in one hundred battles is not the acme of skill; to subdue the enemy without fighting is the acme of skill. – General Sun Tzu, The Art of War, Spring and Autumn Period

Across professions, citizens refused to acknowledge the abundant evidence of CCP influence on lockdown policies, assuming that if the CCP had played a role in them, intelligence agencies would say so. Their faith was misplaced for several reasons, but they all stem from one overarching failure. From the very beginning, western intelligence officials had been operating on the assumption that SARS-CoV-2 might be a supervirus from the Wuhan Institute of Virology.

This assumption was confirmed by the prominent New York Times reporter Donald McNeil: "My colleagues who cover national security were being assured by their Trump administration sources—albeit anonymously and with no hard evidence—that it was a lab leak and the Chinese were covering it up."[374] McNeil's article verified what had long been hinted at. National security officials had gone along with lockdowns based on bad intelligence that SARS-CoV-2 was a potential supervirus from the Wuhan lab. German insiders likewise confirmed that western biosecurity networks had played a crucial role in bringing "lockdown" to Germany in late February 2020:

It is February 24th ... an urgent appointment at the Federal Ministry of the Interior... Heiko Rottmann-Großner accompanies him, Head of Subdivision 61: 'Health Security' ... When the officials from the Ministry of the Interior want to know what exactly 'mitigation' means, Rottmann-Großner takes over. Precautions must be taken to ensure that there are curfews of indefinite duration. One must also, as it will later be said in a note on the conversation, 'paralyze the economy and ask the population to stock up on food and medicines.' Something like this would soon be called 'lockdown.'[375]

Signs of this intelligence failure were everywhere. In spring 2020, the intelligence community grew suddenly hawkish on China, issuing dire warnings about the CCP and investigating hundreds of scientists in chemistry and biology for ties to China—apparently out of a concern about bioweapons.[376] Prominent security officials wrote endlessly about the Wuhan lab.[377] A report later released by the Canadian Armed Forces revealed that military leaders had seen COVID-19 as a unique opportunity to test propaganda techniques on the public, "shaping" and "exploiting" information to bolster government messages about the virus.[378]

The Wuhan lab had indeed played a key role in lockdowns. But not necessarily as a source of the coronavirus, which proved to be fairly ordinary. Rather, the CCP had used the Wuhan lab as a decoy to misdirect their opposition.

The story was perfect. The Wuhan lab had been engaged in "gain-of-function" research on coronaviruses in bats, which meant altering viruses in ways that could make them more dangerous. Worse yet, the Wuhan lab had lax security for one engaged in this kind of research. During gain-of-function research, so the story went, one of these coronaviruses had leaked out, causing mass death in Wuhan about which brave whistleblowers like Li Wenliang had to warn the world. But the CCP had covered it up, allowing the supervirus to spread. World leaders had to implement lockdowns and other cutting-edge measures on the advice of their best scientists and health officials. This was the narrative that preoccupied the intelligence community throughout 2020 and 2021. They knew researchers at the lab had gotten sick. They knew about the virus' unique furin cleavage site. All they had to do was prove SARS-CoV-2 came from that lab, and China could be held responsible. QED.

It was, indeed, the perfect setup. Exactly as Xi Jinping intended.

In the early 13th century, a nomadic chieftain led a band of 6,000 warriors to China's northern border. Baffled, the Jin Emperor sent a dispatch to the chieftain:

> Our Empire is as vast as the sea. Yours is but a handful of sand. What have we to fear of you?[379]

Even if they survived the impassable Gobi Desert, the warriors faced legions of mercenaries in Heilongjiang. Even if they defeated Heilongjiang's mercenaries, they'd be stopped by the forests of Jilin, where the trees stood as tall as mountains. Even if they passed Jilin's forests, they'd be stuck in the muddy silk fields of Liaoning.

But Temüjin was no ordinary chieftain, and in 1213 AD he laid siege to Beijing. Though he'd begun vastly outnumbered, the scores of mercenaries he'd co-opted in Heilongjiang evened the odds. Though Beijing was fortified by stone walls, the wood from Jilin made for excellent ladders and rams. Though Jin archers filled the sky with arrows, the warriors' armor was fortified with silk from Liaoning, trapping the arrows before they met flesh.

This was the end of the Jin empire, and the first of many such conquests by Genghis Khan. It was one of the great military catastrophes of all time, and a lesson China's strategists would never forget. To underestimate one opponent—a single intelligence failure—can be the downfall of even the greatest empires.

Strategy is deeply ingrained in Chinese culture. Whereas the west traditionally played chess, a tactical game, the Chinese played Go, a game of abstract strategy. In Go, even advanced players may initially take many of their opponents' pieces, only to find that they've played into the hands of a more worthy opponent. As Sun Tzu wrote in the 5th century BC:

> All warfare is based on deception. Hence, when we are able to attack, we must seem unable; when using our forces, we must appear inactive; when we are near, we must make the enemy believe we are far away; when far away, we must make him believe we are near... Appear weak when you are strong, and strong when you are weak.

The overtaking of liberal democracies by advanced autocracies in the realm of information warfare is one of the most important stories of the early 21st century. By 2020, the CCP had nearly a century of experience using propaganda to convince intelligent people of absurdities. This was the CCP's biggest strength. By contrast, few living westerners had experienced this level of propaganda firsthand.

The CCP's lockdown operation appears to have had its philosophical origins in the book *Unrestricted Warfare*, magnum opus of China's most influential modern strategist, Qiao Liang, and his comrade Wang Xiangsui.[380] In *Unrestricted Warfare*, Qiao and Wang reimagined warfare for the 21st century. Accepting the reality of mutually-assured destruction in a post-nuclear world, the authors theorized that the rules of warfare were set to fundamentally change. Forces seeking to dominate a superpower would need to do so in an innovative way. Future wars would be waged on "a level that is hard for the common people—or even military men—to imagine." Understanding that even the most sophisticated military force "does not have the ability to control public clamor, and cannot deal with an opponent who does things in an unconventional manner":

> We can point out a number of other means and methods used to fight non-military war, some of which already exist and some of which may exist in the future. Such means and methods include psychological warfare (spreading rumors to intimidate the enemy and break down his will); media warfare (manipulating what people see and hear in order to lead public opinion along) ... economic aid warfare (bestowing favor in the open and contriving to control matters in secret); cultural warfare (leading cultural trends along in order to assimilate those with different views); and international law warfare...

Qiao and Wang foretell of a "weapons revolution," pivoting away from heavy machinery and mass casualties to attacks on the mind. Weapons would be "symbolized by information" and would be powered by psychology:

> Some morning people will awake to discover with surprise that quite a few gentle and kind things have begun to have offensive and lethal characteristics.

In October 2019, just two months before the SARS-CoV-2 virus was revealed in Wuhan, the Gates Foundation, the World Economic Forum (WEF), Bloomberg, and the Johns Hopkins Bloomberg School of Public Health hosted Event 201, a pandemic simulation.[381] Each sponsor was an organization with close ties to China, and each played an outsized role in the world's response to COVID-19.

It's unlikely that many participants at Event 201 realized a coronavirus was sweeping across Asia at the time. But the CCP may have manipulated its fatality data to trigger the emergency responses planned by the China-friendly organizations at Event 201, triggering their apocalyptic response to COVID-19. Event 201 bore an uncanny similarity to the COVID-19 crisis—with one notable exception: The fictional coronavirus at Event 201 had a case fatality rate (CFR) of about 7%, dozens of times higher than the infection fatality rate (IFR) for SARS-CoV-2 of less than 0.2%.[382] Event 201 does not appear to have theorized any significant difference between the hypothetical coronavirus' CFR and IFR, apparently presuming that nearly all infections would be found through testing. Although we now know COVID-19 had an IFR of less than 0.2%, estimates for the case fatality rate coming from China in March 2020, when the world shut down, showed a CFR of over 4%.[383]

Event 201 delegates included George Fu Gao, director of the Chinese Center for Disease Control and Prevention, who oversaw the original article in the New England Journal of Medicine on COVID-19 symptoms.[384] Participants discussed the control of "misinformation" during a coronavirus pandemic, and Gao even raised the point of countering rumors that the virus was man-made.[385] Each participant was gifted a one-of-a-kind Event 201 coronavirus plush (made in China).[386]

From the first reports about a new virus, the Wuhan narrative had overtly suggested a bioweapon. Whistleblowers, residents collapsing, emergency lockdowns, a novel virus, all previous science tossed out. Many of the fake Wuhan fear videos were even captioned as much: "Wuhan China. Dead Bodies waiting 4 pickup. Coronavirus NO ordinary Virus. Is it intentionally released BIO WEAPON?"[387]

By February 2020, independent news sites were filled with tales of a lab-made supervirus causing an emergency lockdown in Wuhan.[388] These stories could be read alongside the fake videos of Wuhan residents falling dead for added flavor. That mainstream websites insisted the virus was natural only made the "lab leak theory" all the more enticing.[389] Add to that the sensational tale of young Li Wenliang, struck down by the virus, and the strange stories of thousands of funeral urns shipped to Wuhan and tens of millions of Chinese cell phone users vanishing.[390] But it was all a lie. Reverse psychology. This was how the CCP, aware of their poor reputation for transparency, made the world believe an ordinary virus was a supervirus.

The fake Wuhan fear videos had set the stage for the psychological blitz that the world would soon see from global institutions. In the fake videos, doctors had to "kill" fake actors to save the world from a "supervirus." Just one month later, elite institutions like the WHO, supposedly dedicated to saving lives, would cite that "supervirus" as necessitating lockdowns that killed millions of real innocent people. In a world with a supervirus—perhaps even an "intentionally released BIO WEAPON"—that was suddenly deemed ethically acceptable. All the elites were doing it. And the actors in the Wuhan fear videos had primed the public with the idea that these murderous decisions were the only way.

There was abundant evidence that SARS-CoV-2 had begun spreading much earlier than December 2019. Wastewater samples found traces of SARS-CoV-2 as far back as March 2019.[391] Later, a widely-published report revealed that orders for PCR tests had soared in China beginning in May 2019, a full seven months before China had reported its first coronavirus case: "Orders doubled from universities, jumped fivefold from the Chinese Center for Disease Control and Prevention and surged tenfold from animal testing bureaus."[392]

These findings were in line with examinations of excess mortality. In late 2018 and 2019, Asian countries experienced higher excess deaths in age groups vulnerable to COVID-19.[393] Then, in 2020, excess deaths in Asian countries dropped a bit, apparently due to prior immunity, while excess deaths in western countries in those age groups increased. These facts are highly indicative that SARS-CoV-2 actually began somewhere in Asia in 2018 or early 2019 at the latest.

From early on, leading scientists including John Ioannidis had estimated COVID-19's true IFR to be less than 0.2%.[394] Given its statistical normality, SARS-CoV-2 really could have originated anywhere. Certainly, the virus could have leaked from the Wuhan lab in 2018 or early 2019. But that would fly in the face of the original imprimatur of the supervirus theory: The collapsing Wuhan residents and whistleblowers, and the CCP's emergency lockdown and "cover-up." What was the relevance of the source of a virus that was not much deadlier than the flu?

That was, of course, the point of the CCP's seeding the lab investigation: There was no point. By seeding the supervirus narrative, the CCP could convince their political opposition to focus on a theory that, even if true, had no especial relevance to their real crime. Worse yet, given that SARS-CoV-2 had begun spreading across Asia in 2018 or early 2019, the CCP could have picked literally any city to shut down for purposes of its lockdown fraud. Xi Jinping had chosen Wuhan because there was a lab there.

In one of the CIA's worst-ever failures, from 2010 to 2012 the CCP dismantled the CIA's entire network in China, executing dozens of agents.[395] A subsequent investigation concluded that at least one double agent had been involved; three CIA officers were later convicted as double agents for the CCP. By 2012, the entire

U.S. intelligence network in China, cultivated over decades, had been eviscerated. CCP agents could operate with newfound impunity.

In 2020, a Chinese real estate billionaire named Guo Wengui funded "War Room: Pandemic," a series dedicated to the bioweapon narrative hosted by media executive Steve Bannon.[396] A well-known figure in the Chinese dissident community, Guo marketed himself as an anti-Beijing crusader. There was just one problem: After years of investigations, intelligence officials had concluded that Guo was not actually an anti-Beijing crusader, but a "dissident-hunter, propagandist, and agent in the service of the People's Republic of China."[397] During courtroom testimony in 2021, Guo refused to answer whether he was still a CCP spy. That is to say, Guo, who had funded an entire series dedicated to the COVID bioweapon narrative, was controlled opposition of the worst kind.

Guo sponsored another "whistleblower" named Li-Meng Yan, who was given significant primetime coverage with her reports that SARS-CoV-2 was a bioweapon. Her reports used misleading credentials, fake co-authors, and provided no new evidence for her claim.[398] Fake whistleblowers like the two Lis—Li Wenliang and Li-Meng Yan—served an additional purpose: They obscured the fact that Wuhan had real whistleblowers like Zhang Zhan, who'd been sentenced to four years in prison for her impassioned criticism of Wuhan's lockdown.[399]

Used throughout history, controlled opposition can disinform and discredit a regime's opponents by convincing them of false information. Second, it can lull opponents into complacency with leaders who give them false hope. Finally, it can misdirect opponents to focus on activities that do not threaten the regime.

By using controlled opposition figures to sponsor the COVID-19 lab leak and bioweapon theories, the CCP advanced each of these goals. First, CCP opponents were wrongfully convinced that

SARS-CoV-2 was exceptionally dangerous—its origins worth investigating. Second, CCP opponents were lulled into complacency, following leaders who promised to find the virus' origin, but who had no real intention of holding the CCP accountable. Finally, opponents of the CCP could be misdirected to pour their energies into a wild goose chase to find SARS-CoV-2's origin, while opposition to lockdowns was silenced.

The CCP used the Wuhan lab as a decoy to distract hawkish officials while laundering totalitarian lockdown policies into "science." But western leaders refused to acknowledge or investigate this disinformation operation, fixating on the origin of the virus.

It may seem strange that world leaders and intelligence officials failed to see the clear signs that the CCP had been promoting lockdowns and fear of COVID-19. The fake videos, the fake whistleblowers, the first WHO official to tell the world to "copy China" being unwilling to say "Taiwan" weeks later—it all looks obvious in hindsight. But intelligence officials were far from the only ones fooled; when the world first shut down in March 2020, there was astonishingly little resistance.

Owing to their secrecy, the public tends to perceive intelligence agencies as omnipotent. But the western intelligence community has experienced several failures in living memory: The Vietnam quagmire, the failure to stop the September 11 attacks, the misidentification of weapons of mass destruction (WMDs) in Iraq, the Afghanistan debacle; echoes of all these failures can be found in the failure to stop the CCP's lockdown fraud. By contrast, for all their inefficiencies, totalitarian regimes are always able to harness their top analytical minds for military strategy.

What's more, intelligence officials tend to be proud. As Vietnam, Iraq, and Afghanistan made clear, intelligence officials can take years to admit an embarrassing mistake. Politicians could also block whatever information the intelligence community produced on the CCP's influence on lockdowns—just as prior administrations had long blocked intelligence about the futility of the Vietnam War or the nonexistence of Iraqi WMDs.

And, simply enough, though the public widely believed it was intelligence officials' job to stop CCP influence on lockdown policies, fraud in scientific policies wasn't technically in their job description. Suffice to say that few people ever considered the use of public health for geopolitical domination. Of course, this oversight is exactly why public health so appealed to the CCP. Public health is the most collaborative field in international relations. Health professionals have a reputation for being a bit gullible, owing to their work in a high-trust environment. At the same time, they enjoy unparalleled public trust. What better conduit to popularize totalitarianism as "science"?

The hard truth is that an enormous portion of the China-watching, human rights, journalism, and think tank community is controlled opposition to the CCP—financially restrained from reporting anything that might be too damaging to China. The result is a mass abdication of responsibility for monitoring the CCP's worst activities, dumping responsibility for such information on independent investigators.[400]

Many who work in the intelligence community, newsrooms, think tanks, and other elite institutions would be shocked to learn they'd been used as controlled opposition. But when their prestigious employers insist they believe something, however absurd—even something obscenely charitable to the CCP, like the idea that the CCP eliminated COVID-19 from China by shutting down Wuhan for two months—they generally believe them. Thus, the CCP was able to extend its Party line to these organizations, and they either supported or stayed silent about the global adoption of lockdown policies.

The CCP knows western intelligence capabilities better than anyone in the world—including the intelligence agencies themselves. Whether by corruption or incompetence, the CCP knew intelligence officials wouldn't stop lockdowns, lulling the public into complacency.

That politicians and media outlets were, by 2021, talking about a lab leak while ignoring the thousands of citizens slaughtered by China's bad guidance on mechanical ventilators was a demonstration of controlled opposition at work. Regardless of one's views on lockdowns, *everyone* should have been outraged by the bad ventilator guidance that killed thousands of innocent patients. Leaders' silence on this subject spoke volumes as to their credibility on holding Beijing accountable for anything, especially complex virological theories.

For the political right, the lab leak theory was a bit like "follow the science" was to the political left. Many of those loyal to the political right saw leaders endorsing the lab leak theory and fell in line. Just as the Soviets had learned through their domination of Eastern Europe, democracy could be subverted more easily by corrupting officials on both the left and the right. Corrupt one side and you can mislead 40 or 50% of the population; corrupt both sides and you can mislead 80 or 90% of the population.

Furthermore, the lab investigation was only necessary because Beijing refused to reveal what they knew about the virus—which refusal was, in itself, an unforgivable crime. The interminable lab investigation presupposed evil on the part of the CCP, as if that evil were a phenomenon the world simply had to accept and work around. That, itself, was a psychological game. Any decent regime would have revealed everything it knew about SARS-CoV-2 voluntarily. This could be added to the CCP's already-long list of crimes, all of which were happening in broad daylight. The CCP's tentacles in the western world reached far deeper than most citizens realized. Their real crime, using collaborators, fraudulent science, and propaganda to transform lockdowns into science, was hiding in plain sight. Anyone honestly concerned with holding the CCP accountable should have been talking about it.

No one was more concerned about what transpired at the Wuhan lab than Xi Jinping. These scientists, playing around with superviruses, putting everyone in danger! Xi was glad his work could shed light on this alarming practice. Now, out of an abundance of caution, the west would have to stay shut down. For years, if possible. Forever? Just as good. After all, there was so much about this virus we didn't know.

Xi was deeply hurt that no one believed him capable of shutting down the world. How many evil deeds must one do to earn these leaders' respect? Would he ever be good enough for them?

But he expected as much. Xi had always admired those westerners who'd won the Second World War, defeating the Nazis and the Japanese invaders. But with that generation gone, now the west was fat and plump, like a small calf waiting to be sliced into a nice veal chop.

Intellectuals had long foreseen the usefulness of disease to tyrants. As CS Lewis wrote in 1949: "If crime and disease are to be regarded as the same thing, it follows that any state of mind which our masters choose to call 'disease' can be treated as crime; and compulsorily cured."[401] Lockdowns further built on the work of Stanley Milgram, whose experiments proved that people can be convinced to commit atrocities when ordered to do so by scientific authorities. Xi's lockdowns were essentially a giant Milgram experiment, with leaders instructed by "experts" in lab coats to immiserate their own people. That only a small handful stood against lockdowns vindicated Milgram's findings.

The CCP's initial "medical guidance" from Wuhan was designed to inflict death in three ways: 1. Excessive use of mechanical ventilators, killing patients outright; 2. Moving still-sick patients to nursing homes, ostensibly to clear up hospital space; and 3. The deprivation of lockdowns themselves, increasing deaths from all other causes.[402] That initial spike in deaths from China's "medical guidance" would be used as proof of COVID-19's danger, sowing the fear that would justify further lockdowns.

PCR tests were calibrated to produce an endless supply of "cases," even if they were picking up nothing more than the residue of ordinary cold viruses, while an endless supply of absurd models could always justify more lockdowns. There was dark humor in Xi's use of a common coronavirus for the lockdown fraud. If the "west" was so spineless as to destroy itself over a cold, was it really worth saving?

Forcing workers into their homes isolated them from their neighbors, initiating the loss of empathy necessary for them to support tyrannical measures. This simultaneously forced them into the CCP's information environment, allowing the CCP to control public opinion through disinformation. Mask mandates ensured individuals bore a constant symbol of submission to the lie of a supervirus necessitating previously-unconstitutional mandates.

Xi was especially proud of his contributions to the field of social distancing. For this purpose, "social distancing rules" were simply any rules to which constitutional principles did not apply. As COVID-19 "cases" increased, more and more "social distancing" rules would be needed. First, protests would be denounced as "inessential."[403] Then snitching—among the most tried-and-true methods of totalitarian regimes—would be introduced, isolating individuals in a world where they could be ratted out anytime.[404]

It's no coincidence that lockdowns were specifically designed to ruin small businesses. They're the one asset the CCP can't easily buy. The shakedown of small businesses increased both the value of CCP's assets and its control of the world's resources. Western oligarchs would quickly intuit that their own self-interest now aligned with the CCP and support lockdowns regardless of any actual data.

In truth, of course, Xi loathed no one more than decadent western oligarchs. In due time they too would discover their services were no longer required, they had no country left to defend them, and now their corporations belonged to Xi.

The CCP's financial ties with social media companies policing "misinformation" would facilitate the censorship necessary to prevent leaders from easing the public's hysteria.[405] Xi was very concerned with issues of racial justice, and especially worried about the spread of racially charged rumors online. The clever Chinaman using "public health" to subvert the liberal order... where did people get these ideas?

As COVID-19 and its endless "variants" flourished unabated, one human right after another would be stripped in the vain hope that it would eliminate the pesky virus as the CCP's "real lockdown" had done in Wuhan. Vaccines would be dangled like cat toys in front of fearful populations, each one proving futile, but ratifying all the human rights abuses on which they'd been premised. Draconian health passports would qualify long-cherished rights on compliance with arbitrary government mandates, laying the groundwork for a social credit system and producing an endless supply of scapegoats in those who refused to consent to the lies and diktats of the new regime.

Lockdowns were, of course, never really meant to end. First it was "flatten the curve," then the "second wave," then "control the virus," then "wait for a vaccine," then "variants." All a bait-and-switch to gradually strip the world of human rights. In time, all such rights would be stripped, information would be censored, and the world would effectively be China. But the "exceptional" virus and its variants would remain, calling for indefinite, previously-unconstitutional measures—the "new normal."

The suspension of all economic activity would mandate unprecedented unemployment subsidies and transfer payments. Under the pretext that COVID-19 called for the indefinite suspension of rights, puppet politicians would keep populations in check as natural resources and public works were stripped from one country after another.

Tracing and government "quarantine centers," first used to arbitrarily quarantine COVID-positive patients, could easily be transitioned to the preemptive monitoring and "quarantine" of those opposed to "public health" mandates. Under the same philosophy of *fangkong* that had inspired lockdowns, entire resistant populations could even be "quarantined" wholesale, just as the Uyghurs had been. Given minority populations tended to be more resistant to public health diktats, were governments quarantining germs or quarantining minorities? Such was the versatility of *fangkong*.

If anyone ever asked how all this could be necessary, the answer would be simple: "The science." And who, one might ask, determined "the science?" That was easy: your leader, Xi Jinping, Chairman of the World.

CHAPTER VIII

TOGETHER APART

Each act, each occasion, is worse than the last, but only a little worse. You wait for the next and the next... But the one great shocking occasion, when tens or hundreds or thousands will join with you, never comes. That's the difficulty. If the last and worst act of the whole regime had come immediately after the first and smallest, thousands, yes, millions would have been sufficiently shocked... In between come all the hundreds of little steps, some of them imperceptible, each of them preparing you not to be shocked by the next...

And one day, too late, your principles, if you were ever sensible of them, all rush in upon you. The burden of self-deception has grown too heavy ... and you see that everything, everything, has changed and changed completely under your nose. The world you live in—your nation, your people—is not the world you were born in at all. The forms are all there, all untouched, all reassuring, the houses, the shops, the jobs, the mealtimes, the visits, the concerts, the cinema, the holidays. But the spirit, which you never noticed because you made the lifelong mistake of identifying it with the forms, is changed. Now you live in a world of hate and fear, and the people who hate and fear do not even know it themselves; when everyone is transformed, no one is transformed. – Milton Mayer, They Thought They Were Free, 1955

Xi Jinping would never forget the day he met Bill Gates. It was May 2012, during Gates's visit to Beijing.[406] Gates was a longtime Sinophile, and he and Xi met twice more in 2013 and 2015, each time seeking deeper scientific collaboration.[407]

Xi felt a connection to Bill unlike anything he'd felt before. The feeling was mutual. "I'm impressed with how hard President Xi works," Gates admired, fascinated by the peculiar interest Xi seemed to show in public health. "He's quite amazing in that he's able to contribute in a number of ways."[408] Xi and Gates met a fourth time during Xi's 2015 trip to Seattle, where Xi announced new collaborations with the University of Washington, home to the Institute for Health Metrics, second-most influential COVID-19 modeler after Imperial College.[409] Bill invited Xi over for dinner, but had to cancel the catering when Xi didn't show up.[410] They were married men, after all.

Gates was a vocal advocate for the global adoption of China's lockdown policies throughout 2020 and 2021, and his broad influence pushed many institutions in a pro-lockdown direction. When COVID-19 broke out, Gates sent tens of millions of dollars to the CCP to assist with China's response, for which Xi wrote him a personal thank you note.[411] Xi would make sure that money went to good use.

Gates expressed exasperation with the west in contrast to China's apparent success, telling CNN: "You know, China did a lot of things right at the beginning."[412] Gates complained that "freedom" was hindering the western response; China, by contrast, "did a very good job of suppressing the virus," thanks, in part, to the "typical, fairly authoritarian" approach and the "individual rights that were violated."[413]

In an August 2021 interview, Gates called for "all countries" to be "more like Australia"; parts of Australia were then exceeding 200 days in strict lockdown, protests had been banned, and the military had been deployed as COVID cases reached all-time highs.[414] Gates went on, suggesting, "People don't like flu and common cold, and we can build tools that, over time, can get rid of those as well," implying that, after eliminating COVID-19, governments could go on to eliminate the flu and common cold through strict lockdown measures.[415]

By mid-2021, Gates's reputation began to spiral following the revelation of his divorce from Melinda, his wife of 27 years. Media reports revealed that Gates had had a close relationship with sex trafficker Jeffrey Epstein and had "pursued women who worked for him at Microsoft and the Bill and Melinda Gates Foundation."[416] Amid these revelations, Chinese interpreter Zhe "Shelly" Wang publicly denied having an affair with Gates, posting an article defending her as "an innocent Chinese girl."[417]

We may never know just how many westerners supported the CCP's COVID-19 narrative because of their relationships with China. But the fact that the pandemic guidelines of the WHO and nearly every developed nation were discarded to make way for lockdowns—and the vast majority of the public was neither consulted nor informed of this decision—suggests that the corruption ran very deep. The CCP's lockdowns were laundered into science with shockingly little debate, and many scientists, health officials, and other professionals showed an unusual sycophancy toward China in advocating their continuation.

In a May 2020 interview for China Central Television, Richard Horton, editor-in-chief of the once-esteemed medical journal The Lancet, emphatically praised China's lockdowns:

> It was not only the right thing to do, but it also showed other countries how they should respond in the face of

such an acute threat. So, I think we have a great deal to thank China for...[418]

In August, Horton doubled down in a full-throated piece that had surprisingly little to do with public health:

> The "century of humiliation," when China was dominated by a colonially-minded west and Japan, only came to an end with the Communist victory in the civil war in 1949... Every contemporary Chinese leader, including Xi Jinping, has seen their task as protecting the territorial security won by Mao and the economic security achieved by Deng.[419]

In March 2020, The Lancet published a "Statement in support of the scientists, public health professionals, and medical professionals of China combatting COVID-19."[420] On October 8, 2020, The Lancet published a ringing endorsement of China's pandemic response: *China's successful control of COVID-19*.[421] This was met with high praise by Chen Weihua, China Daily EU Bureau Chief:

> Despite ignorance by many in the West, this article by The Lancet is a powerful endorsement of China's successful pandemic response. Hate to read stories by those paparazzi journalists who are experts at spinning but have little knowledge of science.[422]

Many top health officials were not only very unqualified but also demonstrated conspicuous pro-China bias. Matt Hancock was an economist with no background in health or science before becoming health secretary of the U.K. Prior to COVID-19, Hancock showed little interest in his role: "For him, it's all about promoting himself and using it as a stepping stone to his next job," said one NHS chief. "His belief that tech can solve many of the NHS's difficulties had led to him being derided by people he needs to respect him."[423] Hancock was especially keen on adopting tech from China, leading a 2018 delegation to China "to look at collaborating with our Chinese counterparts to harness the power of tech & innovation in healthcare."[424]

In April 2020, Hancock and his Chinese counterpart Ma Xioawei discussed collaboration during COVID-19: "Hancock spoke highly of China's commitment to fighting COVID-19 and China-UK cooperation during the pandemic, and said that the UK is willing to enhance exchanges and collaboration with China..."[425] Three weeks later, Hancock and Ma held a digital meeting of high-level officials from China and the U.K. in a bid to increase cooperation—including "lockdown-lifting strategies:"

> Hancock said he appreciated the cooperation so far ... and expressed that the UK is willing to strengthen anti-epidemic cooperation with China and to use the epidemic prevention and control agreements as an opportunity to deepen bilateral health and global health cooperation... They held in-depth discussions on topics including lockdown-lifting strategies and reiterated their willingness to strengthen experience sharing and technical cooperation to jointly safeguard the people of the two countries.[426]

In 2021, Hancock resigned after salacious footage leaked of him breaking his own lockdown rules to commiserate with his married mistress.[427]

Canada's top health minister, Patty Hajdu, who had no apparent background in epidemiology or infectiology, first earned the praise of Chinese foreign spokesperson Hua Chunying in early 2020 for refusing to ban travel from China.[428] In April, Hajdu defended China's COVID-19 data: "There is no indication the data that came out of China in terms of their death rate and infection rate was falsified in any way."[429] When a reporter pointed out a U.S. intelligence report to the contrary, Hajdu scolded, "I would say your question is feeding into conspiracy theories that many people have been perpetuating on the internet."[430] Hajdu was excoriated in Canada's press for "effectively trying to gaslight her own citizens about the conduct of a habitually oppressive and untruthful regime."[431] But Hajdu doubled down, praising China's "historic containment efforts."[432] As one commentator noted, "Propaganda Patty ... appears to be one of the only people on Earth who actually believes China's official virus numbers."[433]

Hajdu continued into September, earning aplomb from Chen Weihua for defending China: "Canadian Health Minister Hajdu is a role model. She is a disappointment to those paparazzi journalists and fearmongers."[434] Hajdu even earned a special nod from China's Ministry of Foreign Affairs: "We noticed relevant reports and applaud the Canadian health minister's objective and fair remarks."[435]

Daniel Andrews, Premier of Victoria, Australia, home to the city of Melbourne, had several advisors with ties to the CCP involved in his uniquely draconian lockdowns—among the strictest in the world.[436] Andrews had previously signed onto Xi Jinping's Belt and Road initiative without informing Australia's Prime Minister, for which he was roundly rebuked.[437] FOIA'd documents show Andrews pitching for money in China in October 2019, with a promise to "facilitate" access to Victoria as "China's gateway to Australia."[438]

Danny Pearson, the MP who led Andrews' Belt and Road negotiations, lauded China's handling of COVID-19.[439] Andrews' long-time staffer, Nancy Yang, attended a course in propaganda at a high-level CCP academy and helped spread disinformation early in the COVID-19 crisis.[440] Both Yang and Andrews' senior advisor on China, Marty Mei, were members of the CCP's foremost United Front organization in Victoria.[441] Arthur Wu and Su Junxi, senior figures linked to the CCP's foreign influence operations, served as COVID-19 "community ambassadors" in Andrews' government.[442]

Former CDC director Tom Frieden was another prominent lockdown advocate with long-time ties to China. In 2015, "Frieden praised the public health partnership between China and the United States," according to Global Times.[443] In 2017, Frieden joined China in backing Tedros Adhanom as director of the WHO: "Tedros is an excellent choice to lead WHO. He succeeded in Ethiopia, making remarkable health progress..."[444] On the contrary, as was widely known at the time, Tedros had helped Ethiopia's regime cover up three cholera epidemics during his time as Minister of Public Health.[445] As a senior member of the Tigray People's Liberation Front, Tedros "was a crucial decision maker in relation to security service actions that included killing, arbitrarily detaining and torturing Ethiopians" and was "personally responsible for brutal repression of the Amhara people, using aid money selectively to starve them out and deny them access to basic services"—war crimes for which charges of genocide were submitted against him at The Hague.[446]

Susan Michie, a leading member of the U.K.'s Scientific Advisory Group for Emergencies and a 40-year member of the British Communist Party, was very impressed with the CCP's Wuhan lockdown: "Exemplary response to home confinement of children due to #COVID19 in China. Could UK Government do this?"[447] By June 2021, Michie was advocating for the U.K.'s lockdown policies to last forever: "Test, trace and isolate system, border controls are really essential ... social distancing ... wearing face masks ... we'll need to keep these going in the long term ... I think forever."[448]

When asked on Good Morning Britain whether her membership in the Communist Party might inform her draconian policy preferences, Michie expressed outrage: "I've come on your program as a scientist... You don't ask other scientists about politics, so I'm very happy to speak about science, which is what my job is, and to limit it to that."[449] Michie was a behavioral psychologist with no background in epidemiology or infectious disease.

Jorge Cuyubamba popularized lockdowns in Peru. Cuyubamba was widely believed to be one of Peru's leading experts based on 10 years he spent as a "doctor" in China, but it was later revealed that he actually had no science or health background; he'd spent 10 years in China studying filmmaking.[450]

Dr. Leana Wen, a frequent CNN medical contributor and one of the most influential voices in the U.S. response to COVID-19, became famous for her frequent, vocal advocacy of coercive vaccination measures. In July 2021, Wen suggested: "It needs to be hard for people to remain unvaccinated... Mandates by workplaces, by schools, I think it will be important to say ... you have to sign these forms, have to get twice weekly testing ... make getting vaccinated the easy choice."[451] Wen was a WEF Young Global Leader and a fellow at the heavily China-centric Brookings Institution. Her family had been granted political asylum from the CCP to come to the U.S.—but that didn't appear to stop her from returning to work in China; Wen "served as a consultant to the WHO, Brookings Institution, and the China Medical Board, and ... conducted international health systems research in ... China."[452]

Eric Feigl-Ding, a WEF Global Shaper, became a major pro-lockdown celebrity with his long series of wildly-inaccurate COVID tweets. This led to several interview spots with CNN and the New York Times, despite his evident lack of qualifications and his being denounced as a "charlatan" by prominent scientists on all sides.[453] In one example, Ding admired a CCP publicity

stunt in which China sent its hockey team to Sweden in hazmat
suits to emphasize Sweden's lack of COVID restrictions—though
Sweden had among the fewest COVID-19 cases of any country at
the time:

> Behold—Chinese hockey players upon arrival in the
> dangerous land of mask-resistant, no-kids-under-16-
> vaccination, pro-natural-mass-infection, let folks-get-
> infected, record excess death country... also known as
> Sweden (where its COVID chief Tegnell is anti-
> mainstream-science).[454]

From the earliest possible date, physicist Yaneer Bar-Yam urged
the global adoption of China's lockdowns. Bar-Yam launched the
website www.endcoronavirus.org in February 2020, quickly
translated into 17 languages.[455] In March 2020, Bar-Yam
defended China's data in contrast to the U.S.: "Actually, the
numbers in the US are underreported because of limited testing.
This is known. Many said the numbers in China are
underreported, nobody has shown evidence. If you have it show
it or take a seat."[456] "Speculations about the problems in China
with data are projections."[457] Bar-Yam spent over a year
advocating China's lockdowns—including the CCP's murderous
"wartime" lockdown in Xinjiang: "17 new cases, shut the city
down. Don't give it a chance. China coronavirus: 'Wartime state'
declared for Urumqi in Xinjiang."[458]

In 2021, a clique of woefully-unqualified scientists and
influencers—led in part by Eric Feigl-Ding, Tomas Pueyo, and
Yaneer Bar-Yam—joined in the cause of advocating lockdowns as
long and strict as necessary to supposedly eliminate COVID-19
under the banner of "#ZeroCovid."[459] The stated goal of
ZeroCovid was, of course, impossible. The group's imprimatur
was thus continuing public dedication to the lie that China had,
in fact, eliminated COVID-19 through its strict lockdown of
Wuhan. In meetings, at no point would ZeroCovid supporters

concern themselves with epidemiology or whether lockdowns were moral, legal, necessary, or even effective. Rather, the sole concern of ZeroCovid "science" was psychological: How to get the public to comply.[460] Without fail, ZeroCovid supporters—whether "scientists," influencers, or otherwise—would insist that China's manifestly-fraudulent data was real. When asked to define a "real" lockdown—one which had succeeded in a mainland country—they could point to only one example: China.

These scientists and health officials were far from alone in their admiration for the CCP. The co-founders of CanSino Biologics, a Chinese vaccine company working with Canada, were found to be members of the CCP's Thousand Talents Plan for co-opting scientists.[461] According to the Harvard Crimson, the largest gift in the history of Harvard's Chan School of Public Health came in part from a "pawn of the CCP," a "cheerleader for a government responsible for significant humanitarian crises" through a series of shell companies.[462]

In June 2020, the U.S. National Institutes of Health (NIH) disclosed that 189 of its grantees, including Charles Lieber, chair of Harvard's chemistry department, had received undisclosed funding from foreign governments.[463] By April 2021, the number of NIH grantees under investigation by the FBI had grown to over 500; 90% of the foreign ties were with China.[464]

No one toed the CCP's lines on COVID-19 more reliably than NIH Director Anthony Fauci. In 2021, a series of leaked emails shed light on Fauci's endorsement of a national shutdown of the United States. Fauci was generally dismissive of scientists who reached his inbox. In one example, on March 18, 2020, a physicist and CEO named Erik Nilsen sent Fauci a prophetic email accurately describing key aspects of China's lockdown fraud and predicting how it would transpire:

I'm a physicist and have been modeling this outbreak since January... I'm confident that China stop counting dead COVID-19 infected bodies since January 7, 2020. They've been adding fabricated data daily to show ... an impressive flattening of China outbreak curve. It's easy to prove this via data analysis because, for example, improbable coincidences occurred in much of the data. My suspicions were eventually confirmed by at least two of my sources in China... The data posted by China is not only garbage, it has misled the world...

I also have lots of information about USA. Here is some: I believe that many COVID-19 deaths were incorrectly labelled at 2019-2020 flu deaths. The spreading in the USA is almost certainly already homogeneous, because it's been going on since last year without any containment whatsoever. Once massive testing finally starts, this truth/reality will, unfortunately, become obvious. It will manifest itself as hyper exponential (hyperbolic) growth starting a day or two after the millions of testing kits arrive and start being used... I'm 99% sure that SARS-CoV-2 been spreading in the USA since late November / early December last year.

Fauci wrote of Nilsen's email: "Too long for me to read"; the email was 1,700 words.[465]

In sharp contrast, Fauci showed particular affinity for prominent New York Times reporter Donald McNeil—an early advocate of China's lockdown policies.[466] In a February 2020 New York Times podcast, McNeil compared COVID-19 to the Spanish flu and expressed his preferred method to fight it: "You can't leave. You can't see your families. All the flights are canceled. All the trains are canceled. All the highways are closed. You're going to stay inside there. And you're locked in with a deadly disease. We can do it."[467] The next day, the New York Times published

McNeil's article, *To Take on the Coronavirus, Go Medieval on It*, in which he urged the world to follow WHO leader Bruce Aylward's advice and copy China's response to COVID-19:

> The Chinese leader, Xi Jinping, was able to seal off the city of Wuhan, where the Covid-19 outbreak began, because China is a place where a leader can ask himself, 'What would Mao do?' and just do it... The head of the W.H.O. team that visited China said this week that China 'took one of the most ancient strategies and rolled out one of the most ambitious, agile and aggressive disease-containment efforts in history.'[468]

"What would Mao do" indeed. The leaked emails reveal McNeil's target audience: Fauci himself. Fauci had been in constant contact with McNeil throughout the early weeks of the COVID-19 crisis. On February 25, McNeil wrote to Fauci on how impressed he was with the Wuhan lockdown:

> In China, we in the media tend to report the horrors and the lockdown and the government's early lies... But the truth is that a lot of average Chinese behaved incredibly heroically in the face of the virus... Meanwhile, in America, people tend to act like selfish pigs interested only in saving themselves.

"You make some very good points Donald," Fauci replied.[469]

McNeil expressed great admiration for Bruce Aylward. On March 4, 2020, McNeil published Aylward's Q&A on the Wuhan lockdown: "I know there's suspicion, but ... I didn't see anything that suggested manipulation of numbers. A rapidly escalating outbreak has plateaued, and come down faster than would have been expected." Fauci congratulated McNeil on the article: "Your interview with Bruce Aylward was the best discussion of COVID-19 that I have seen thus far. Great job!"[470]

But even more telling than what is in Fauci's emails is what isn't. At no point does Fauci explain his March 15 decision to endorse a national shutdown. Instead, through February and early March, Fauci wrote that he was well aware SARS-CoV-2 was flu-like, the healthy weren't at risk, store-bought masks weren't effective, asymptomatic spread was rare, the virus "may diminish as weather gets warmer," and "social distancing is not really geared to wait for a vaccine."[471] On February 28, 2020, Fauci even published an article in the New England Journal of Medicine stating that "the overall clinical consequences of Covid-19 may ultimately be more akin to those of a severe seasonal influenza (which has a case fatality rate of approximately 0.1%) or a pandemic influenza (similar to those in 1957 and 1968) rather than a disease similar to SARS or MERS."[472] On March 9, Fauci said it was okay for healthy people to board cruise ships, and as late as March 13, Fauci questioned draconian measures.[473] Then, two days later, he nonchalantly shut America down.[474]

Both the New York Times and celebrity author Michael Lewis endorsed a narrative in which U.S. lockdowns were based on the work of Richard Hatchett, Carter Mecher, and Robert Glass, inspired by a science fair project by Glass's 14-year-old daughter.[475] Their work had culminated in the document *Community Mitigation Guidelines to Prevent Pandemic Influenza – United States, 2017.*[476] But this narrative is false. Fauci's emails show no indication that the work of Hatchett, Mecher, and Glass played any role in his call for a national shutdown. Nor are the *Community Mitigation Guidelines* ever mentioned. Indeed, as Judge Stickman noted in *Cnty. of Butler v. Wolf*, nothing even remotely approximating lockdowns is mentioned in the *Community Mitigation Guidelines*, which recommend only "*voluntary* home isolation of ill persons," and "*voluntary* home quarantine of exposed household members," even for a "Very High Severity pandemic."[477]

Contrary to the narrative promoted by the New York Times, Fauci's decision to shut down America appears to have been influenced almost entirely by the endorsement of the CCP's Wuhan lockdown by Bruce Aylward and Donald McNeil—both of whom expressed admiration for China's leaders and one of whom disconnected a live interview when asked to acknowledge Taiwan.[478]

Fauci continued to endorse one COVID-19 mandate after another. First it was a two-week national shutdown, then indefinite school closures, then mask mandates, then lockdowns until vaccines were available, then two masks, then masking years into the future due to the sudden onset of "variants." In a March 2021 hearing, Senator Rand Paul finally took Fauci to task:

> Fauci: 'You're not hearing what I'm saying about variants. We're talking about wild type versus variants...'
>
> Paul: 'You're making policy based on conjecture. You have the conjecture that we're going to get variants, so you want people to wear a mask for another couple years ... you're defying everything we know about immunity ... People don't want to hear it and there's no science behind it.'[479]

Just two months later, Fauci made an abrupt U-turn on post-immunity masking, indicating he'd actually agreed with Paul the whole time:

> Before the CDC made the recommendation change, I didn't want to look like I was giving mixed signals, but being a fully vaccinated person, the chances of my getting infected in an indoor setting is extremely low, and that's the reason why in indoor settings now I feel comfortable about not wearing a mask because I'm fully vaccinated.[480]

The idiosyncrasy of Fauci's policies could perhaps be explained by a University of Edinburgh panel in which he participated alongside Chinese CDC Director Zhong Nanshan. Chinese state media had often described Zhong as "China's Fauci." As Chinese foreign spokesperson Hua Chunying wrote:

> China's #Fauci Dr. Zhong Nanshan was awarded Medal of the Republic for his outstanding contributions to China's fight against #COVID19. He was the first to warn of human-to-human transmission. We are so sad to learn Dr. Fauci got harassment, even death threats.[481]

In the University of Edinburgh panel, Zhong shared a wealth of false information about China's COVID-19 response.[482] Zhong's slides presented China as having had the world's best COVID-19 response and the U.S. as having had the world's worst response, which he attributed to the Wuhan lockdown, repeating the lie that it had eliminated the virus from China. Zhong concluded by urging other countries not to reopen and to instead wait until the entire world was vaccinated, describing natural immunity as "less scientific." Fauci endorsed Zhong's comments, saying he "would underscore everything that Professor Zhong said."[483] "To emphasize something that both of us said; if we do not completely suppress this, we will continue to be challenged by variants which have a way of coming back to bite us."

As late as May 2021, Fauci was advising the government of India to "learn from China's experience fighting Covid-19" and to implement a complete national lockdown for "a few weeks."[484] By that time, lockdowns had already killed more than 228,000 children in South Asia.[485]

When life for many Americans ground to a halt by virtue of the strange diktats coming from the likes of Fauci and his admirers, many flocked to Florida.[486] Governor Ron DeSantis had initially shut Florida down on the advice of health authorities, but was one of the few politicians who quickly and publicly recognized his error. By August 2020, DeSantis had vowed Florida "will never do one of these lockdowns again."[487]

DeSantis became a vocal opponent of COVID-19 mandates, urging local governments to repeal them.[488] As Florida's health outcomes proved no worse than states that had long enforced draconian measures, DeSantis became an early front-runner for the 2024 Republican presidential nomination.[489] In 2021, DeSantis became the first major political leader to publicly share his belief that the CCP had influenced the world's lockdown policies, stating as much in a series of interviews:

> The west did a lot of damage to itself by adopting some of these policies, which have proven to not work to stop the spread, but to be very economically destructive. I do think there was an information operation angle to this, where they really believed that if they could get these other countries to lock down, and they were willing to do some propaganda along the way, particularly in Europe, that ultimately would help China. And I think it has helped China.[490]

DeSantis told Newsweek that "the CCP was one of the largest proponents for lockdowns during the pandemic and that those ideas were supported through interference from Big Tech."[491] As he explained to Fox News's Maria Bartiromo in June:

> You look at how big tech has handled the CCP, they are very deferential to the Communist Party of China. And I think that China was very much invested in promoting lockdowns as we started getting into 2020, February, March. Obviously, Italy, those Italy lockdowns were very much patterned off what we saw in Wuhan. And Facebook and some of these big companies, they were really serving to elevate the lockdown hysteria and to absolutely suppress people who were raising questions

and concerns about lockdowns. And the reason why that's so galling is because, up until COVID, public health guidance was never, in a pandemic, to just lock down indefinitely. This was kind of a new invention that was really fueled by the Chinese experience.[492]

Throughout the COVID-19 crisis, western nations experienced the greatest backslide in civil liberties since the Second World War. No one described this madness more articulately than former U.K. Supreme Court Justice Jonathan Sumption. In February 2021, Lord Sumption wrote:

> Ministers discarded a decade of planning in a few hours and embarked on a sinister and untried experiment with the lives of millions. They ordered a national lockdown which was both coercive and indiscriminate. That decision, I believe, was nothing to do with the science. They were panicked to act by seeing recently ordered lockdowns in Italy, France and Spain, following the lead of totalitarian China.[493]

Lord Sumption went on:

> The problem is perfectly encapsulated in a recent interview with Professor Neil Ferguson, whose projections were used to justify the first lockdown last March. Before that, as Prof Ferguson related in that interview, Sage had concluded that the Chinese lockdown had worked but was out of the question in Europe. 'It's a communist, one-party state, we said. We couldn't get away with it in Europe, we thought. And then Italy did it. And we realised we could ... If China had not done it, the year would have been very different.'
>
> China is not a liberal democracy. It is a totalitarian state. It treats human beings as so many tools of state policy. There is no personal space which the state cannot invade

at will. Liberal democracies have good reasons of political morality for not wishing to be like China... Many people believe that it is OK to be like China for a time, because when the crisis ends we can go back to being like Britain again. These people are making a serious mistake. We cannot switch in and out of totalitarianism at will. Because a free society is a question of attitude, it is dead once the attitude changes.[494]

Later, Lord Sumption continued:

Now, actually the reasons why we did not behave like China before March 2020 were not just pragmatic reasons. It wasn't that we thought it wouldn't work. The reasons were essentially moral... Well, now there are disputes about whether it does work... The result has been that what began as a public health crisis is still a public health crisis, but it's an economic crisis, an educational crisis, a moral crisis, and a social crisis on top of that. The last four aspects of this crisis, which are much the worst aspects, are entirely manmade.[495]

Of course, every COVID-19 restriction was *per se* unconstitutional. The lockdown operation was never meant to be legal. The initial lockdowns had been intended as a psychological blitz that overwhelmed normal legal and ethical processes through shock, coercion, and groupthink. And the world's high courts had largely stepped aside and let it all happen.

Opinions by the United States Supreme Court shed light on the predominant thinking of judges at the time. To justify all the draconian measures to which Americans had been subject, the Supreme Court and its followers used *Jacobson v. Massachusetts*, a 1905 case in which a man was fined $5 (about $150 today) for refusing a smallpox vaccine.[496] A man of principle, Mr. Jacobson had taken his case all the way to

Washington, where the fine was upheld; he paid the five bucks
and went on his way. A single paragraph written by Chief Justice
John Roberts in *South Bay United Pentecostal Church v. Gavin
Newsom* is essentially all the Supreme Court ever wrote about
COVID-19 mandates:

> The precise question of when restrictions on particular
> social activities should be lifted during the pandemic is a
> dynamic and fact-intensive matter subject to reasonable
> disagreement. Our Constitution principally entrusts
> '[t]he safety and the health of the people' to the politically
> accountable officials of the States 'to guard and protect.'
> *Citing Jacobson v. Massachusetts.*[497]

Roberts' opinion is problematic in several respects. First,
Jacobson had been overruled many times, not least because it
was subsequently used to justify eugenics in *Buck v. Bell*, a
decision that was then cited by several Nazi leaders at the
Nuremberg trials.[498] The resurrection of *Jacobson* has been
compared to "resurrecting *Dred Scott*, *Plessy v. Ferguson*, or
Korematsu"—historical Supreme Court cases referred to as
"anticanon" owing to not only their lack of intellectual rigor but
to the awful human tragedies they precipitated.[499]

U.S. federal courts apply certain standards to determine the
constitutionality of actions affecting individual rights. "Strict
scrutiny" is used where fundamental rights are concerned—not
least of which is the right to bodily autonomy: "No right is held
more sacred, or is more carefully guarded by the common law,
than the right of every individual to the possession and control of
his own person, free from all restraint or interference of
others."[500] Even where the affected rights are not considered
fundamental, the policies are subject to "rational basis scrutiny."
Instead of applying strict or rational basis scrutiny, the Supreme
Court appears to have applied "zero scrutiny"—exerting precisely
zero effort to determine if any of these COVID mandates actually

advanced their purported goal of reducing viral transmission. Roberts waves off this question as a "dynamic and fact-intensive matter," as if expert testimony is out of the question.

Roberts asserts that "medical and scientific" actions of "politically accountable officials" should not be second-guessed by an "unelected federal judiciary"—apparently forgetting that not only are health officials unelected, but "second guessing" the actions of officials is the sole purpose of judicial review. Courts are meant to uphold rights in spite of the whims of officials, precisely because political accountability is such a lengthy and imperfect process. Further, Roberts' opinion depends on a specific word: "Pandemic." "Pandemic" had no legal definition; it was determined by the same officials issuing lockdown mandates, and lobbyists were actively lobbying for a "permanent pandemic."[501]

Finally, whereas the fine at issue in Jacobson was $5, lockdown policies cost the United States upwards of $16 trillion.[502] But with that one paragraph in *South Bay*, Roberts set a superprecedent, signaling that U.S. courts should essentially never interfere in deciding what orders were constitutional during a "pandemic."[503] The Supreme Court simply declined to review virtually any challenges to COVID mandates, effectively suspending all legal accountability as lockdowns unfolded.

Roberts' decision in *South Bay* differs from *Dred Scott*, *Plessy v. Ferguson*, or *Korematsu* in that whereas they contained lengthy, obtuse analyses, *South Bay* is an inadequate analysis in which the Court failed to recognize the gravity of the issue altogether. One of the greatest suspensions of civil liberties in American history was occurring, and the Supreme Court simply abdicated its duty out of deference to wolves cloaked in the sheepskin of "science." Insofar as human tragedies are concerned, no Supreme Court case comes close to *Dred Scott*, one of many avoidable decisions that rended a nation in two, taking a toll that would recoup every drop of blood drawn with the lash and consign vast swathes of the Antebellum South to ashes in the wind. But in light of lockdowns' unimaginable toll and the ease with which the Supreme Court could have stopped them, it's no exaggeration to compare the Court's one-paragraph dismissal of the Bill of Rights in *South Bay* to the ranks of "anticanon."

The Court's overarching error is the implicit assumption that "restrictions on particular social activities" are legitimately grounded in science. Whether out of diffidence, indifference, complacency, laziness, or simply the same spell of groupthink that had bewitched much of the population, the Supreme Court apparently believed it was not their job to determine whether the pretense of COVID-19 restrictions as "science" was fraudulent.

Roberts could have simply asked his fellow judges on lower courts, some of whom were not so easily fooled. Early in the crisis, the Wisconsin Supreme Court struck down the state's stay-at-home order. Justice Rebecca Bradley described in blistering detail the legal atrocities taking place:

> We mention cases like *Korematsu* in order to test the limits of government authority, to remind the state that urging courts to approve the exercise of extraordinary power during times of emergency may lead to extraordinary abuses of its citizens... These cases, among other similarly despicable examples, illustrate rather painfully why the judiciary cannot dispense with constitutional principles, even in response to a dire emergency... These repugnant cases must be cited to explain the fundamental importance of judicial resistance to popular pressures, which in times of crisis implore judges to cast aside the law in the name of emergency... The DHS secretary-designee bases her authority to enter the Safer at Home Order ... which she characterizes as a

law that 'simply empowers DHS to act'—unilaterally, and with no input from the legislature or the people... In a particularly chilling exchange with this court during oral arguments, the attorney for the state representing the DHS secretary-designee claimed the authoritarian power to authorize the arrest and imprisonment of the people of Wisconsin for engaging in lawful activities proscribed by the DHS secretary-designee in her sole discretion...[504]

Judge William Stickman issued the first U.S. federal court decision striking down a stay-at-home order, having discovered that lockdown measures vastly exceeded anything in the CDC's pandemic guidelines and intuiting that "lockdowns in Wuhan and other areas of China—a nation unconstrained by concern for civil liberties and constitutional norms—started a domino effect where one country, and state, after another imposed draconian and hitherto untried measures on their citizens":

The orders are such an inversion of the usual American experience that the Court believes that no less than the highest scrutiny should be used. However, the Court holds that the stay-at-home orders would even fail scrutiny under the lesser intermediate scrutiny... Defendants' orders subjected every Pennsylvanian to a lockdown where he or she was involuntarily committed to stay-at-home unless he or she was going about an activity approved as an exception ... This broad restructuring of the default concept of liberty of movement in a free society eschews any claim to narrow tailoring... Broad population-wide lockdowns are such a dramatic inversion of the concept of liberty in a free society as to be nearly presumptively unconstitutional...[505]

Kentucky Judge Richard Brueggemann ruled all his state's COVID-19 orders unconstitutional following expert testimony to the effect that non-pharmaceutical interventions had netted zero results in stopping the virus:

> Mr. Petty explained that the field of his expertise is 'to anticipate and recognize and control things that could hurt people, everything from making them sick to killing them.' ... He testified that both the six-foot-distancing rule, and mask mandates, are wholly ineffective at reducing the spread of this virus... According to Dr. Stack, federal regulation prohibits labs from reporting to the public the number of cycles it took to yield a positive result during the test... This invites many questions, such as why ... a federal government agency has ordered labs to 'not include Ct values on laboratory reports.'[506]

In Germany, the district court in Weimar issued a devastating ruling that Germany's ban on contact for healthy persons had exceeded what was advised by German public health authorities even in nightmare scenarios. In his conclusion, the Weimar district judge noted the unimaginable damage lockdowns were doing all over the world:

> Having said that, there can be no doubt that the number of deaths caused by the lockdown policy alone is many times the number of deaths prevented by the lockdown... Added to this are the direct and indirect restrictions on freedom, the gigantic financial damage, the immense damage to health and ideal. The word 'disproportionate' is too colorless to even suggest the dimensions of what is happening.[507]

Soon after, the Weimar family court rejected the entire foundation of Germany's COVID-19 measures. The court held that PCR testing was an insufficient basis for determining infection, and found it inappropriate for schools to impose masks or distancing as it conferred no benefit on children, harmed their well-being, hindered their development, and infringed on their rights:

> '100,000 primary school pupils would be forced to suffer all the side effects of wearing masks for a week to prevent just one infection per week.' To call this result merely disproportionate would be a completely inadequate description. Rather, it shows the State legislature regulating this area has become removed from the facts to an extent that seems historic.[508]

The Court of Appeal of Lisbon concluded, "In view of current scientific evidence, this [PCR] test shows itself to be unable to determine beyond reasonable doubt that such positivity corresponds, in fact, to the infection of a person by the SARS-CoV-2 virus," and that "the probability of … receiving a false positive is 97% or higher."[509] A group of scientists sought to have the judges disciplined by the Superior Council for their decision; they were cautioned, but not punished.[510]

These judges' efforts were met with mixed success, and executives complied with their rulings to varying degrees. In El Salvador, President Nayib Bukele enforced a strict lockdown in defiance of both El Salvador's Congress and Supreme Court.[511] But by and large, like the U.S. Supreme Court, the high courts of most countries failed in spectacular fashion. Businessman Simon Dolan led a challenge to the U.K. Government's lockdown measures in May 2020, arguing that the measures were contrary to the Human Rights Act of 1998.[512] Echoing the U.S. Supreme Court, the U.K. Court of Appeal held that the Government should not face a judicial review because "the margin of judgement to be afforded to the executive is particularly wide in this context."[513]

The result was a collective shirking of responsibility for considering whether the pretense of these draconian restrictions as "science"—and the information from China on which they had been based—were fraudulent. When judges actually examined the policies, none withstood even the slightest scrutiny. But the superficial, cosmopolitan cutesiness of public health ensured that by and large, no scrutiny took place.

Perhaps these judges believed that investigating lockdowns from a forensic perspective was someone else's job—either scientists or intelligence agencies, who were largely distracted by the Wuhan lab. Or perhaps lockdowns were such a shameless inversion of enlightenment principles that judges were cowed, thinking they had to be missing something. Whatever the reason, western governments proved unprepared to cope with or even comprehend wide-scale scientific fraud. The judges deferred to the politicians. The politicians deferred to the health officials. The health officials deferred the WHO. The WHO deferred to China. And China deferred to Xi.

In George Orwell's 1984, the four Ministries of Oceania—Ministries of Truth, Love, Peace, and Plenty—are each satirically responsible for perpetuating the exact opposite of that which their names purport. Likewise, virtually every aspect of the "science" the world employed in response to COVID-19 effected the opposite of its stated purpose.

Ventilators, supposedly meant to save patients, actually killed them. Masks, allegedly meant to relieve public anxiety, actually sowed it.[514] Lockdowns, supposedly intended to prevent deaths, actually caused them. Mass PCR testing, declared as necessary to "reopen" the economy, created the endless cases necessary to keep it shut down.[515]

Delaying medical operations, allegedly to protect patients, simply killed them. Stopping the economy was supposed to save it, but actually destroyed it. Anti-lockdown activists fighting for human rights were compared to "neo-Nazis." The "novel" nature of the virus supposedly meant that it could spread asymptomatically and rendered immunity and seasonality irrelevant, but it was actually an ordinary coronavirus.

"The science" flew in the face of all pre-existing science, and forcibly resisted testing and debate—the literal antithesis of real science. And censorship, supposedly to prevent "misinformation," actually prevented the public from learning that none of these policies were based on any real science at all.

Xi Jinping frequently stressed global cooperation in the fight against COVID-19.[516] In turn, the world began to look a lot like China. Autocracies grew more oppressive, and democracies took on autocratic characteristics.[517] Countries unveiled new fleets of surveillance drones; Chinese company DJI, the world's largest drone manufacturer, donated drones to 22 U.S. states to help enforce lockdown rules.[518] DJI was later blacklisted by the U.S. for having "enabled wide-scale human rights abuses within China through abusive genetic collection and analysis or high-technology surveillance, and/or facilitated the export of items by China that aid repressive regimes."[519]

Big tech companies established policies for censoring medical information that ran contrary to the WHO.[520] It was an overtly Orwellian policy; from the earliest days of the crisis, it was widely known that the WHO was in the pocket of the CCP.[521] The renowned Harvard professor and epidemiologist Martin Kulldorff, one of the world's most qualified individuals to opine on public health policies, had his account locked by Twitter for weeks for opining about the unintended consequences of masks.[522] YouTube censored a panel of leading health experts opposed to the masking of children, banning a video that bore directly on democratic accountability.[523]

Health officials grew accustomed to voicing draconian opinions on virtually all aspects of social policy, while silencing those who disagreed. In April 2021, British health officials demanded that the Prime Minister punish Helena Morrissey, a member of the House of Lords, for mentioning the viral fake videos of Wuhan residents falling dead in the streets and for stating—very truthfully—that COVID-19 no longer qualified as a pandemic.[524] In its official denouncement of Dr. Kulvinder Kaur for her vocal criticism of lockdowns in 2021, Ontario's regulator admitted that "information coming from public health" was still relying on "China":

> The lockdowns in China and South Korea provide evidence that lockdowns can and did work in reducing the spread of COVID-19. For the Respondent to state otherwise is misinformed and misleading and furthermore an irresponsible statement to make on social medial during a pandemic.[525]

South Korea never had a lockdown. Paired with Ontario Premier Doug Ford's statement that "there's no politician in this country that's gonna disagree with their chief medical officer," it was no wonder Ontario had some of the world's longest, strictest lockdowns.[526]

In March 2020, Italy had gone into lockdown, followed shortly after by France and then by Germany. In March 2021, Italy again went into lockdown, followed shortly after by France and then by Germany. In April 2021, German Chancellor Angela Merkel held a phone call with Xi Jinping; later that same day, she called for stricter lockdowns in Germany.[527] Incredibly, the German Government's Federal Ministry of Education and Research even produced a study on the implementation of a "social credit system like in China": "In view of the successful use of the social credit system in China, other countries are also discussing the use of such a system."[528]

By 2021, the WHO was not pretending they ever intended for the "pandemic" to end. In August 2020, Tedros stated: "A vaccine on its own will not end the pandemic. Surveillance will need to continue. People will still need to be tested ... contacts will still need to be traced and quarantined."[529] In June 2021, David Nabarro, the WHO's special envoy on coronavirus, officially stated that variants and the WHO's "COVID-ready strategy"—i.e. social distancing—"is going to be the pattern for the foreseeable future."[530] In October 2021, Spain's Minister of Health announced that mask mandates would be kept in place for as long as there was still a seasonal flu: "The masks are here to stay, at least as long we have influenza or other autumn viruses."[531]

For two years, the world watched its political class play dumb about the fact that they'd imported a totalitarian "public health" regime from China. The lockdown fraud held the unique status of being both taboo conspiracy theory and widely-known reality at the same time. In a little over a year, western leaders had introduced lockdowns, mandatory masks, drones, tracing apps, censorship, propaganda, the WEF's "great reset," the "new normal," quarantine centers, vaccine mandates, and "health passes," and expected their citizens to pretend they saw no indication of CCP influence on any of this.

It was tyranny in franchise form. The CCP supplied the lockdown policies, the marketing, the propaganda, and the lie of a supervirus that could be contained and eliminated through illiberal measures. All local politicians had to do was sign the obligatory pronouncements and manage the locals.

Even as elites supported lockdown mandates, few really believed in them. This could be said for certain because, by 2021, it was hard to find any scientists and politicians who hadn't been caught breaking their own COVID rules.[532] It's difficult to explain these actions without concluding that, despite the immiseration of their own people, they just didn't see lockdown restrictions as a very big deal—perhaps owing to how easily they, personally, could break them. The only thing more frightening than the fact that some of them were surely on the CCP's payroll, either directly or indirectly, is that so many of them were not.

At the opening of the 2021 G7 summit, a meeting of seven leading democracies, the leaders made a show of wearing masks, forgoing handshakes, and staying six feet apart for their photo ops.[533] But the very next day, the same leaders posed for photo ops in which they congregated, unmasked, in tight groups.[534] From these photos, it might have seemed like they were sending mixed messages. Not so. The message was loud and clear: "We know you know we're lying about COVID-19. To be one of us, you need to keep lying as well."

Journalist Gerhard Wisnewski characterized the governments' policies as a series of "completely nonsensical and contradictory measures":

> There is a method behind this madness. It is actually a method of torture. Keeping people in constant confusion and plunging them into uncertainty, completely leaving people in the lurch and totally destroying lifestyles... I have found a significant amount of information about these methods, and interestingly enough, they were developed in China... These prisoners of war were permanently harassed with contradictory measures. They could never be sure if they were doing everything right or not ... they are trying to destroy people psychologically, in my opinion.[535]

In April 2021, the Chinese government began downplaying the effectiveness of their own vaccine.[536] This was an extraordinary step, as the CCP hardly ever admits error or fault for anything. Just days later, first the WHO, then Anthony Fauci, Boris Johnson, and Canadian PM Justin Trudeau followed, dramatically downplaying the effectiveness of vaccines and calling for more lockdowns.[537]

The Washington Post floated the possibility of digital vaccine passports in the United States.[538] Early on, China had rolled out a COVID-19 vaccine pass system using color codes for vaccination status; sure enough, the proposed system in the United States used this same color code system.[539] The proposal was widely seen as a political trial balloon by lobbyists and quickly scrapped. But Europe wasn't so lucky. In June 2021, the European Parliament approved digital COVID-19 vaccine passports for travel within the European Union.[540]

Lithuania implemented Europe's strictest vaccine pass system, in which the unvaccinated were banned from nearly all public spaces and employment outside their homes; the few shops where they could purchase bare essentials had to post large red signs on their doors indicating that unvaccinated persons could be present.[541] Six weeks after implementing this system, new COVID cases per capita in Lithuania had soared to record highs, while new cases per capita in Sweden, just 200 miles away, where all restrictions had ended, were the lowest in Europe.[542]

For all their inhumanity, it's unclear that any of these vaccine mandates actually increased vaccine uptake. After Italy mandated a vaccine pass for nearly all workers to access their places of work, the number of Italians choosing to get vaccinated declined sharply.[543] Out of solidarity, many citizens refused to get COVID vaccines for as long as governments tied them to infringements on civil liberties. Regardless of whether they were safe or effective, assenting to human rights restrictions from which they could be released only by waiting for and accepting the latest vaccine was not a precedent many were willing to accept.

In cities across Europe, Australia, and Canada, protesters took to the streets in the tens of thousands to protest against lockdowns, vaccine passes, and other vestiges of CCP-style medical tyranny.[544] The media silence on these protests seemed only to encourage them. The people weren't sure exactly what was going on, but they could tell that something was off and they were being lied to.

A number of grassroots organizations launched challenges to the restrictions. In Switzerland, activists filed criminal charges against the Swiss Corona Task Force, alleging implausible prognoses, manipulation of ICU data, false statements on deaths and hospitalizations, and shifting rationale for lockdown measures.[545] In Germany, a number of investigators found that German hospitals had knowingly underreported ICU capacity to obtain federal funding; Merkel's government was aware of this, but went along with it to drive consent for lockdowns.[546]

Pennsylvania became the first U.S. state to amend its constitution to curtail emergency powers in light of COVID-19.[547] Following French President Emanuel Macron's announcement that a health pass would be required in all "bars, restaurants, amusement parks, shopping centers, trains, coaches and planes," hundreds of thousands of protesters took to the streets in cities across France for several consecutive months.[548]

Police brutality flared as law-enforcement personnel faced protesters angry at the suspension of human rights through policies justified only by the exaggerated fears the policies themselves sowed, and which therefore had no endpoint. In 2021, as cases rose to all-time highs in Australia despite some of the world's strictest lockdowns, the military was deployed to the streets; police fired rubber bullets and teargas at protesters, including at the Shrine of Remembrance in Melbourne; and a young man was sentenced to eight months in prison for organizing protests.[549]

From the beginning, moderates had rationalized their silence about the suspension of civil liberties on the basis that lockdown measures were temporary, and if the policies crossed some unspecified line they would speak up. To some degree, that did occur. When Australia banned protests, announced indefinite restrictions, and unveiled a new tracking app for lockdown compliance, many began to push back, and The Atlantic published an influential article titled *Australia Traded Away Too Much Liberty*.[550] When Greek police attacked demonstrators protesting against vaccine passes with tear gas, flash grenades, and truck-mounted water cannons, Amnesty International—having remained largely silent about lockdown restrictions for over a year—finally spoke up.[551]

But it was too little and too late. As is their perennial error, western moderates failed to timely recognize the ethical, scientific, and legal indefensibility of the pro-lockdown position. The ultimate red line had already been crossed in March 2020 when the entire world was shut down and millions condemned to starve for no good reason at all; from that point on, the thinking of moderates was purely within the context of the degree that they would accommodate previously-unthinkable human rights abuses. Catastrophic and irreparable damage had been done to global economies, psyches, legal institutions, and trust in political and scientific leadership. The belated conversions of moderates, while essential in bringing an end to lockdown measures, could not undo this damage.

Worse yet, all of these results were foreseeable from the countless historical examples in which governments had stopped their countries' economies. Lockdowns had saved no lives, killed millions, cast hundreds of millions into poverty, strained the mental health of billions, and transferred trillions of dollars from the world's poorest to the very richest, and all of these horrifying results had been entirely predictable to anyone who did the required reading.

Xi Jinping always did the required reading. He lived by the principle that those who would give up essential liberty for a little temporary safety deserved neither, and he always made sure that's exactly what they got. He'd be right there with those protesters, fighting to cast off the jackboot of tyranny. That is, if it wasn't his own jackboot.

No one appreciated the sorry predicament of these embattled western leaders better than Xi Jinping. How could their people ever forgive them for being so vacuous as to employ his evil policies? Getting your public health advice from Xi was like getting your relationship advice from Jack the Ripper. Monsters looked for Xi under their beds before going to sleep at night. Drug lords prayed to the Virgin to protect them from Xi.

The lockdown fraud was mostly textbook, but Xi claimed two major breakthroughs in the art of tyranny. One: Tanks, planes, and boats don't matter if one's system of propaganda and censorship is embraced directly by the enemy. Two: Those who talk a big talk about freedom and human rights are often the most willing to sell them cheap.

Lockdown was never about a virus. It was about sending a message: That stripped of all disguise, the illusion of virtue, competence, and commitment to human rights among the western political class was nothing but conformity with easily-subvertible norms and institutions passed down by prior generations. Since the original egalitarian propaganda of communism no longer fooled most people, the system had to be rebooted with a new lie that would justify the indefinite suspension of the rule of law. Xi had found it in the form of a "virus."

CHAPTER IX

THE YEAR OF THE RAT

The simple act of an ordinary brave man is not to participate in lies, not to support false actions. Let your credo be this: Let the lie come into the world. Let it even triumph. But not through me.

But it is within the power of writers and artists to do much more: To defeat the lie! For in the struggle with lies, art has always triumphed and shall always triumph. Visibly, irrefutably for all! Lies can prevail against much in this world, but never against art. And no sooner will the lies be dispersed than the repulsive nakedness of violence will be exposed—and age-old violence will topple in defeat...

The favorite proverbs in Russian are about truth. They give voice to a long and tortured national experience, sometimes with staggering clarity:

ONE WORD OF TRUTH SHALL OUTWEIGH THE WHOLE WORLD. – Aleksandr Solzhenitsyn, 1970

By April 2020, more than half the world's population—3.9 billion people—was under some form of lockdown. In a matter of weeks, hundreds of millions of lives had been upended and destroyed in the largest man-made famine since Mao's Great Leap Forward. An entire generation of children would miss out on years of education, their futures tossed aside for the perception of a little bit of safety. Journalists and officials were largely desensitized to these consequences, feeling they were under unspoken orders to drum up support for lockdown policies regardless of any harms they might cause. Nonetheless, these harms were all too real.

Data showed that over 60% of business closures during the COVID-19 crisis were permanent, amounting to more than 97,000 businesses lost in the U.S. alone.[552] Half of Black-owned small businesses in the U.S. were wiped out.[553] Nearly 5% of the population of the U.K. went hungry during the first three weeks of lockdown.[554] 150,000 Ontario nursing home residents were confined for as long as 15 months. "We did nothing wrong," one resident recalled, "we're not guilty of any crime. If vaccinations don't end the rules, if no one having COVID doesn't end the restrictions, then what does it take?"[555]

A survey found that 22% of Canadians were experiencing high anxiety levels, a four-fold increase from before lockdowns, while the number reporting symptoms of depression doubled to 13%.[556] U.S. drug-overdose deaths soared nearly 30%.[557] Though at little risk from the virus itself, young people bore an outsized share of the burden of lockdowns. More than seven in ten adults aged 18-23 said they experienced common symptoms of depression.[558] The CDC revealed that young adults aged 25-44 saw the largest increase in excess deaths from previous years, a stunning 26.5% jump, despite accounting for *fewer than 3%* of deaths from COVID-19.[559] This increase *surpassed* the increase in excess mortality of older Americans, who were at much higher risk of COVID-19 fatality. Since young people were at very low risk for COVID-19 fatality—20-49-year-olds had a 99.98% chance of surviving the virus, per CDC data—this shocking increase in deaths was largely attributable to deaths of "despair," in other words, deaths by lockdown.[560]

According to the CDC, despite mass PCR testing and the enormous number of false positives, at least 100,947 excess deaths in 2020 were not linked to COVID-19 at all.[561] A simple review of excess mortality confirms these findings and paints a grim picture of the toll lockdowns took. In 2020, the United States had over 200,000 more excess deaths than it would have had if excess deaths per capita by age had been the same as Sweden's.[562] The fact that these deaths were heavily skewed toward younger age brackets—whereas deaths from COVID-19 were heavily skewed toward the oldest age brackets— corroborates the conclusion that these were excess deaths caused by government policy.[563] Furthermore, other developed countries that implemented lockdown mandates, such as the U.K. and France, experienced ratios of excess deaths by age that resembled those in the U.S. rather than those in Sweden.[564] In other words, the U.S. appears to have had over 200,000 more deaths than it would have if it had followed Sweden's approach instead of the CCP's, and followed its own pandemic plan instead of implementing strict lockdown mandates.

And, despite being at virtually no risk from COVID-19, as a result of lockdowns, children suffered the most of all. Nearly one in four children living under COVID-19 lockdowns and school closures dealt with anxiety, with many at risk of lasting psychological distress.[565] In surveys by Save the Children, up to 65% of children struggled with feelings of isolation.[566] According to the University of Wisconsin, American children over the age of ten engaged in 50% less physical activity during the crisis.[567] Per the CDC, the proportion of mental health–related emergency visits for children aged 5–11 and 12–17 years increased approximately 24% and 31%, respectively.[568]

Children's intellectual development regressed. Achievement gaps widened and early literacy declined.[569] Some who were potty-trained before lockdowns reverted to diapers, and others forgot basic numbers or how to use a knife and fork.[570] One study estimated that approximately three million of the most educationally marginalized students in the United States had "simply fallen off the grid, not showing up for online or in-person instruction, their whereabouts unknown by school officials."[571] Though COVID-19 posed almost no risk to children, lockdowns took an enormous toll on their physical health. By 2021, children were falling ill in record numbers, their immune systems having suffered during lockdowns; in New Zealand, wards were flooded with babies with a potentially-deadly non-COVID respiratory virus.[572] One study found a 1493% rise in the incidence of abusive head trauma among children during the first month of lockdown in the U.K.[573]

In the words of Stanford Professor Scott Atlas, "The consequences of the lockdowns have been enormously harmful and they will last for decades after this pandemic is completely finished... It's a disgrace. It's a heinous abuse of the power of public health experts to do what was done."[574] His colleague Jay Bhattacharya agreed: "Historians will look back on this and say this was the single biggest public health mistake, possibly of all history... Every single poor person on the face of the Earth has faced ... sometimes catastrophic harm from this lockdown policy."[575]

These are not statistics. They're friends, neighbors, and citizens, whose lives were needlessly destroyed by government policies. But while these numbers in the developed world are terrifying enough, they pale in comparison to the suffering of untold millions in the developing world who were cast into starvation and poverty as a result of lockdown policies. Every single poor person on the face of the earth faced harm from lockdowns, and these harms were often catastrophic.

In India, more than 100 million workers, many of whom lived hand to mouth, were thrown out of work and forced to return to villages sometimes thousands of miles away.[576] About 230 million Indians fell into poverty—defined as living on less than $5 a day—in the first year of the crisis. Around 15%—including

47% of female workers—had failed to find employment by the end of 2020.[577] By 2021, millions of migrant workers from West Bengal were still stranded and starving, their work having evaporated along with any way to sustain their families.[578]

By summer 2021, India had experienced close to five million excess deaths. India's GDP fell by a record 7.3%, and surveys in Uttar Pradesh showed that household incomes had slumped by an average of 75% over that timeframe.[579] Research has long shown that life expectancy and GDP are closely connected in poor countries: A slight increase in GDP can greatly increase life expectancy, whereas a decrease in GDP will decrease it. The near-five million increase in India's excess deaths in 2020 was a consequence of the lockdowns implemented in spring 2020 and the panic that followed.[580]

In the early months of lockdown, India restricted access to clinics even for direly ill patients, leaving hundreds of thousands of tuberculosis, HIV, cancer, malaria, diabetes, and obstetrics patients without much-needed medical attention. By one accounting, missed treatments caused an additional 400,000 tuberculosis deaths.[581] Globally, over one million additional tuberculosis patients who should have been diagnosed and treated were missed as a result of the lack of access to health facilities in lockdown.[582]

The situation was even more catastrophic in Peru, where officials imposed some of the world's longest and strictest lockdowns, scrupulously following the advice of the WHO. In Peru, 2020 all-cause mortality increased 96% over the running 3-year average—dwarfing increases elsewhere in Latin America.[583]

Food lines in Africa stretched for miles, and by 2021 South Africa was experiencing its worst civil unrest since Apartheid.[584] The United Nations estimated that the crisis had "pushed an additional 150 million children into multidimensional poverty—

deprived of education, health, housing, nutrition, sanitation or water."[585] On a global scale, UNICEF forecast 1.2 million child deaths as a result of lockdowns, not the virus itself.[586] All this for a virus that caused little to no above-average mortality in countries without lockdowns—and which the WHO estimated had already infected 10% of the world's population by October 2020.[587] In other words, all for nothing.

According to the International Monetary Fund, the economy of just one G20 country grew during 2020: China.[588]

What made this crime so singularly despicable was that it was never intended to end. The cycle of lockdowns and vaccinations was meant to be normalized. Every year or so, when respiratory-virus season came around, the public health machine would unveil the latest strains and "variants," the charts and models would come back out, and the lockdowns would begin anew. Small businesses would shut down and the unemployment rolls would swell—the middle class shaken down for any money they might have saved along the way.

For the general public, the idea that anyone might accept some outside incentive to support such devastating policies while knowing them to be ineffective was, quite simply, too dark. Most supported lockdowns because the alternative—that they might have been implemented without proper cause—was too evil to contemplate.

In the 20th century, the term *totalitarian* was born to describe regimes that used modern technology to control every aspect of citizens' lives, binding them to the state by breaking all pre-existing social bonds. These regimes would utilize any and all means in their monopolization of power. Though they delivered an exceptionally poor quality of life to their citizens, totalitarian states were advanced political organisms, punching above their weight in geopolitics with their unparalleled ability to keep secrets and execute complex operations—the archetypal example being Germany's clandestine rearmament in the 1930s.

As with all effective totalitarianism, the dark genius of the CCP's lockdown policies could be found in their universal language. "Just stay home" was an Orwellian euphemism for indefinite house arrest and a blanket suspension of human rights. The lockdown policy thus transformed every petty official into a tyrant, and well-meaning, intelligent people into unwitting propagandists versed in the newspeak of "social distancing."

From its earliest days in power, the CCP had distinguished itself from other regimes by the extent to which it viewed its own people as the enemy. By convincing world leaders to likewise view their people as enemies impeding the goal of Zero Covid, the CCP had turned world governments into one tyranny after another.

The lockdown fraud was similar to German rearmament, early Soviet communism, or the Vietnam War in that the contemporary narrative among western elites was simply very, very wrong. Xi Jinping didn't care if leaders thought his policies cruel. (He knew). He cared only that they were sufficiently frightened, and thought his policies effective.

Totalitarianism is a virus. It starts with a single aberrant individual or cell, and pathologically corrupts, replicates, and kills by any available means. Any policy from a totalitarian China, including lockdowns, should have been presumed to be advancing that singular goal. Instead, two years on, the states and countries that most assiduously implemented the "best practices" of lockdowns and masks recommended by China, the WHO, and their sycophants were poorer, weaker, and more miserable than those that had done little or nothing. Snake oil.

The Chinese Communist Party is not Chinese, not communist, and not a party. The CCP is the world's largest criminal organization, with no racial or geographic boundaries, which happens to have begun in China—led by an extraordinarily small number of extraordinarily evil people.

From the time Henry Kissinger first opened the west's doors to China in 1971, the CCP had wrapped itself like a tapeworm through elite institutions and networks, methodically warping reality to further its interest in power. The foundations of the CCP's lockdown fraud were laid over decades by funneling elites into positions of power who were either gullible or corrupt enough to treat information from China as real. It succeeded in large part because CCP influence seemed so innocuous for decades. But as time passed, western elites grew more and more accustomed to treating the outrageous fictions propagated by China's propaganda machine as reality—in economics, history, science, human rights, and public health.

The CCP knew they had far more influence over western institutions and leaders than almost anyone realized. Under China's moderate leaders, this influence was so gradual as to be practically invisible. But Xi Jinping was just insane enough to put the lockdown operation into action.

The lockdown fraud exploited the identities and loyalties that citizens had constructed over their entire lives. Loyalty to their governments and leaders, loyalty to their scientists and universities—all tracked by the CCP and used to ensnare them. The mechanics of the fraud were simple, but intelligent people had built up trust in the global order, and it was hard for most to dissociate from that despite clear evidence that it was a lie.

With the fall of the Soviet Union, westerners had become blasé about dictators, seeing them as tin-pot bullies who crossed the headlines now and then. Xi's lockdown fraud was the first time in living memory that most westerners had experienced the hell dictators could unleash upon ordinary citizens. To paraphrase Churchill, there never was a crime more easy to stop. In March 2020, if just one prominent leader had pointed out that the WHO chief who'd told the world to copy China's lockdowns was unwilling to say "Taiwan" weeks later, the entire fraud may well have unraveled.

At the heart of lockdown policies was the mainstream indulgence of science fiction: A supervirus that could be stopped by indefinitely suspending human rights. It caused spontaneous death in Wuhan (but nowhere else) until Xi's two-month lockdown of Wuhan eliminated it from all of China (but nowhere else) where "variants" now demanded indefinite lockdowns. The real story was straight out of ancient Rome: The tyrant instructed his cronies to suspend everyone's rights, and they did.

The fraud capitalized on a confluence of anti-democratic forces in the 21st century: Information monopolies, digital atomization, and unaccountable foundations and global institutions, without which it would not have been possible. Having been sold initially on supporting lockdowns in early 2020, elites' cognitive resistance to accepting guilt triggered a collective rejection of information indicating that lockdowns had, in fact, been a crime. The result was a false reality wherein public health officials and any advice they gave must not be scrutinized, for fear of what that scrutiny might reveal about lockdowns.

The interests of global elites were thus aligned with the CCP in perpetuating the lie that lockdowns had been good and necessary. Under these conditions, international organizations, technology companies, and public health foundations began to perversely propagate a totalitarian hygiene regime of mass testing and restrictions. When the professionals who worked for these organizations perceived that their livelihoods depended on it, they too bought into the lie.

Everything after "15 days to slow the spread"—from the fear propaganda and masks to the school closures and vaccine passes—was a cover-up of the catastrophe of the original lockdowns and denialism about the insanity of treating information from China as real. By May 2020, it was abundantly clear that the world had been lied to. World leaders and media elites then had two choices: Either call out the CCP's information warfare, or join the CCP as accomplices to the fraud. With few exceptions, they joined the CCP.

Those who questioned any aspect of lockdowns' origins were dismissed as "anti-science," and those who resisted were denounced as fringe radicals. But where would the world be today if no one had fought back against lockdowns in 2020, when doing so provoked scorn, derision, and ostracism?

As lockdowns dragged on, the biggest shock was not the incalculable toll they'd taken, though it confirmed activists' worst fears. The real shock was discovering, one by one, why all the world's so-called leaders had let it happen—and feeling the same sting of betrayal every time.

"15 days to slow the spread" began in March 2020: The Year of the Rat. No year was ever more fitting of the name. Never in history had the people of the western world been betrayed so callously and flagrantly by their own supposed leaders.

They were betrayed by their WHO representatives, their national health authorities, and their medical journals. They were betrayed their by their elite journalists. They were betrayed by universities, professors, scientists, economists, and the entire public health profession.

They were betrayed by the WHO, the WEF, the UN, the NIH, the CDC, and the NHS. They were betrayed by doctors and nurses, millionaires and billionaires. They were betrayed by philanthropists and tech executives. They were betrayed by mayors, governors, premiers, legislators, health ministers, and judges. They were betrayed by presidents, chancellors, and prime ministers.

They were betrayed by their own intelligence agencies, and the armed forces who swore to protect them. They were betrayed by leaders on both the left and the right. Most deeply of all, they were betrayed by the enablers of the Chinese Communist Party.

Lockdowns have been too great a crime, and the lies on which they were based too brazen, for their origins to stay hidden. To abandon truth and force the people to conform to the lies of the powerful is the very nature of totalitarianism. Totalitarianism is not and never will be science, no matter how forcefully the political class insists it is and how much they're paid to say so.

In good times, citizens can live their lives and let journalists, academics, and officials hash out geopolitics. But like Germany in the 1930s, the western political class does not have the China situation under control. Lockdowns are proof that this problem has grown deadly serious. Citizens must identify the leaders known to *not* be connected to the CCP and empower them to investigate the ones who are.

In the words of Simon Leys, summarizing the work of László Ladány: The Chinese Communist Party is in essence a secret society. In its methods and mentality it presents a striking resemblance to an underworld mob. Communist legality is a contradiction in terms, since the Party is above the law; but whereas the Soviet tyrant merely practiced inhumanity, the CCP gave it a theoretical foundation, expounding the notion—without parallel in other communist countries—that the proletariat alone is fully endowed with human nature. To deny the humanity of the individual is the very essence of terrorism.

Before securing power, the Party thrives on political chaos. When confronted by a deliquescent government, it can succeed through organization and propaganda, even when it operates from a minuscule base. It fears daylight, feeds on deception and conspiracy, and rules by intimidation and terror.[589]

When Xi Jinping's Vice Premier visited Wuhan in March 2020, the city's residents erupted in a rare act of protest: "Fake, fake, everything is fake!"[590] As the lockdown fraud dragged on, significant weight was lent to their words.

Fake alarm had invited a fake public health response. Fake rules were enforced, fake videos were leaked, and fake hospitals were built. Fake heroes were born.

Fake infection data led to a fake WHO report. A fake WHO representative gave the world fake public health advice. Fake social media accounts posed as fake citizens posting fake comments. Fake intelligence officials conducted fake investigations of a fake lab, tipped off by fake whistleblowers.

The CCP extended the world a hand of fake friendship, providing fake aid in a fake show of concern. Fake ventilators were distributed in a display of fake humanitarianism. Fake modelers produced fake models, giving the world fake hope. Fake epidemiologists acted on fake pandemic plans funded by fake philanthropists. Fake scientists signed off on fake tests producing fake death counts, justifying a fake state of emergency. Fake journalists reported fake news, moderated by fake fact checkers. Fake politicians and fake health officials enforced fake public health policies.

The Chinese Communist Party is a fake party and a fake government. It enforces fake laws, signs fake treaties, nurtures fake friendships and opposes fake enemies in service to a fake ideology. And its entire machinery was set into lethal motion by one, very fake leader.

ENDNOTES

[1] Mark Purdy, *China's Economy, in Six Charts*, Harvard Bus. Review, Nov. 29, 2013, https://hbr.org/2013/11/chinas-economy-in-six-charts.
[2] PBS, China, A Century of Revolution: Born Under the Red Flag 1976–1997 (Video), Jul. 9, 1997.
[3] Lee, Khoon Choy, Pioneers of Modern China: Understanding the Inscrutable Chinese, 2005, ISBN 981-256-464-0.
[4] Kristof, Nicholas D. *Hu Yaobang, Ex-Party Chief in China, Dies at 73* (Obituary), N.Y. Times, Apr. 16, 1989, https://www.nytimes.com/1989/04/16/obituaries/hu-yaobang-ex-party-chief-in-china-dies-at-73.html.
[5] Thomas, Antony, The Tank Man (Video), PBS, 2006.
[6] PBS, China, A Century of Revolution: Born Under the Red Flag 1976–1997 (Video), Jul. 9, 1997.
[7] Philip P. Pan, Out of Mao's shadow, 2008, ISBN 978-1-4165-3705-2.
[8] Wu, Renhua, *The release of Tiananmen Square clearance order*, Boxun blog, May 4, 2010, https://web.archive.org/web/20190331042756/https://blog.boxun.com/hero/201004/wurenhua/10_1.shtml.
[9] Thomas, Antony, The Tank Man (Video), PBS, 2006.; N.Y. Times, *TURMOIL IN CHINA; Student Tells the Tiananmen Story: And Then, 'Machine Guns Erupted'*, Jun. 12, 1989, https://www.nytimes.com/1989/06/12/world/turmoil-in-china-student-tells-the-tiananmen-story-and-then-machine-guns-erupted.html.
[10] John Pomfret, *A Massacre, Erased*, Wash. Post, May 30, 2019, https://www.washingtonpost.com/graphics/2019/opinions/global-opinions/tiananmen-square-a-massacre-erased/.
[11] The Economist, *Strike less hard*, Aug. 3, 2013, https://www.economist.com/china/2013/08/03/strike-less-hard.
[12] Andrew J. Bacevich, American Empire: The Realities and Consequences of U.S. Diplomacy (2002), ISBN 978-0674013759.
[13] Amanda Price, *Xi Jinping versus the world*, Korea Times, May 31, 2020, https://www.koreatimes.co.kr/www/opinion/2020/08/137_290399.html.
[14] Tanner Greer, *Xi Jinping Knows Who His Enemies Are*, Foreign Policy, Nov. 21, 2019, https://foreignpolicy.com/2019/11/21/xi-jinping-china-communist-party-francois-bougon/; Tanner Greer, *China's Plans*

to Win Control of the Global Order, Tablet, May 17, 2020, https://www.tabletmag.com/sections/news/articles/china-plans-global-order; Choi Chi-yuk, *Xi Jinping's anti-graft drive has caught so many officials that Beijing's elite prison is running out of cells*, S. China Morning Post, Feb. 14, 2018, https://www.scmp.com/news/china/policies-politics/article/2133251/xi-jinpings-anti-graft-drive-has-caught-so-many; Francis Fukuyama, *What Kind of Regime Does China Have?*, The American Interest, May 18, 2020, https://www.the-american-interest.com/2020/05/18/what-kind-of-regime-does-china-have/; Shibani Mahtani and Eva Dou, *China's security law sends chill through Hong Kong, 23 years after handover*, Wash. Post, Jun. 30, 2020, https://www.washingtonpost.com/world/asia_pacific/hong-kong-national-security-law-ends-freedom-democracy-china/2020/06/30/c37e5a4a-ba8b-11ea-97c1-6cf116ffe26c_story.html; Wash. Post, *New evidence of China's concentration camps shows its hardening resolve to wipe out the Uighurs*, Sep. 3, 2020, https://www.washingtonpost.com/opinions/global-opinions/new-evidence-of-chinas-concentration-camps-shows-its-hardening-resolve-to-wipe-out-the-uighurs/2020/09/03/aeeb71b4-ebb2-11ea-99a1-71343d03bc29_story.html; Tom Phillips, *Dictator for life': Xi Jinping's power grab condemned as step towards tyranny*, The Guardian, Feb. 26, 2018, https://www.theguardian.com/world/2018/feb/26/xi-jinping-china-presidential-limit-scrap-dictator-for-life.

[15] Victims of Communism, *The Coronavirus Cover-up: A Timeline*, Apr. 10, 2020, https://victimsofcommunism.org/publication/chinese-communist-party-world-health-organization-culpability-in-coronavirus-pandemic/; Nick Givas, *WHO haunted by old tweet saying China found no human transmission of coronavirus*, N.Y. Post, Mar. 20, 2020, https://nypost.com/2020/03/20/who-haunted-by-old-tweet-saying-china-found-no-human-transmission-of-coronavirus/.

[16] Scott w. Atlas, John R. Birge, Ralph L Keeney and Alexander Lipton, *The COVID-19 shutdown will cost Americans millions of years of life*, The Hill, May 25, 2020, https://thehill.com/opinion/healthcare/499394-the-covid-19-shutdown-will-cost-americans-millions-of-years-of-life; Alan Rappeport and Jeanna Smialek, *I.M.F. Predicts Worst Downturn Since the Great Depression*, N.Y. Times, Apr. 14, 2020, https://www.nytimes.com/2020/04/14/us/politics/coronavirus-economy-recession-depression.html; Lori Hinnant and Sam Mednick, *Virus-linked hunger tied to 10,000 child deaths each month*, Assoc. Press, Jul. 27, 2020, https://apnews.com/5cbee9693c52728a3808f4e7b4965cbd; Matthew Haag, *One-Third of New York's Small Businesses May Be Gone Forever*, N.Y. Times, August 3, 2020,

https://www.nytimes.com/2020/08/03/nyregion/nyc-small-businesses-closing-coronavirus.html.
[17] Jack Healy, *It's 'People, People, People' as Lines Stretch Across America*, N.Y. Times, Apr. 12, 2020, https://www.nytimes.com/2020/04/12/us/coronavirus-long-lines-america.html.
[18] Rajesh Roy, *India Tries to Stem Migrant Worker Exodus Amid Coronavirus Lockdown*, Wall St. J., Mar. 29, 2020, https://www.wsj.com/articles/india-tries-to-stem-migrant-worker-exodus-amid-coronavirus-lockdown-11585499312.
[19] Reuters, *Miles-long lines for food in South Africa* (Video), YouTube, Apr. 30, 2020, https://www.youtube.com/watch?v=pl-R7KeUm50&fbclid=IwAR3P1MPAPWDNk3uDM3uPOq_qMjE-3WW3gVqMD0eTTMn3tQYl29hdIPvjDBQ; Assoc. Press, *Tear gas, rubber bullets: coronavirus lockdown in Africa*, S. China Morning Post, Mar. 28, 2020, https://www.scmp.com/news/world/africa/article/3077415/tear-gas-rubber-bullets-coronavirus-lockdown-africa.
[20] Will Brown and Zecharias Zelalem, *Investigation: African migrants 'left to die' in Saudi Arabia's hellish Covid detention centres*, The Telegraph, Aug. 30, 2020, https://www.telegraph.co.uk/global-health/climate-and-people/investigation-african-migrants-left-die-saudi-arabias-hellish/.
[21] Fiona Harvey, *Coronavirus pandemic 'will cause famine of biblical proportions'*, Guardian, Apr. 21, 2020, https://www.theguardian.com/global-development/2020/apr/21/coronavirus-pandemic-will-cause-famine-of-biblical-proportions.
[22] Buck Institute, *COVID Webinar Series (TRANSCRIPT): Robert Redfield, MD*, Jul. 14, 2020, https://www.buckinstitute.org/covid-webinar-series-transcript-robert-redfield-md/; Mike Valerio, *Excess deaths in DC rise 40%, as residents avoid hospitals during coronavirus pandemic*, WUSA9, Jul. 9, 2020, https://www.wusa9.com/article/news/health/coronavirus/deaths-from-treatable-diseases-rise-in-dc-fear-of-hospitals-coronavirus/65-caf65ac3-3903-4791-b933-c891f1f62bcb.
[23] Simon Leys, *The Art of Interpreting Nonexistent Inscriptions Written in Invisible Ink on a Blank Page*, ChinaFile, Oct. 11, 1990, https://www.chinafile.com/library/nyrb-china-archive/art-interpreting-nonexistent-inscriptions-written-invisible-ink-blank.
[24] Schram, Stuart, Mao Tse-Tung, 1966, ISBN 978-0-14-020840-5.
[25] The Economist, *Merry Mao-mas*, Dec. 7, 2013, https://www.economist.com/china/2013/12/07/merry-mao-mas.

26 Simon Leys, *The Art of Interpreting Nonexistent Inscriptions Written in Invisible Ink on a Blank Page*, ChinaFile, Oct. 11, 1990, https://www.chinafile.com/library/nyrb-china-archive/

27 *Id.*

28 *Id.*

29 21CN, *Wang Zhen behind the dismissal of Xinjiang Zhenjiang*, Jul. 7, 2009, https://web.archive.org/web/20110817121418/http://www.news.21cn.com/junshi/jsh/2009/07/07/6541691.shtml.

30 Pramit Pal Chaudhuri, *Tibet's conquest of China's Xi Jinping family*, Hindustan Times, Feb. 4, 2013, https://web.archive.org/web/20130213111900/http://www.hindustantimes.com/India-news/NewDelhi/Tibet-s-conquest-of-China-s-Xi-Jinping-family/Article1-1005946.aspx.

31 Alice Su, *Dreams of a Red Emperor: The relentless rise of Xi Jinping*, L.A. Times, Oct. 22, 2020, https://www.latimes.com/world-nation/story/2020-10-22/china-xi-jinping-mao-zedong-communist-party.

32 Andrew Higgins, *In China, a long path of writing the Communist Party's history*, Wash. Post, May 26, 2011, https://www.washingtonpost.com/in-china-a-long-path-of-writing-the-communist-partys-history/2011/05/26/AG5a1ECH_story.html.

33 Chris Buckley and Didi Kirsten Tatlow, *Cultural Revolution Shaped Xi Jinping, From Schoolboy to Survivor*, N.Y. Times, Sep. 24, 2015, https://www.nytimes.com/2015/09/25/world/asia/xi-jinping-china-cultural-revolution.html.

34 *Id.*

35 Christina Zhou and Sean Mantesso, *Chinese President Xi Jinping's astonishing rise to become one of the world's most powerful people*, ABC News, Mar. 5, 2019, https://www.abc.net.au/news/2019-03-06/the-astonishing-rise-of-chinese-president-xi-jinping/10794486.

36 Evan Osnos, *Born Red*, New Yorker, Mar. 30, 2015, https://www.newyorker.com/magazine/2015/04/06/born-red.

37 Tanner Greer, *Xi Jinping Knows Who His Enemies Are*, Foreign Policy, Nov. 21, 2019, https://foreignpolicy.com/2019/11/21/xi-jinping-china-communist-party-francois-bougon/.

38 Evan Osnos, *Born Red*, New Yorker, Mar. 30, 2015, https://www.newyorker.com/magazine/2015/04/06/born-red.

39 Barbara Demick And David Pierson, *China political star Xi Jinping a study in contrasts*, L.A. Times, Feb. 11, 2012, https://www.latimes.com/world/la-xpm-2012-feb-11-la-fg-china-xi-20120212-story.html.

40 Katsuji Nakazawa, *Why Xi honored a deposed reformer*, Nikkei, Dec. 4, 2015, https://asia.nikkei.com/Politics/Why-Xi-honored-a-deposed-reformer2.

⁴¹ Evan Osnos, *Born Red*, New Yorker, Mar. 30, 2015,
https://www.newyorker.com/magazine/2015/04/06/born-red.
⁴² *Id.*
⁴³ Tanner Greer, *China's Plans to Win Control of the Global Order*,
Tablet, May 17, 2020,
https://www.tabletmag.com/sections/news/articles/china-plans-global-order.
⁴⁴ *Id.*
⁴⁵ *Id.*
⁴⁶ Hal Brands, *What does China really want? To dominate the world*,
Japan Times, May 22, 2020,
https://www.japantimes.co.jp/opinion/2020/05/22/commentary/worl
d-commentary/china-really-want-dominate-world/.
⁴⁷ Tanner Greer, *China's Plans to Win Control of the Global Order*,
Tablet, May 17, 2020,
https://www.tabletmag.com/sections/news/articles/china-plans-global-order.
⁴⁸ Daniel Tobin, *How Xi Jinping's "New Era" Should Have Ended U.S.
Debate on Beijing's Ambitions*, CSIS, May 8, 2020,
https://www.csis.org/analysis/how-xi-jinpings-new-era-should-have-ended-us-debate-beijings-ambitions.
⁴⁹ Tanner Greer, *Xi Jinping in Translation: China's Guiding Ideology*,
Palladium, May 31, 2019, https://palladiummag.com/2019/05/31/xi-jinping-in-translation-chinas-guiding-ideology/.
⁵⁰ Tanner Greer, *China's Plans to Win Control of the Global Order*,
Tablet, May 17, 2020,
https://www.tabletmag.com/sections/news/articles/china-plans-global-order.
⁵¹ Shannon Tiezzi, *Xi Jinping Continues His Quest for Absolute Party
Control*, The Diplomat, Jul. 10, 2019,
https://thediplomat.com/2019/07/xi-jinping-continues-his-quest-for-absolute-party-control/.
⁵² Javier C. Hernández, *China's 'Chairman of Everything': Behind Xi
Jinping's Many Titles*, N.Y. Times, Oct. 25, 2017,
https://www.nytimes.com/2017/10/25/world/asia/china-xi-jinping-titles-chairman.html.
⁵³ Andrew J. Nathan, *Who is Xi?*, ChinaFile, May 12, 2016,
https://www.chinafile.com/nyrb-china-archive/who-xi.
⁵⁴ Michael Forsythe, *Database Tracks 'Tigers and Flies' Caught in Xi
Jinping's Corruption Crackdown*, N.Y. Times, Jan. 21, 2016,
https://www.nytimes.com/2016/01/22/world/asia/china-database-tigers-and-flies-xi-jinping.html.
⁵⁵ Evan Osnos, *Born Red*, New Yorker, Mar. 30, 2015,
https://www.newyorker.com/magazine/2015/04/06/born-red.

⁵⁶ Choi Chi-yuk, *Xi Jinping's anti-graft drive has caught so many officials that Beijing's elite prison is running out of cells*, S. China Morning Post, Feb. 14, 2018, https://www.scmp.com/news/china/policies-politics/article/2133251/xi-jinpings-anti-graft-drive-has-caught-so-many.

⁵⁷ Evan Osnos, *Born Red*, New Yorker, Mar. 30, 2015, https://www.newyorker.com/magazine/2015/04/06/born-red.

⁵⁸ Andrew J. Nathan, *Who is Xi?*, ChinaFile, May 12, 2016, https://www.chinafile.com/nyrb-china-archive/who-xi.

⁵⁹ Tanner Greer, *Xi Jinping Knows Who His Enemies Are*, Foreign Policy, Nov. 21, 2019, https://foreignpolicy.com/2019/11/21/xi-jinping-china-communist-party-francois-bougon/.

⁶⁰ *Id.*

⁶¹ Andrew J. Nathan, *Who is Xi?*, ChinaFile, May 12, 2016, https://www.chinafile.com/nyrb-china-archive/who-xi.

⁶² Francis Fukuyama, *What Kind of Regime Does China Have?*, The American Interest, May 18, 2020, https://www.the-american-interest.com/2020/05/18/what-kind-of-regime-does-china-have/.

⁶³ Steven W. Mosher, *How China's Xi Jinping destroyed religion and made himself God*, N.Y. Post, Feb. 1, 2020, https://nypost.com/2020/02/01/how-chinas-xi-jinping-destroyed-religion-and-made-himself-god/.

⁶⁴ Evan Osnos, *Born Red*, New Yorker, Mar. 30, 2015, https://www.newyorker.com/magazine/2015/04/06/born-red.

⁶⁵ Tanner Greer, *Xi Jinping Knows Who His Enemies Are*, Foreign Policy, Nov. 21, 2019, https://foreignpolicy.com/2019/11/21/xi-jinping-china-communist-party-francois-bougon/.

⁶⁶ Tanner Greer, *China's Plans to Win Control of the Global Order*, Tablet, May 17, 2020, https://www.tabletmag.com/sections/news/articles/china-plans-global-order.

⁶⁷ William Knee, *China's 709 Crackdown Is Still Going On*, The Diplomat, Jul. 9, 2021, https://thediplomat.com/2021/07/chinas-709-crackdown-is-still-going-on/.

⁶⁸ Javier C. Hernández, *'We're Almost Extinct': China's Investigative Journalists Are Silenced Under Xi*, N.Y. Times, Jul. 12, 2019, https://www.nytimes.com/2019/07/12/world/asia/china-journalists-crackdown.html.

⁶⁹ Tom Phillips, *Liu Xiaobo, Nobel laureate and political prisoner, dies at 61 in Chinese custody*, The Guardian, https://www.theguardian.com/world/2017/jul/13/liu-xiaobo-nobel-laureate-chinese-political-prisoner-dies-61.

⁷⁰ BBC, The World About Us: Tibet (Video), Jun. 18, 1984, *available at* https://www.youtube.com/watch?v=V3j_fgI_VS8; BBC, The Lost World of Tibet (Video), Nov. 2006.

[71] Jason Lansdell, Tibet Situation Critical (Video), May 26, 2013, *available at* https://www.youtube.com/watch?v=ga96oaVtOaA.

[72] Melvyn C. Goldstein, A history of modern Tibet, 1913-1951, the demise of the lamaist state, 1991, ISBN 978-0520075900.

[73] The Guardian, *The Dalai Lama: The lost horizons*, May 7, 1999, https://www.theguardian.com/books/1999/may/08/books.guardianrevi ew9.

[74] France 3, Tibet, the Story of a Tragedy (Video), 1995, *available at* https://www.youtube.com/watch?v=CUMBFKegowI.

[75] *Id.*

[76] Bruce A. Elleman and S. C. M. Paine, Modern China: Continuity and Change, 1644 to the Present, Dec. 27, 2009, ISBN 978-0136000600.

[77] France 3, Tibet, the Story of a Tragedy (Video), 1995, *available at* https://www.youtube.com/watch?v=CUMBFKegowI.

[78] *Id.*

[79] Ellen Bork, *Making the Case for Tibet*, The American Interest, Dec. 20, 2018, https://www.the-american-interest.com/2018/12/20/making-the-case-for-tibet/; Jason Lansdell, Tibet Situation Critical (Video), May 26, 2013, *available at* https://www.youtube.com/watch?v=ga96oaVtOaA.

[80] Jason Lansdell, Tibet Situation Critical (Video), May 26, 2013, *available at* https://www.youtube.com/watch?v=ga96oaVtOaA.

[81] Didi Tang, *China accused of imprisoning 500k Tibetans in labour camps*, Times of London, Sep. 25, 2020, https://www.thetimes.co.uk/article/china-accused-of-imprisoning-500k-tibetans-in-labour-camps-rh3mvjkvb.

[82] Lee Smith, *The Thirty Tyrants*, Tablet, Feb. 3, 2021, https://www.tabletmag.com/sections/news/articles/the-thirty-tyrants.

[83] Lee Smith, *China Queen Dianne Feinstein Used Her Senate Power to Push Most-Favored-Nation Status for the CCP's Corrupt Dictatorship. Why?*, Tablet, Apr. 20, 2020, https://www.tabletmag.com/sections/news/articles/lee-smith-china-coronavirus-1.

[84] Lee Smith, *The Thirty Tyrants*, Tablet, Feb. 3, 2021, https://www.tabletmag.com/sections/news/articles/the-thirty-tyrants.

[85] *Id.*

[86] *Id.*

[87] Scott Neuman and Cory Turner, *Harvard, Yale Accused Of Failing To Report Hundreds Of Millions In Foreign Donations*, NPR, Feb. 13, 2020, https://www.npr.org/2020/02/13/805548681/harvard-yale-targets-of-education-department-probe-into-foreign-donations; Lee Smith, *The Thirty Tyrants*, Tablet, Feb. 3, 2021, https://www.tabletmag.com/sections/news/articles/the-thirty-tyrants.

[88] Lee Smith, *The Thirty Tyrants*, Tablet, Feb. 3, 2021, https://www.tabletmag.com/sections/news/articles/the-thirty-tyrants.

[89] Caylan Ford, *Why Did Liberal Elites Ignore a 21st-Century Genocide?*, Medium, Feb. 3, 2021, https://medium.com/arc-digital/why-did-liberal-elites-ignore-a-21st-century-genocide-17ab88bc5adb.

[90] Caylan Ford, *Why Did Liberal Elites Ignore a 21st-Century Genocide?*, Medium, Feb. 3, 2021, https://medium.com/arc-digital/why-did-liberal-elites-ignore-a-21st-century-genocide-17ab88bc5adb.

[91] Elizabeth M. Lynch, *Self-Censorship or Survival? If so, Bloomberg is Not Alone*, China Law & Policy, Dec. 4, 2013, https://chinalawandpolicy.com/2013/12/04/self-censorship-or-survival-if-so-bloomberg-is-not-alone/.

[92] Colin Freeze, CBC pulls Falun Gong documentary, Nov. 8, 2007, The Globe and Mail, https://www.theglobeandmail.com/news/national/cbc-pulls-falun-gong-documentary/article697294/.

[93] Falun Dafa Info Center, *HRW: Excerpts about Falun Gong from: We Could Disappear At Any Time: Retaliation and Abuses Against Chinese Petitioners (December 2005)*, http://web.archive.org/web/20210122072732/https://faluninfo.net/hrw-excerpts-about-falun-gong-from-we-could-disappear-at-any-time-retaliation-and-abuses-against-chinese-petitioners-december-2005/.

[94] Caylan Ford, *Why Did Liberal Elites Ignore a 21st-Century Genocide?*, Medium, Feb. 3, 2021, https://medium.com/arc-digital/why-did-liberal-elites-ignore-a-21st-century-genocide-17ab88bc5adb.

[95] *Id.*

[96] @AMFChina, Twitter, May 17, 2021, https://threadreaderapp.com/thread/1394278157541384193.html.

[97] Sarah Cook, *Beijing's Global Megaphone*, Freedom House, 2020, https://freedomhouse.org/report/special-report/2020/beijings-global-megaphone.

[98] Anne-Marie Brady, *China's Foreign Propaganda Machine*, J. of Democracy 26, no. 4 (October 2015).

[99] Socialbakers, *Facebook Statistics—Media*, http://web.archive.org/web/20200102165154/https://www.socialbakers.com/statistics/facebook/pages/total/media/.

[100] Tom Uren, Elise Thomas, and Jacob Wallis, *Tweeting through the Great Firewall*, Australian Strategic Policy Institute, Sep. 3, 2019, https://www.aspi.org.au/report/tweeting-through-great-firewall; Raymond Zhong, Steven Lee Myers, and Jin Wu, *How China Unleashed Twitter Trolls to Discredit Hong Kong's Protesters*, New York Times, Sep. 18, 2019, https://www.nytimes.com/interactive/2019/09/18/world/asia/hk-twitter.html.

[101] Ben Cohen, Georgia Wells, and Tom McGinty, *How One Tweet Turned Pro-China Trolls Against the NBA*, Wall St. J., Oct. 16, 2019,

https://www.wsj.com/articles/how-one-tweet-turned-pro-china-trolls-against-the-nba-11571238943.

[102] Paul D. Shinkman, *Government Feuds With Twitter Over Claims China is Exploiting Coronavirus*, U.S. News, May 11, 2020, https://www.usnews.com/news/national-news/articles/2020-05-11/government-feuds-with-twitter-over-claims-china-is-exploiting-coronavirus.

[103] DFC Research, *A Bot Network Arrived In Serbia Along With Coronavirus*, Apr. 13, 2020, https://dfcme.me/en/dfc-finds-out-a-botnet-arrived-in-serbia-along-with-coronavirus/.

[104] Michael Kan, *Pro-China Propaganda Act Used Fake Followers Made With AI-Generated Images*, PCMag, Aug. 13, 2020, https://www.pcmag.com/news/pro-china-propaganda-act-used-fake-followers-made-with-ai-generated-images.

[105] Nick Arama, *The Mysterious Blue-Checked Twitter Account of 'Dr. Jialun' Who Blamed Trump After Capitol Ramming Attack*, Apr. 3, 2021, RedState, https://redstate.com/nick-arama/2021/04/03/the-mysterious-blue-checked-twitter-account-of-dr-jialun-who-blamed-trump-after-capitol-ramming-attack-n355015.

[106] Juan Pablo Cardenal, *Sharp Power: Rising Authoritarian Influence*, National Endowment for Democracy, Dec 2017, https://www.ned.org/wp-content/uploads/2017/12/Sharp-Power-Rising-Authoritarian-Influence-Full-Report.pdf; David Shullman ed., *Chinese Malign Influence and the Corrosion of Democracy*, International Republican Institute, 2019, https://www.iri.org/sites/default/files/chinese_malign_influence_report.pdf.

[107] Cathy He and Nicole Hao, *Chinese Internet Trolls Attack Shen Yun in Bid to Influence Public Opinion*, Epoch Times, Nov. 27, 2019, https://www.theepochtimes.com/chinese-internet-trolls-attack-shen-yun-in-bid-to-shift-public-opinion_3157694.html.

[108] Sarah Cook, *Worried about Huawei? Take a Closer Look at Tencent*, Diplomat, Mar. 26, 2019, https://thediplomat.com/2019/03/worried-about-huawei-take-a-closer-look-at-tencent/; Nathan Vanderklippe, *Huawei Providing Surveillance Tech to China's Xinjiang Authorities, Report Finds*, Globe and Mail, November 29, 2019, https://www.theglobeandmail.com/world/article-huawei-providing-surveillance-tech-to-chinas-xinjiang-authorities/; Sean Mantesso and Christina Zhou, *China's Multibillion-Dollar Media Campaign 'a Major Threat for Democracies' around the World*, ABC News, Feb. 7, 2019, https://www.abc.net.au/news/2019-02-08/chinas-foreign-media-push-a-major-threat-to-democracies/10733068.

[109] Sarah Cook, *The Long Shadow of Chinese Censorship*, Freedom House, Oct. 22, 2013,

https://freedomhouse.org/sites/default/files/2020-02/Special_Report_Long_Shadow_Chinese_Censorship_2013.pdf.
[110] Martin Hala, *CEFC: Economic Diplomacy with Chinese Characteristics*, Sinopsis, Feb. 8, 2018, https://sinopsis.cz/en/cefc-economic-diplomacy-with-chinese-characteristics/; Emily Baumgaertner and Jacqueline Williams, *In Australia, Fears of Chinese Meddling Rise on U.N. Bribery Case Revelation*, New York Times, May 22, 2018, https://www.nytimes.com/2018/05/22/world/australia/bribery-un-china-chau-chak-wing.html.
[111] Donnelle Eller, *Chinese-Backed Newspaper Insert Tries to Undermine Iowa Farm Support for Trump, Trade War*, The Des Moines Register, Sep. 24, 2018, https://www.desmoinesregister.com/story/money/agriculture/2018/09/24/china-daily-watch-advertisement-tries-sway-iowa-farm-support-trump-trade-war-tariffs/1412954002/.
[112] Bill Marczak and others, *China's Great Cannon*, Citizen Lab, Apr. 10, 2015, https://citizenlab.ca/2015/04/chinas-great-cannon/.
[113] Sarah Cook, *Beijing's Global Megaphone*, Freedom House, 2020, https://freedomhouse.org/report/special-report/2020/beijings-global-megaphone.
[114] James Griffiths, *Buzzfeed's China reporter says she was forced to leave the country*, CNN, Aug. 23, 2018, https://money.cnn.com/2018/08/23/media/buzzfeed-china-reporter-visa/index.html; David Martin, *Chinese Authorities Detain Relatives of Radio Free Asia's Uighur Reporters*, Deutsche-Welle, Mar. 2, 2018, https://www.dw.com/en/chinese-authorities-detain-relatives-of-radio-free-asias-uighur-reporters/a-42803793; Committee to Protect Journalists, *Wife of Critical Chinese-American Journalist Disappears in China*, Jan. 18, 2018, https://cpj.org/2018/01/wife-of-critical-chinese-american-journalist-disap/.
[115] Sarah Cook, *Beijing's Global Megaphone*, Freedom House, 2020, https://freedomhouse.org/report/special-report/2020/beijings-global-megaphone.
[116] East Turkistan Government in Exile, *The Second East Turkistan Republic (1944-1949)*, Nov. 10, 2019, https://east-turkistan.net/second-east-turkistan-republic-1944-1949/.
[117] Andrew D. W. Forbes, Warlords and Muslims in Chinese Central Asia: a Political History of Republican Sinkiang 1911–1949, 1986, ISBN 0-521-25514-7.
[118] Allen S. Whiting and General Sheng Shih-ts'ai, *Sinkiang: Pawn or Pivot?*, East Lansing: Mich. State Univ. Press, 1958.
[119] Uyghur Culture and History Studies, *A brief introduction of Uyghur history*, https://web.archive.org/web/20140714223258/http://www.bbk.ac.uk/~aisa01/infma/uyghur-history.html.

120 Allen S. Whiting and General Sheng Shih-ts'ai, *Sinkiang: Pawn or Pivot?*, East Lansing: Mich. State Univ. Press, 1958.
121 21CN, *Wang Zhen behind the dismissal of Xinjiang Zhenjiang*, Jul. 7, 2009, https://web.archive.org/web/20110817121418/http://www.news.21cn.com/junshi/jsh/2009/07/07/6541691.shtml.
122 Austin Ramzy and Chris Buckley, 'Absolutely No Mercy': Leaked Files Expose How China Organized Mass Detentions of Muslims, N.Y. Times, Nov. 16, 2019, https://www.nytimes.com/interactive/2019/11/16/world/asia/china-xinjiang-documents.html.
123 Lee Smith, *The Thirty Tyrants*, Tablet, Feb. 3, 2021, https://www.tabletmag.com/sections/news/articles/the-thirty-tyrants.
124 Austin Ramzy and Chris Buckley, 'Absolutely No Mercy': Leaked Files Expose How China Organized Mass Detentions of Muslims, N.Y. Times, Nov. 16, 2019, https://www.nytimes.com/interactive/2019/11/16/world/asia/china-xinjiang-documents.html.
125 *Id.*
126 *Id.*
127 *Id.*
128 *Id.*
129 *Id.*
130 *Id.*
131 Regina Ip, *Hong Kong Is China, Like It or Not*, N.Y. Times, Oct. 1, 2020, https://www.nytimes.com/2020/10/01/opinion/hong-kong-china-security-law.html.
132 Chester Yung, *China Reminds Hong Kong of Its Control*, Wall St. J., Jun. 10, 2014, https://www.wsj.com/articles/china-reminds-hong-kong-of-its-control-1402411342.
133 Jonathan Kaiman, *Hong Kong pro-democracy march attracts tens of thousands*, The Guardian, Jul. 1, 2014, https://www.theguardian.com/world/2014/jul/01/hong-kong-students-occupation-business-district; BBC, *Hong Kong lawmakers reject Beijing poll plan*, Jun. 18, 2015, https://www.bbc.com/news/world-asia-33179247.
134 Jonathan Kaiman, *Hong Kong's umbrella revolution - the Guardian briefing*, The Guardian, Sep. 30, 2014, https://www.theguardian.com/world/2014/sep/30/-sp-hong-kong-umbrella-revolution-pro-democracy-protests.
135 Adam Connors, *Hong Kong's umbrella movement: A timeline of key events one year on*, ABC News, Jun. 15, 2019, https://www.abc.net.au/news/2015-09-28/timeline-hong-kong-umbrella-movement-one-year-on/6802388?nw=0&r=Gallery.

[136] Reuters, *Timeline: Key dates in Hong Kong's anti-government protests*, May 29, 2020, https://www.reuters.com/article/us-hongkong-protests-timeline/timeline-key-dates-in-hong-kongs-anti-government-protests-idUSKBN23608O.

[137] South China Morning Post, *As it happened: A historic day in Hong Kong concludes peacefully as organisers claim almost 2 million people came out in protest against the fugitive bill*, Jun. 16, 2019, https://www.scmp.com/news/hong-kong/politics/article/3014695/sea-black-hong-kong-will-march-against-suspended.

[138] Austin Ramzy and Mike Ives, *Hong Kong Protests, One Year Later*, N.Y. Times, Jun. 9, 2020, https://www.nytimes.com/2020/06/09/world/asia/hong-kong-protests-one-year-later.html.

[139] *Id.*

[140] Keith Bradsher, Austin Ramzy and Tiffany May, *Hong Kong Election Results Give Democracy Backers Big Win*, N.Y. Times, Nov. 24, 2019, https://www.nytimes.com/2019/11/24/world/asia/hong-kong-election-results.html.

[141] Russell Goldman and Elaine Yu, *Hong Kong Protesters Return to Streets as New Year Begins*, N.Y. Times, Dec. 31, 2019, https://www.nytimes.com/2020/01/01/world/asia/hong-kong-protest.html.

[142] Revolver, *How Phony Coronavirus "Fear Videos" Were Used as Psychological Weapons to Bring America to Her Knees*, Feb. 4, 2021, https://www.revolver.news/2021/02/how-phony-coronavirus-fear-videos-were-used-as-psychological-weapons-to-bring-america-to-her-knees/.

[143] @1nfodaily, Twitter, Feb. 26, 2020, https://twitter.com/1nfodaily/status/1232719653983617026.

[144] Jane Lytvynenko, *Chinese State Media Spread A False Image Of A Hospital For Coronavirus Patients In Wuhan*, BuzzFeed News, Jan. 27, 2020, https://www.buzzfeednews.com/article/janelytvynenko/china-state-media-false-coronavirus-hospital-image.

[145] Brendan McFadden, *Coronavirus: Infected people seen 'dead in streets' in Chinese city dubbed 'zombieland'*, Daily Mirror, Jan. 24, 2020, https://www.mirror.co.uk/news/world-news/infected-people-seen-dead-streets-21347952; Simon Osborne, *'Like Walking Dead' Coronavirus hell as corpses litter hospitals while people drop dead*, Daily Express, Jan. 24, 2020, https://www.express.co.uk/news/world/1232931/coronavirus-outbreak-wuhan-hospital-footage-corpses-corridors-china.

[146] @MichaelPSenger, Twitter, Aug. 2, 2020, https://twitter.com/MichaelPSenger/status/1290134603412508673.

[147] Revolver, *How Phony Coronavirus "Fear Videos" Were Used as Psychological Weapons to Bring America to Her Knees*, Feb. 4, 2021, https://www.revolver.news/2021/02/how-phony-coronavirus-fear-

videos-were-used-as-psychological-weapons-to-bring-america-to-her-knees/.
[148] Arijeta Lajka, *Video falsely claims to show bodies of virus victims in China*, Assoc. Press, February 21, 2020, https://apnews.com/article/archive-fact-checking-8509320385.
[149] Cristina Tardáguila, *Photos and videos allegedly showing the coronavirus are now challenging fact-checkers*, Poynter, Jan. 30, 2020, https://www.poynter.org/fact-checking/2020/photos-and-videos-allegedly-showing-the-coronavirus-are-now-challenging-fact-checkers/.
[150] Liselotte Mas, *Did police kill a woman escaping a COVID-19 quarantine in China?*, France 24, Feb. 19, 2020, https://observers.france24.com/en/20200219-china-police-kill-woman-escape-quarantine-covid-19.
[151] Michael Thau, *'Investigate China's Global Lockdown Fraud!' Demand Lawyers, Retired Brig. Gen. in Open Letter to FBI*, RedState, Jan. 12, 2021, https://redstate.com/michael_thau/2021/01/12/308650-n308650.
[152] Yu Jinyi, *Wuhan Municipal Health Commission notified the outbreak of pneumonia*, Hubei Daily News, Jan. 1, 2020, http://web.archive.org/web/20210911233625/https://epaper.hubeidail y.net/pc/content/202001/01/content_15040.html; Michael Thau, *The 'Whistleblower' Who Told Tucker Carlson COVID-19 Is a Chinese Bioweapon May Be Playing a Very Devious Game*, RedState, Sep. 17, 2020, https://redstate.com/michael_thau/2020/09/17/920958-n254575.
[153] Hou Liqiang and Zhou Lihua, *27 quarantined in Wuhan due to viral pneumonia*, People's Daily, Jan. 1, 2020, https://web.archive.org/web/20210909080445/https://peoplesdaily.pd news.cn/2020/01/01/china/27-quarantined-in-wuhan-due-to-viral-pneumonia-113538.html.
[154] Yanan Wang and Mike Stobbe, *Chinese report says illnesses may be from new coronavirus*, Assoc. Press, Jan. 8, 2020, https://apnews.com/article/asia-pacific-health-china-wuhan-international-news-1565541fb13b6a2f0c871e0eae02bd7d.
[155] Reuters, *Chinese officials investigate cause of pneumonia outbreak in Wuhan*, SaltWire, Dec. 31, 2019, http://web.archive.org/web/20211002205324/https://www.saltwire.co m/prince-edward-island/news/chinese-officials-investigate-cause-of-pneumonia-outbreak-in-wuhan-393011/; CrofsBlog, *China: 27 quarantined in Wuhan due to viral pneumonia*, Dec. 31, 2019, http://web.archive.org/web/20210126190916/https://crofsblogs.typepa d.com/h5n1/2019/12/china-27-quarantined-in-wuhan-due-to-viral-pneumonia.html.

[156] BBC, *China pneumonia outbreak: Mystery virus probed in Wuhan*, Jan. 3, 2020, https://www.bbc.com/news/world-asia-china-50984025.

[157] World Health Organization, *COVID-19 – China*, Jan. 5, 2020, http://web.archive.org/web/20210923155454/https://www.who.int/emergencies/disease-outbreak-news/item/2020-DON229.

[158] Jim Geraghty, *The Comprehensive Timeline of China's COVID-19 Lies*, National Review, Mar. 23, 2020, https://www.nationalreview.com/the-morning-jolt/chinas-devastating-lies/.

[159] Han Qian, *Trained Wuhan doctor: 11 days later, he was infected by the patient and was admitted to the isolation ward. The previous comments in the group were taken out of context | In-depth dialogue*, Beijing Youth Daily, Jan. 27, 2020, https://web.archive.org/web/20200127104707/https://mp.weixin.qq.com/s/YRIjgJ6oNdIYVqUMiLgoRg; Han Qian, *Beijing Youth Daily | Trained Wuhan doctor: 11 days later, he was infected by the patient and was admitted to the isolation ward*, China Digital Times, Jan. 27, 2020, https://chinadigitaltimes.net/chinese/633323.html.

[160] *Id.*

[161] Chris Buckley and Steven Lee Myers, *As New Coronavirus Spread, China's Old Habits Delayed Fight*, N.Y. Times, Feb. 1, 2020, https://www.nytimes.com/2020/02/01/world/asia/china-coronavirus.html.

[162] @EmilyZFeng, Twitter, Jan. 30, 2020, https://twitter.com/EmilyZFeng/status/1223121276849385477.

[163] New York Times, *Guidelines on Integrity*, May 7, 1999, https://nytimes.com/editorial-standards/guidelines-on-integrity.html; Francine Du Plessix Gray, *The Journalist and The Dictator*, N.Y. Times, Jun. 24, 1990, https://www.nytimes.com/1990/06/24/books/the-journalist-and-the-dictator.html.

[164] Caixin, *New crown pneumonia "whistleblower" Li Wenliang: the truth is most important*, Feb. 7, 2020, https://china.caixin.com/2020-02-07/101509761.html.

[165] Han Qian, *Trained Wuhan doctor: 11 days later, he was infected by the patient and was admitted to the isolation ward. The previous comments in the group were taken out of context | In-depth dialogue*, Beijing Youth Daily, Jan. 27, 2020, https://web.archive.org/web/20200127104707/https://mp.weixin.qq.com/s/YRIjgJ6oNdIYVqUMiLgoRg.

[166] @GlobalTimesBiz, Twitter, Feb. 6, 2020, http://web.archive.org/web/20200316110526/https://twitter.com/GlobalTimesBiz/status/1225434548269223938.

[167] Chris Buckley, *Chinese Doctor, Silenced After Warning of Outbreak, Dies From Coronavirus*, Feb. 6, 2020, N.Y. Times, https://www.nytimes.com/2020/02/06/world/asia/chinese-doctor-Li-Wenliang-coronavirus.html.

[168] *E.g.*, Emily Badger and Quoctrung Bui, *Cities That Went All In on Social Distancing in 1918 Emerged Stronger for It*, N.Y. Times, Apr. 3, 2020, https://www.nytimes.com/interactive/2020/04/03/upshot/coronavirus -cities-social-distancing-better-employment.html.

[169] *Citing* Howard Markel *et al.*, *Nonpharmaceutical Interventions Implemented by US Cities During the 1918-1919 Influenza Pandemic*, 298 JAMA 644 (2007); Greg Ip, *New Thinking on Covid Lockdowns: They're Overly Blunt and Costly*, Wall St. J., Aug. 24, 2020, https://www.wsj.com/articles/covid-lockdowns-economy-pandemic-recession-business-shutdown-sweden-coronavirus-11598281419.

[170] Cnty. of Butler v. Wolf, 486 F. Supp. 3d 883 (W.D. Pa. 2020), https://casetext.com/case/cnty-of-butler-v-wolf-1.

[171] *Citing* Noreen Quails *et al.*, *Community Mitigation Guidelines to Prevent Pandemic Influenza*, United States, 2017.

[172] Thomas V. Inglesby, Jennifer B. Nuzzo, Tara O'toole, and D. A. Henderson, *Disease Mitigation Measures in the Control of Pandemic Influenza*, Biosecurity and Bioterrorism: Biodefense Strategy, Practice, and Science Vol. 4 No. 4, 2006, http://citeseerx.ist.psu.edu/viewdoc/download?doi=10.1.1.552.1109&rep=rep1&type=pdf.

[173] Amy Qin, *China's Leader, Under Fire, Says He Led Coronavirus Fight Early On*, N.Y. Times, Feb. 15, 2020, https://www.nytimes.com/2020/02/15/world/asia/xi-china-coronavirus.html.

[174] Sheena Chestnut Greitens and Julian Gewirtz, *China's Troubling Vision for the Future of Public Health*, Foreign Affairs, Jul. 10, 2020, https://www.foreignaffairs.com/articles/china/2020-07-10/chinas-troubling-vision-future-public-health; Austin Ramzy and Chris Buckley, *'Absolutely No Mercy': Leaked Files Expose How China Organized Mass Detentions of Muslims*, N.Y. Times, Nov. 16, 2019, https://www.nytimes.com/interactive/2019/11/16/world/asia/china-xinjiang-documents.html; Tanner Greer, *China's Plans to Win Control of the Global Order*, Tablet Magazine, May 17, 2020, https://www.tabletmag.com/sections/news/articles/china-plans-global-order.

[175] Amy Qin, *China's Leader, Under Fire, Says He Led Coronavirus Fight Early On*, N.Y. Times, Feb. 15, 2020, https://www.nytimes.com/2020/02/15/world/asia/xi-china-coronavirus.html.

[176] Josh Rudolph, *Translation: Essay by Missing Property Tycoon Ren Zhiqiang*, China Digital Times, Mar. 13, 2020, https://chinadigitaltimes.net/2020/03/translation-essay-by-missing-property-tycoon-ren-zhiqiang/.

[177] Chris Buckley, *China's 'Big Cannon' Blasted Xi. Now He's Been Jailed for 18 Years*, N.Y. Times, Sep. 22, 2020, https://www.nytimes.com/2020/09/22/world/asia/china-ren-zhiqiang-tycoon.html.

[178] Sinéad Baker, *China extended its Wuhan coronavirus quarantine to 2 more cities, cutting off 19 million people in an unprecedented effort to stop the outbreak*, Bus. Insider, Jan. 23, 2020, https://www.businessinsider.com/china-wuhan-coronavirus-quarantine-extended-cities-cut-off-2020-1.

[179] *E.g.*, Frances Eve, *China's reaction to the coronavirus outbreak violates human rights*, The Guardian, Feb. 2, 2020, https://www.theguardian.com/world/2020/feb/02/chinas-reaction-to-the-coronavirus-outbreak-violates-human-rights.

[180] Michael Levenson, *Scale of China's Wuhan Shutdown Is Believed to Be Without Precedent*, N.Y. Times, Jan. 22, 2020, https://www.nytimes.com/2020/01/22/world/asia/coronavirus-quarantines-history.html.

[181] World Health Organization, *Statement on the second meeting of the International Health Regulations (2005) Emergency Committee regarding the outbreak of novel coronavirus (2019-nCoV)*, Jan. 30, 2020, https://www.who.int/news/item/30-01-2020-statement-on-the-second-meeting-of-the-international-health-regulations-(2005)-emergency-committee-regarding-the-outbreak-of-novel-coronavirus-(2019-ncov).

[182] World Health Organization, *WHO Director-General's statement on IHR Emergency Committee on Novel Coronavirus (2019-nCoV)*, Jan. 30, 2020, https://www.who.int/dg/speeches/detail/who-director-general-s-statement-on-ihr-emergency-committee-on-novel-coronavirus-(2019-ncov).

[183] Xinhua, *China deserves "gratitude and respect" for efforts to fight virus outbreak: WHO chief*, Jan. 30, 2020, http://www.xinhuanet.com/english/2020-01/30/c_138742332.htm.

[184] James Griffiths, *China goes into emergency mode as number of confirmed Wuhan coronavirus cases reaches 2,700*, CNN, Jan. 27, 2020, https://www.cnn.com/2020/01/26/asia/wuhan-coronavirus-update-intl-hnk/index.html.

[185] @DrEricDing, Twitter, Jan. 25, 2020, https://threader.app/thread/1220919589623803905.

[186] Tom Bartlett, *This Harvard Epidemiologist Is Very Popular on Twitter. But Does He Know What He's Talking About?*, The Chronicle of Higher Educ., Apr. 17, 2020, https://www.chronicle.com/article/this-harvard-epidemiologist-is-very-popular-on-twitter-but-does-he-know-what-hes-talking-about/.

[187] World Health Organization, *Report of the WHO-China Joint Mission on Coronavirus Disease 2019 (COVID-19)*, Feb. 16–24, 2020,

https://www.who.int/docs/default-source/coronaviruse/who-china-joint-mission-on-covid-19-final-report.pdf.

[188] World Health Organization, *Subject: Press Conference of WHO-China Joint Mission on COVID-19*, Feb. 24, 2020, https://www.who.int/docs/default-source/coronaviruse/transcripts/joint-mission-press-conference-script-english-final.pdf?sfvrsn=51c90b9e_2; Tom Grundy, *Video: Top WHO doctor Bruce Aylward ends video call after journalist asks about Taiwan's status*, Hong Kong Free Press, Mar. 29, 2020, https://hongkongfp.com/2020/03/29/video-top-doctor-bruce-aylward-pretends-not-hear-journalists-taiwan-questions-ends-video-call/.

[189] Daniel Harries, *'Copy China's response to COVID-19,' WHO expert urges rest of the world*, CGTN, Feb. 26, 2020, https://newseu.cgtn.com/news/2020-02-26/-Copy-China-s-response-to-COVID-19-WHO-expert-urges--OnNfwORI3u/index.html.

[190] True North, *WHO forbids Canadian official from testifying before health committee*, Aug. 19, 2020, https://tnc.news/2020/08/19/who-forbids-canadian-official-from-testifying-before-health-committee/.

[191] Stacey Rudin, *What's Behind The WHO's Lockdown Mixed-Messaging*, American Institute for Economic Research, Oct. 14, 2020, https://www.aier.org/article/whats-behind-the-whos-lockdown-mixed-messaging/.

[192] *Id.*; World Health Organization, *Report of the WHO-China Joint Mission on Coronavirus Disease 2019 (COVID-19)*, Feb. 16–24, 2020, https://www.who.int/docs/default-source/coronaviruse/who-china-joint-mission-on-covid-19-final-report.pdf.

[193] World Health Organization, *Non-pharmaceutical public health measures for mitigating the risk and impact of epidemic and pandemic influenza*, 2019, https://apps.who.int/iris/bitstream/handle/10665/329438/9789241516839-eng.pdf?ua=1.

[194] @yaneerbaryam, Twitter, Apr. 26, 2020, https://twitter.com/yaneerbaryam/status/1254455465200816134.

[195] Donald G. McNeil Jr., *To Take On the Coronavirus, Go Medieval on It*, N.Y. Times, Feb. 28, 2020, https://www.nytimes.com/2020/02/28/sunday-review/coronavirus-quarantine.html.

[196] Ryan Pickrell, *China says admonishing doctor and coronavirus whistleblower Li Wenliang was 'improper,' calls for punishing local officials*, Bus. Insider, Mar. 19, 2020, https://www.businessinsider.com/china-admits-punishing-coronavirus-whistleblower-li-wenliang-inappropriate-2020-3.

[197] Wikipedia, *2015 Xi Jinping visit to the United Kingdom*, https://en.wikipedia.org/wiki/2015_Xi_Jinping_visit_to_the_United_Kingdom.

[198] Andrew Scheuber, *Chinese President sees UK-China academic partnerships at Imperial*, Imperial College London, Oct. 21, 2015, https://www.imperial.ac.uk/news/168497/chinese-president-sees-uk-china-academic-partnerships/.

[199] *Id.*

[200] Neil M Ferguson *et al.*, *Report 9: Impact of non-pharmaceutical interventions (NPIs) to reduce COVID-19 mortality and healthcare demand*, Imperial College COVID-19 Response Team, Mar. 16, 2020, https://www.imperial.ac.uk/media/imperial-college/medicine/sph/ide/gida-fellowships/Imperial-College-COVID19-NPI-modelling-16-03-2020.pdf.

[201] Neil M Ferguson *et al.*, *Report 12: The Global Impact of COVID-19 and Strategies for Mitigation and Suppression*, Imperial College COVID-19 Response Team, Mar. 16, 2020, https://www.imperial.ac.uk/media/imperial-college/medicine/mrc-gida/2020-03-26-COVID19-Report-12.pdf.

[202] Centers for Disease Control and Prevention, *Provisional Death Counts for Coronavirus Disease 2019 (COVID-19)*, https://www.cdc.gov/nchs/nvss/vsrr/covid19/index.htm; National Health Service, *COVID-19 Daily Deaths*, https://www.england.nhs.uk/statistics/statistical-work-areas/covid-19-daily-deaths/.

[203] Neil M Ferguson and Steven Riley *et al.*, *Report 11 - Evidence of initial success for China exiting COVID-19 social distancing policy after achieving containment*, Imperial College COVID-19 Response Team, Mar. 24, 2020, https://www.imperial.ac.uk/mrc-global-infectious-disease-analysis/covid-19/report-11-china-exiting-social-distancing/.

[204] Sonam Sheth and Isaac Scher, *The US intelligence community has reportedly concluded that China intentionally misrepresented its coronavirus numbers*, Bus. Insider, Apr. 1, 2020, https://www.businessinsider.com/us-intelligence-found-china-misrepresented-coronavirus-stats-report-2020-4.

[205] Tom Whipple, *Professor Neil Ferguson: People don't agree with lockdown and try to undermine the scientists*, Times of London, Dec. 25, 2020, https://www.thetimes.co.uk/article/people-don-t-agree-with-lockdown-and-try-to-undermine-the-scientists-gnms7mp98.

[206] Joseph Friedman *et al.*, *Predictive performance of international COVID-19 mortality forecasting models*, Nov. 19, 2020, https://doi.org/10.1101/2020.07.13.20151233.

[207] The Spectator, *Five experts who predicted daily Covid cases would hit 100,000*, Jul. 27, 2021, https://www.spectator.co.uk/article/five-experts-who-predicted-covid-cases-would-hit-100-000.

[208] Government of the United Kingdom, *Coronavirus (COVID-19) in the UK: Cases*, as of Oct. 2, 2021, https://coronavirus.data.gov.uk/details/cases.

209 Tomas Pueyo, *Coronavirus: Why You Must Act Now*, Medium, Mar. 10, 2020, https://tomaspueyo.medium.com/coronavirus-act-today-or-people-will-die-f4d3d9cd99ca.

210 @tomaspueyo, Twitter, Mar. 11, 2020, https://twitter.com/tomaspueyo/status/1237678288367005697.

211 Warren Pearce, *What does Covid-19 mean for expertise? The case of Tomas Pueyo*, U. of Sheffield, Feb. 9, 2021, https://www.sheffield.ac.uk/ihuman/covid-19-blog/what-does-covid-19-mean-expertise-case-tomas-pueyo.

212 @sapinker, Twitter, Mar. 11, 2020, https://twitter.com/sapinker/status/1237761514989289472.

213 L.S. Mech, Comment on *Tomas Pueyo, Coronavirus: Why You Must Act Now*, Medium, Mar. 10, 2020, as of Oct. 2, 2021, https://tomaspueyo.medium.com/coronavirus-act-today-or-people-will-die-f4d3d9cd99ca.

214 Margaret Menzin, Comment on *Tomas Pueyo, Coronavirus: Why You Must Act Now*, Medium, Mar. 10, 2020, as of Oct. 2, 2021, https://tomaspueyo.medium.com/coronavirus-act-today-or-people-will-die-f4d3d9cd99ca.

215 Don Planck, Comment on *Tomas Pueyo, Coronavirus: Why You Must Act Now*, Medium, Mar. 10, 2020, as of Oct. 2, 2021, https://tomaspueyo.medium.com/coronavirus-act-today-or-people-will-die-f4d3d9cd99ca.

216 @tomaspueyo, Twitter, Mar. 25, 2020, https://twitter.com/tomaspueyo/status/1242711009254506497.

217 World Health Organization, *Archived: WHO Timeline - COVID-19*, Apr. 27, 2020, https://www.who.int/news/item/27-04-2020-who-timeline---covid-19.

218 Tomas Pueyo, *Coronavirus: The Hammer and the Dance*, Medium, Mar. 19, 2020, https://tomaspueyo.medium.com/coronavirus-the-hammer-and-the-dance-be9337092b56.

219 Anette Dowideit, *Interior Ministry hired scientists to justify corona measures*, Welt, Feb. 7, 2021, https://www.welt.de/politik/deutschland/article225864597/Interner-E-Mail-Verkehr-Innenministerium-spannte-Wissenschaftler-ein.html.

220 German Society for Epidemiology, *Statement by the German Society for Epidemiology (DGEpi) on the Dissemination of the New Coronavirus (SARS-CoV-2)*, Mar. 20, 2020, https://www.dgepi.de/assets/Stellungnahmen/Stellungnahme2020Corona_DGEpi-21032020-v2.pdf.

221 Parliamentwatch, *The Interior Ministry's Internal Strategy Paper on the Corona Pandemic*, Apr. 7, 2020, https://www.abgeordnetenwatch.de/blog/informationsfreiheit/das-interne-strategiepapier-des-innenministeriums-zur-corona-pandemie.

222 Federal Ministry of the Interior, *How We Get COVID-19 Under Control, Strategy Paper of the Federal Ministry of the Interior*, FragDenStaat, Mar. 22, 2020, https://fragdenstaat.de/dokumente/4123-wie-wir-covid-19-unter-kontrolle-bekommen/.

223 Google Trends, *Hammer and Dance*, as of Oct. 3, 2021, https://trends.google.com/trends/explore?date=all&q=%22hammer%2 0and%20dance%22; Google Trends, *Hammer and the Dance*, as of Oct. 3, 2021, https://trends.google.com/trends/explore?date=all&q=%22hammer%2 0and%20the%20dance%22.

224 Federal Ministry of the Interior, *Letter: Freedom of Information Act Strategy Paper of the Federal Ministry of the Interior "How we can get COVID-19 under control"*, Jun. 9, 2020, https://clubderklarenworte.de/wp-content/uploads/2020/06/BMI-Dokument-incl.-Autoren.pdf.

225 Université de Lausanne Faculté des lettres Section d'allemand, *Kölbl Otto*, https://web.archive.org/web/20201230040127/https://www.unil.ch/all /fr/home/menuinst/mitarbeitende-1/assoziierte-mitarbeitende/kolbl-otto.html.

226 Otto Kölbl, *Hong Kong – An extreme example of parasitic development*, https://web.archive.org/web/20201230040346/http://rainbowbuilders .org/china-development/hong-kong-economy; Otto Kölbl, *Have Tibetans benefited from recent economic development?*, https://web.archive.org/web/20201230040016/http://rainbowbuilders .org/tibet-development/tibet-development-aid.

227 Federal Ministry of the Interior, *Letter: Freedom of Information Act Strategy Paper of the Federal Ministry of the Interior "How we can get COVID-19 under control"*, Jun. 9, 2020, https://clubderklarenworte.de/wp-content/uploads/2020/06/BMI-Dokument-incl.-Autoren.pdf.

228 University of Munich, *Dr. Maximilian Mayer*, https://web.archive.org/web/20201230034459/https://www.mcts.tum. de/en/people/maximilian-mayer/.

229 *Id.*

230 Anette Dowideit and Alexander Nabert, *When the State Secretary calls on scientists to "collaborate as much as possible"*, Welt, Feb. 8, 2021, https://www.welt.de/politik/deutschland/plus225868061/Corona-Politik-Wie-das-Innenministerium-Wissenschaftler-einspannte.html.

231 @eugyppius1, Twitter, Mar. 14, 2021, https://twitter.com/eugyppius1/status/1371103407558291460.

232 @nhaerting, Twitter, Feb. 8, 2021, https://threadreaderapp.com/thread/1358791154330980354.html.

[233] Joshua Philipp, *Leaked Emails Show Chinese Regime Employs 500,000 Internet Trolls*, Epoch Times, Dec. 15, 2014, https://www.theepochtimes.com/leaked-emails-show-chinese-regime-employs-500000-internet-trolls_1142634.html; Gary King, Jennifer Pan and Margaret E. Roberts, *How the Chinese Government Fabricates Social Media Posts for Strategic Distraction, not Engaged Argument*, Harvard, Apr. 9, 2017, https://gking.harvard.edu/files/gking/files/50c.pdf?m=1463587807.

[234] Terry Glavin, *The coronavirus pandemic is the breakthrough Xi Jinping has been waiting for*, Maclean's, Apr. 3, 2020, https://www.macleans.ca/opinion/the-coronavirus-pandemic-is-the-breakthrough-xi-jinping-has-been-waiting-for-and-hes-making-his-move/.

[235] Jack Nicas, *Does Facebook Really Know How Many Fake Accounts It Has?*, N.Y. Times, Jan. 30, 2019, https://www.nytimes.com/2019/01/30/technology/facebook-fake-accounts.html.

[236] Gary King, Jennifer Pan and Margaret E. Roberts, *How the Chinese Government Fabricates Social Media Posts for Strategic Distraction, not Engaged Argument*, Harvard, Apr. 9, 2017, https://gking.harvard.edu/files/gking/files/50c.pdf?m=1463587807.

[237] Huffington Post, *"Ci sono ancora troppe persone per strada e comportamenti da migliorare"*, Mar. 14, 2020, https://www.huffingtonpost.it/entry/ci-sono-ancora-troppe-persone-per-strada-e-comportamenti-da-migliorare_it_5e6cc3b5c5b6dda30fc9dcd0.

[238] James Patterson, *Italy Coronavirus Lockdown 'Not Enough,' Says China, Healthcare Staff Stop Counting Bodies*, Int'l Bus. Times, Mar. 20, 2020, https://www.ibtimes.com/italy-coronavirus-lockdown-not-enough-says-china-healthcare-staff-stop-counting-2943402.

[239] Francesco Bechis and Gabriele Carrer, *How China unleashed Twitter bots to spread COVID-19 propaganda in Italy*, Formiche, Mar. 31, 2020, https://formiche.net/2020/03/china-unleashed-twitter-bots-covid19-propaganda-italy/.

[240] Michael P. Senger, *China's Global Lockdown Propaganda Campaign*, Tablet, Sep. 15, 2020, https://www.tabletmag.com/sections/news/articles/china-covid-lockdown-propaganda.

[241] Raymond Zhong *et al.*, *Behind China's Twitter Campaign, a Murky Supporting Chorus*, N.Y. Times, Jun. 8, 2020, https://www.nytimes.com/2020/06/08/technology/china-twitter-disinformation.html.

[242] @Mr_Zaheed, Twitter, Mar. 16, 2020, https://web.archive.org/web/20210203093335/https://twitter.com/Mr_Zaheed/status/1239494611497889795; @PolySarkcess, Twitter, Mar.

18, 2020,
https://web.archive.org/web/20210120044349/https://twitter.com/Pol
ySarkcess/status/1240209649024016384; @SipheleleQalaba, Twitter,
Mar. 22, 2020,
https://web.archive.org/web/20210116071915/https://twitter.com/Siph
eleleQalaba/status/1241634533176377344; @jaysibalatani, Twitter, Mar.
15, 2020,
https://web.archive.org/web/20200316013345/https://twitter.com/jay
sibalatani/status/1239363614722621446; @King_Mindu, Twitter, Mar.
14, 2020,
https://web.archive.org/web/20200314101350/https://twitter.com/Kin
g_Mindu/status/1238765666053865473; @LDNSOM, Twitter, Mar. 15,
2020,
https://web.archive.org/web/20210111085203/https://twitter.com/LD
NSOM/status/1239127435532255232; @juanitoalimagna, Twitter, Mar.
15, 2020,
https://web.archive.org/web/20200315115123/https://twitter.com/juan
itoalimagna/status/1239154669743738881; @chez_art, Twitter, Mar.
15, 2020,
https://web.archive.org/web/20210113090946/https://twitter.com/che
z_art/status/1239224144308420609; @dedeteodoro, Twitter, Mar. 14,
2020,
https://web.archive.org/web/20210203094815/https://twitter.com/de
deteodoro/status/1238914168251723779; @yycjfl_yycguy, Twitter, Mar.
13, 2020,
https://web.archive.org/web/20200313151545/https://twitter.com/yycj
fl_yycguy/status/1238481375356784640; @cxrdelias, Twitter, Mar. 16,
2020,
https://web.archive.org/web/20210122182437/https://twitter.com/cxr
delias/status/1239520104687099904; @DheerajShah_, Twitter, Mar.
15, 2020,
https://web.archive.org/web/20200315150718/https://twitter.com/Dhe
erajShah_/status/1239202305976619009; @dirkregido, Twitter, Mar.
13, 2020,
https://web.archive.org/web/20210203100703/https://twitter.com/dir
kregido/status/1238566874503413760; @DeanTweets_, Twitter, Mar.
25, 2020,
https://web.archive.org/web/20210320073754/https://twitter.com/De
anTweets_/status/1242829376447746049; @MoToTheMO94, Twitter,
Mar. 16, 2020,
https://web.archive.org/web/20210127172341/https://twitter.com/MoT
oTheMO94/status/1239729692325773312.
243 Kate Conger, *Twitter Removes Chinese Disinformation Campaign*,
N.Y. Times, Jun. 11, 2020,
https://www.nytimes.com/2020/06/11/technology/twitter-chinese-
misinformation.html.

[244] Twitter, Search: "https://www.youtube.com/watch?v=o_cImRzKXOs future until:2020-03-20", as of Oct. 2, 2021, https://twitter.com/search?q=future%20https%3A%2F%2Fwww.youtub e.com%2Fwatch%3Fv%3Do_cImRzKXOs%20until%3A2020-03-20&src=typed_query&f=live.

[245] A Thing By, *Italians record messages for "themself from 10 days ago" during Coronavirus pandemic* (Video), YouTube, Mar. 15, 2020, https://www.youtube.com/watch?v=o_cImRzKXOs.

[246] Chris McGreal, *'I believe in our freedoms': the governor who resists lockdown and stresses American liberty*, The Guardian, Apr. 21, 2020, https://www.theguardian.com/us-news/2020/apr/21/south-dakota-covid-19-coronavirus-freedom.

[247] Michael P. Senger, *China's Global Lockdown Propaganda Campaign*, Tablet, Sep. 15, 2020, https://www.tabletmag.com/sections/news/articles/china-covid-lockdown-propaganda.

[248] *Id.*

[249] *Id.*

[250] Laurence Dodds, *China floods Facebook with undeclared coronavirus propaganda ads blaming Trump*, Daily Telegraph, Apr. 5, 2020, https://www.telegraph.co.uk/technology/2020/04/05/china-floods-facebook-instagram-undeclared-coronavirus-propaganda/.

[251] @HuXijin_GT, Twitter, Mar. 14, 2020, https://twitter.com/HuXijin_GT/status/1238864397713305600.

[252] Michael P. Senger, *China's Global Lockdown Propaganda Campaign*, Tablet, Sep. 15, 2020, https://www.tabletmag.com/sections/news/articles/china-covid-lockdown-propaganda.

[253] David Hutt, *Sweden-China ties grow ever icier over Hong Kong and coronavirus*, Nikkei, Jun. 11, 2020, https://asia.nikkei.com/Politics/International-relations/Sweden-China-ties-grow-ever-icier-over-Hong-Kong-and-coronavirus.

[254] Edward Lucas, *Sweden's China Problem*, CEPA, Jan. 7, 2020, https://www.cepa.org/swedens-china-problem.

[255] Leng Shumei, *Sweden's herd immunity strategy coldblooded, indifferent: netizens*, Global Times, Apr. 25, 2020, https://www.globaltimes.cn/content/1186720.shtml.

[256] World Health Organization, *Coronavirus disease (COVID-19): Herd immunity, lockdowns and COVID-19*, Oct. 15, 2020, https://web.archive.org/web/20201214195732/https://www.who.int/news-room/q-a-detail/herd-immunity-lockdowns-and-covid-19, *contra* World Health Organization, *Coronavirus disease (COVID-19): Serology*, Jun. 9, 2020, https://web.archive.org/web/20201105013101/https://www.who.int/news-room/q-a-detail/coronavirus-disease-covid-19-serology.

[257] Pien Huang, *What We Know About The Silent Spreaders Of COVID-19*, NPR, Apr. 13, 2020,
https://www.npr.org/sections/goatsandsoda/2020/04/13/831883560/c
an-a-coronavirus-patient-who-isnt-showing-symptoms-infect-others.
[258] World Health Organization, *Transmission of SARS-CoV-2: implications for infection prevention precautions*, Jul. 9, 2020,
https://www.who.int/news-room/commentaries/detail/transmission-of-sars-cov-2-implications-for-infection-prevention-precautions.
[259] World Health Organization, *Report of the WHO-China Joint Mission on Coronavirus Disease 2019 (COVID-19)*, Feb. 16–24, 2020,
https://www.who.int/docs/default-source/coronaviruse/who-china-joint-mission-on-covid-19-final-report.pdf.
[260] World Health Organization, *Transmission of SARS-CoV-2: implications for infection prevention precautions*, Jul. 9, 2020,
https://www.who.int/news-room/commentaries/detail/transmission-of-sars-cov-2-implications-for-infection-prevention-precautions; Lei Luo *et al.*, *Modes of contact and risk of transmission in COVID-19 among close contacts*, Mar. 26, 2020,
https://doi.org/10.1101/2020.03.24.20042606; Lei Huang *et al.*, *Rapid asymptomatic transmission of COVID-19 during the incubation period demonstrating strong infectivity in a cluster of youngsters aged 16-23 years outside Wuhan and characteristics of young patients with COVID-19: A prospective contact-tracing study*, J Infect Vol. 80(6), Apr. 10, 2020, https://doi.org/10.1016/j.jinf.2020.03.006; Quan-Xin Long *et al.*, *Clinical and immunological assessment of asymptomatic SARS-CoV-2 infections*, Nat Med Vol. 26, Jun. 18, 2020, https://doi.org/10.1038/s41591-020-0965-6.
[261] Hao-Yuan Cheng, MD, MSc *et al.*, *Contact Tracing Assessment of COVID-19 Transmission Dynamics in Taiwan and Risk at Different Exposure Periods Before and After Symptom Onset*, JAMA Intern Med Vol. 180(9), May 1, 2020,
https://www.ncbi.nlm.nih.gov/pmc/articles/PMC7195694/; Shin Young Park *et al.*, *Coronavirus Disease Outbreak in Call Center, South Korea*, Emerg Infect Dis Vol. 26(8), Apr. 23, 2020,
https://wwwnc.cdc.gov/eid/article/26/8/20-1274_article.
[262] Christian Drosten, *et al.*, *Transmission of 2019-nCoV Infection from an Asymptomatic Contact in Germany*, N Engl J Med Vol. 382, Jan. 30, 2020, https://www.nejm.org/doi/full/10.1056/NEJMc2001468; Kai Kupferschmidt, *Study claiming new coronavirus can be transmitted by people without symptoms was flawed*, Science, Feb. 3, 2020,
https://www.sciencemag.org/news/2020/02/paper-non-symptomatic-patient-transmitting-coronavirus-wrong.
[263] Mercedes Yanes-Lane *et al.*, *Proportion of asymptomatic infection among COVID-19 positive persons and their transmission potential: A systematic review and meta-analysis*, PLoS One, Nov. 3, 2020,
https://doi.org/10.1371/journal.pone.0241536.

[264] Jordan Schachtel, *'First Choice': How China and the WHO created mass ventilator hysteria*, The Dossier, Sep. 30, 2020, https://dossier.substack.com/p/first-choice-how-china-and-the-who.
[265] World Health Organization, *Clinical management of severe acute respiratory infection (SARI) when COVID-19 disease is suspected*, Mar. 13, 2020, https://www.who.int/docs/default-source/coronaviruse/clinical-management-of-novel-cov.pdf.
[266] Philippe Rola *et al.*, *Rethinking the early intubation paradigm of COVID-19: time to change gears?*, Clin Exp Emerg Med Vol. 7(2), Jun. 10, 2020, https://www.ncbi.nlm.nih.gov/pmc/articles/PMC7348679/.
[267] Fujun Peng *et al.*, *Management and Treatment of COVID-19: The Chinese Experience*, Can J Cardiol Vol. 36(6), Apt. 17, 2020, https://www.ncbi.nlm.nih.gov/pmc/articles/PMC7162773/.
[268] Melanie Evans, *Hospitals Retreat From Early Covid Treatment and Return to Basics*, Wall Street Journal, Dec. 20, 2020, https://www.wsj.com/articles/hospitals-retreat-from-early-covid-treatment-and-return-to-basics-11608491436.
[269] Jordan Schachtel, *'First Choice': How China and the WHO created mass ventilator hysteria*, Sep. 30, 2020, https://jordanschachtel.substack.com/p/first-choice-how-china-and-the-who.
[270] Cameron Kyle-Sidell, *From NYC ICU: Does Covid-19 Really Cause ARDS??!!* (Video), YouTube, Mar. 31, 2020, https://www.youtube.com/watch?v=k9GYTc53r20&feature=youtu.be.
[271] Sharon Begley, *With ventilators running out, doctors say the machines are overused for Covid-19*, Stat, Apr. 8, 2020, https://www.statnews.com/2020/04/08/doctors-say-ventilators-overused-for-covid-19/.
[272] Safiya Richardson, MD, MPH, *et al.*, *Presenting Characteristics, Comorbidities, and Outcomes Among 5700 Patients Hospitalized With COVID-19 in the New York City Area*, JAMA 2020 323(20), Apr. 22, 2020, https://jamanetwork.com/journals/jama/fullarticle/2765184.
[273] World Health Organization, *Non-pharmaceutical public health measures for mitigating the risk and impact of epidemic and pandemic influenza*, 2019, https://apps.who.int/iris/bitstream/handle/10665/329438/9789241516839-eng.pdf; Thomas V. Inglesby, Jennifer B. Nuzzo, Tara O'toole, and D. A. Henderson, *Disease Mitigation Measures in the Control of Pandemic Influenza,* Biosecurity and Bioterrorism: Biodefense Strategy, Practice, and Science Vol. 4 No. 4, 2006, http://citeseerx.ist.psu.edu/viewdoc/download?doi=10.1.1.552.1109&rep=rep1&type=pdf.; UK Department of Health, UK Influenza Pandemic

Preparedness Strategy, 2011,
https://assets.publishing.service.gov.uk/government/uploads/system/u
ploads/attachment_data/file/213717/dh_131040.pdf; Australia
Department of Health, Australian Health Management Plan for
Pandemic Influenza, Aug. 2019,
https://www1.health.gov.au/internet/main/publishing.nsf/Content/519
F9392797E2DDCCA257D47001B9948/$File/w-AHMPPI-2019.PDF.
[274] Elisa Black, *For good health*, U. of Adelaide, Sep. 16, 2021,
https://www.adelaide.edu.au/alumni/news/list/2021/08/30/for-good-health.
[275] UK Department of Health, *Coronavirus action plan: a guide to what
you can expect across the UK*, Mar. 3, 2020,
https://gov.uk/government/publications/coronavirus-action-plan/coronavirus-action-plan-a-guide-to-what-you-can-expect-across-the-uk.
[276] New Zealand Ministry of Health, *Aotearoa/New Zealand's COVID-19
elimination strategy: an overview*, Apr. 7, 2020,
http://web.archive.org/web/20210218222052/https:/www.health.govt.
nz/system/files/documents/pages/aotearoa-new_zealands_covid-
19_elimination_strategy-_an_overview17may.pdf.
[277] Adam Creighton, *Suppression plans straight from CCP play book*,
The Australian, Jul. 20, 2021,
https://www.theaustralian.com.au/commentary/suppression-plans-straight-from-ccp-play-book/news-story/71242afe71048b13dd88fe3f4c2fafd9.
[278] Federal Ministry of the Interior, *Necessary Measures for Germany to
Contain the COVID-19 Pandemic and to Avoid Collateral Damage to
Society*, Mar. 24, 2020, https://2020news.de/wp-content/uploads/2021/03/Strategiepapier-BMI-24.03.2020_online.pdf.
[279] Bas Soetenhorst, *Ministry of Economic Affairs Opposed 'Intelligent'
Lockdown*, Het Parool, Jun. 22, 2021,
https://www.parool.nl/nederland/ministerie-van-economische-zaken-verzette-zich-tegen-intelligente-lockdown~b8f9bffb/.
[280] James Hamblin, *You're Likely to Get the Coronavirus*, The Atlantic,
Feb. 24, 2020,
https://www.theatlantic.com/health/archive/2020/02/covid-vaccine/607000/.
[281] Motoko Rich, Ben Dooley and Makiko Inoue, *Japan Shocks Parents
by Moving to Close All Schools Over Coronavirus*, N.Y. Times, Feb. 27,
2020, https://www.nytimes.com/2020/02/27/world/asia/japan-schools-coronavirus.html.
[282] Victor Corman and Christian Drosten *et al.*, *Diagnostic detection of
2019-nCoV by real-time RT-PCR*, Eurosurveillance European
Communicable Disease Bulletin Vol. 25(3), Jan. 23, 2020,
https://www.ncbi.nlm.nih.gov/pmc/articles/PMC6988269/.

[283] Victor Corman and Christian Drosten *et al.*, *Diagnostic detection of 2019-nCoV by real-time RT-PCR*, World Health Organization, Jan. 17, 2020, https://www.who.int/docs/default-source/coronaviruse/protocol-v2-1.pdf.

[284] Victor Corman and Christian Drosten *et al.*, *Diagnostic detection of 2019-nCoV by real-time RT-PCR*, Eurosurveillance European Communicable Disease Bulletin Vol. 25(3), Jan. 23, 2020, https://www.ncbi.nlm.nih.gov/pmc/articles/PMC6988269/.

[285] Wouter Aukema, *Meta-data Analysis at eurosurveillance.org*, Aukema.org, Dec. 8, 2020, http://www.aukema.org/2020/12/meta-data-analysis-at.html.

[286] Eurosurveillane, *Editorial Board*, https://web.archive.org/web/20201224033649/https://www.eurosurveillance.org/board.

[287] Eurosurveillance, *Response to retraction request and allegations of misconduct and scientific flaws*, Feb. 4, 2021, https://www.ncbi.nlm.nih.gov/pmc/articles/PMC7863229/.

[288] Pieter Borger *et al.*, *External peer review of the RTPCR test to detect SARS-CoV-2 reveals 10 major scientific flaws at the molecular and methodological level: consequences for false positive results*, Nov. 27, 2020, https://cormandrostenreview.com/report/.

[289] Stefan Nicola, *A Berlin Biotech Company Got a Head Start on Coronavirus Tests*, Bloomberg Businessweek, Mar. 12, 2020, https://www.bloomberg.com/news/articles/2020-03-12/a-berlin-biotech-company-got-a-head-start-on-coronavirus-tests.

[290] R.E. Hope-Simpson, The Transmission of Epidemic Influenza, 1992, ISBN 978-1-4899-2385-1.

[291] World Health Organization, *Laboratory testing for coronavirus disease (COVID-19) in suspected human cases*, Mar. 19, 2020, https://apps.who.int/iris/bitstream/handle/10665/331501/WHO-COVID-19-laboratory-2020.5-eng.pdf?sequence=1&isAllowed=y.

[292] Otto Kölbl and Maximilian Mayer, *Learning from Wuhan — There is No Alternative to the Containment of COVID-19*, ResearchGate, March 4, 2020, https://www.researchgate.net/publication/339721905_Learning_from_Wuhan_-_there_is_no_Alternative_to_the_Containment_of_COVID-19.

[293] Daniel Payne, *In little noticed July interview, Fauci warned that widely used COVID tests may pick up 'dead' virus*, Just the News, Dec. 10, 2020, https://justthenews.com/politics-policy/coronavirus/newly-surfaced-video-july-fauci-tests-dead-virus.

[294] World Health Organization, *Laboratory testing for coronavirus disease (COVID-19) in suspected human cases*, Mar. 19, 2020, https://apps.who.int/iris/bitstream/handle/10665/331501/WHO-COVID-19-laboratory-2020.5-eng.pdf?sequence=1&isAllowed=y.

295 Qun Li *et al.*, *Early Transmission Dynamics in Wuhan, China, of Novel Coronavirus-Infected Pneumonia*, N Engl J Med Vol. 382(13), Jan. 29, 2020, https://www.ncbi.nlm.nih.gov/pmc/articles/PMC7121484/; *Clinical Characteristics of Coronavirus Disease 2019 in China*, N Engl J Med Vol. 382, Feb. 28, 2020, https://www.nejm.org/doi/10.1056/NEJMoa2002032; Wei Zhang *et al.*, *Molecular and serological investigation of 2019-nCoV infected patients: implication of multiple shedding routes*, Emerg Microbes Infect Vol. 9(1), Feb. 17, 2020, https://www.ncbi.nlm.nih.gov/pmc/articles/PMC7048229/.

296 Apoorva Mandavilli, *Your Coronavirus Test Is Positive. Maybe It Shouldn't Be.*, N.Y. Times, Aug. 29, 2020, https://www.nytimes.com/2020/08/29/health/coronavirus-testing.html.

297 *Id.*

298 Court of Appeal of Lisbon, judgment of 11–11–2020 in Proceedings No1783/20.7T8PDL.L1–3, https://translate.google.com/translate?hl=&sl=pt&tl=en&u=http%3A%2F%2Fwww.dgsi.pt%2Fjtrl.nsf%2F33182fc732316039802565fa00497eec%2F79d6ba338dcbe5e28025861f003e7b30.

299 Chris Lonsdale, *The COVID-19 gaslighting express*, China Daily, May 20, 2021, https://www.chinadailyhk.com/article/168617; Clive Richardson, *Kary Mullis explains why his PCR test is not a diagnostic test* (Video), YouTube, Oct. 1, 2020, https://www.youtube.com/watch?app=desktop&v=rXm9kAhNj-4.

300 *E.g.*, Reuters, *Fact check: Inventor of method used to test for COVID-19 didn't say it can't be used in virus detection*, Nov. 13, 2020, https://www.reuters.com/article/uk-factcheck-pcr/fact-check-inventor-of-method-used-to-test-for-covid-19-didnt-say-it-cant-be-used-in-virus-detection-idUSKBN24420X.

301 Clive Richardson, *Kary Mullis explains why his PCR test is not a diagnostic test* (Video), YouTube, Oct. 1, 2020, https://www.youtube.com/watch?app=desktop&v=rXm9kAhNj-4.

302 Chris Lonsdale, *The COVID-19 gaslighting express*, China Daily, May 20, 2021, https://www.chinadailyhk.com/article/168617.

303 Gary Null, Interview with Kary Mullis (Video), 1996, *available at* https://www.youtube.com/watch?v=nuWH1zFfX5A.

304 World Health Organization, *COVID-19 coding in ICD-10*, Mar. 25, 2020, https://www.who.int/classifications/icd/COVID-19-coding-icd10.pdf; *Iain Davis, A Deceptive Construction - Why We Must Question The COVID 19 Mortality Statistics*, UK Column, Mar. 28, 2021, https://www.ukcolumn.org/article/deceptive-construction-why-we-must-question-covid-19-mortality-statistics.

305 World Health Organization, *International Guidelines for Certification and Classification (Coding) of Covid-19 as Cause of Death,*

Apr. 20, 2020,
https://web.archive.org/web/20200713234711/https://www.who.int/cl
assifications/icd/Guidelines_Cause_of_Death_COVID-19-20200420-
EN.pdf.

[306] *Id.*

[307] *Id.*

[308] *Id.*

[309] UK National Health Service, *Coronavirus Act – excess death
provisions: information and guidance for medical practitioners*, Mar.
31, 2020,
https://web.archive.org/web/20200512135005/https://improvement.n
hs.uk/documents/6590/COVID-19-act-excess-death-provisions-info-
and-guidance-31-march.pdf.

[310] Nicole Grigg, *New report suggests there are thousands of
unaccounted deaths in Arizona*, ABC 15, Aug. 24, 2020,
https://www.abc15.com/news/region-phoenix-metro/central-
phoenix/new-report-suggests-there-are-thousands-of-unaccounted-
deaths-in-arizona.

[311] John Tierney, *Death and Lockdowns*, City J., Mar. 21, 2020,
https://www.city-journal.org/death-and-lockdowns.

[312] Jack Davis, *CDC Says 'Comorbidities' Present in 94% of COVID
Deaths*, The Western J., Aug. 30, 2020,
https://www.westernjournal.com/cdc-now-says-94-covid-deaths-
underlying-condition/.

[313] U.S. CDC, *Weekly Updates by Select Demographic and Geographic
Characteristics*, as of September 23, 2021,
https://www.cdc.gov/nchs/nvss/vsrr/covid_weekly/index.htm.

[314] U.S. CDC, *COVID-19 Vaccine Breakthrough Infections Reported to
CDC — United States, January 1–April 30, 2021*, May 28, 2021,
https://www.cdc.gov/mmwr/volumes/70/wr/pdfs/mm7021e3-H.pdf.

[315] Shaun Lintern, *NHS told to identify patients actually sick from
Covid-19 separately to those testing positive*, The Independent, Jun. 10,
2021, https://www.independent.co.uk/news/health/coronavirus-
hospitals-nhs-england-data-b1862804.html.

[316] NPR, *The CDC Issues A Reversal Of Its Masking Policy For Fully
Vaccinated People*, Jul. 28, 2021,
https://www.npr.org/2021/07/28/1021600447/the-cdc-issues-a-
reversal-of-its-masking-policy-for-fully-vaccinated-people.

[317] CNN, *Transcripts: Interview With CDC Director Dr. Rochelle
Walensky. Aired 9-10a ET*, May 16, 2021,
http://transcripts.cnn.com/TRANSCRIPTS/2105/16/sotu.01.html.

[318] Michael Finney, *FEMA program offers up to $9,000 reimbursement
for COVID-19 funerals*, ABC 7, Apr. 23, 2021, https://abc7news.com/7-
on-your-side-7oys-michael-finney-fema/10537752/.

319 @SpokespersonCHN, Twitter, Apr. 5, 2020,
https://twitter.com/SpokespersonCHN/status/1246665952139198464.
320 Christopher Wray, *The Threat Posed by the Chinese Government and
the Chinese Communist Party to the Economic and National Security of
the United States*, FBI, Jul. 7, 2020,
https://www.fbi.gov/news/speeches/the-threat-posed-by-the-chinese-
government-and-the-chinese-communist-party-to-the-economic-and-
national-security-of-the-united-states.
321 David Cyranoski, *What China's coronavirus response can teach the
rest of the world*, Nature, Mar. 17, 2020,
https://www.nature.com/articles/d41586-020-00741-x; Vanessa Molter
and Renee Diresta, *Pandemics & propaganda: How Chinese state
media creates and propagates CCP coronavirus narratives*,
Misinformation Review, Harvard, Jun. 8, 2020,
https://misinforeview.hks.harvard.edu/article/pandemics-propaganda-
how-chinese-state-media-creates-and-propagates-ccp-coronavirus-
narratives/.
322 Zhang Tengjun, *US political elites attempt to save economy before
people's lives*, Global Times, Mar. 28, 2020,
http://www.globaltimes.cn/content/1184026.shtml.
323 Helen Raleigh, *Why On Earth Should Anyone Believe Communist
China's Coronavirus Statistics?*, The Federalist, Mar. 23, 2020,
https://thefederalist.com/2020/03/23/why-on-earth-should-anyone-
believe-communist-chinas-coronavirus-statistics/; Sonam Sheth and
Isaac Scher, *The US intelligence community has reportedly concluded
that China intentionally misrepresented its coronavirus numbers*, Bus.
Insider, Apr. 1, 2020, https://www.businessinsider.com/us-intelligence-
found-china-misrepresented-coronavirus-stats-report-2020-4.
324 Peter Hessler, *How China Controlled the Coronavirus*, New Yorker,
Aug. 10, 2020,
https://www.newyorker.com/magazine/2020/08/17/how-china-
controlled-the-coronavirus.
325 Kaylee McGhee White, *Don't trust China's coronavirus numbers*,
Wash. Examiner, Mar. 30, 2020,
https://www.washingtonexaminer.com/opinion/dont-trust-chinas-
coronavirus-numbers; Michael Meyer-Resende, *How reliable is WHO
coronavirus data?*, EU Observer, Mar. 19, 2020,
https://euobserver.com/opinion/147776.
326 Geremie R. Barmé, *The Good Caucasian of Sichuan & Kumbaya
China*, China Heritage, Sep. 20, 2020,
http://chinaheritage.net/journal/the-good-caucasian-of-sichuan-
kumbaya-china/.
327 University of Chicago Booth School of Business, *Policy for the
COVID-19 Crisis*, Mar. 27, 2020,
https://www.igmchicago.org/surveys/policy-for-the-covid-19-crisis/.

³²⁸ @RamyInocencio, Twitter, Jun. 29, 2020, https://twitter.com/RamyInocencio/status/1277523571162648577; Sui-Lee Wee, *China Uses Quarantines as Cover to Detain Dissidents, Activists Say*, N.Y. Times, Jul. 30, 2020, https://www.nytimes.com/2020/07/30/world/asia/coronavirus-china-quarantine.html; Assoc. Press, *China cancels Hong Kong vigil for Tiananmen Square anniversary*, MarketWatch, Jun. 3, 2020, https://www.marketwatch.com/story/china-cancels-hong-kong-vigil-for-tiananmen-square-anniversary-2020-06-03; Austin Ramzy, *Hong Kong Delays Election, Citing Coronavirus. The Opposition Isn't Buying It.*, N.Y. Times, Jul. 31, 2020, https://www.nytimes.com/2020/07/31/world/asia/hong-kong-election-delayed.html.

³²⁹ Darren Byler, *Sealed doors and 'positive energy': COVID-19 in Xinjiang*, SupChina, Mar. 4, 2020, https://supchina.com/2020/03/04/sealed-doors-and-positive-energy-covid-19-in-xinjiang/; Josh Rogin, *The coronavirus brings new and awful repression for Uighurs in China*, Feb. 26, 2020, https://www.washingtonpost.com/opinions/2020/02/26/coronavirus-brings-new-awful-repression-uighurs-china/; Dake Kang, *In China's Xinjiang, forced medication accompanies lockdown*, Wash. Post, Aug. 31, 2020, https://www.washingtonpost.com/world/asia_pacific/in-chinas-xinjiang-forced-medication-accompanies-lockdown/2020/08/31/dc9a8430-eb4c-11ea-bd08-1b10132b458f_story.html; Bang Xiao and Michael Walsh, *China's Xinjiang residents yell from balconies as strict coronavirus lockdown drags on*, ABC News, Aug. 25, 2020, https://www.abc.net.au/news/2020-08-25/xinjiang-yell-from-balconies-over-strict-coronavirus-lockdown/12589440; Kelly Wynne, *Countless City Residents Scream Together at Severe Chinese Lockdown Restrictions*, Newsweek, Aug. 24, 2020, https://www.newsweek.com/countless-city-residents-scream-together-severe-chinese-lockdown-restrictions-1527216.

³³⁰ Laura Dodsworth, A State of Fear: How the UK government weaponised fear during the Covid-19 pandemic, 2021, ISBN 978-1780667201.

³³¹ Gordon Rayner, *Use of fear to control behaviour in Covid crisis was 'totalitarian', admit scientists*, The Telegraph, May 14, 2021, https://www.telegraph.co.uk/news/2021/05/14/scientists-admit-totalitarian-use-fear-control-behaviour-covid/.

³³² Andrew T. Levin and William P. Hanage *et al.*, *Assessing the age specificity of infection fatality rates for COVID-19: systematic review, meta-analysis, and public policy implications*, European J. of Epidemiology, Dec. 8, 2020, https://link.springer.com/article/10.1007%2Fs10654-020-00698-1.

333 USC Center for Economic and Social Research, *Understanding Coronavirus in America*, as of Oct. 3, 2021, https://covid19pulse.usc.edu/.

334 John P A Ioannidis, *Infection fatality rate of COVID-19 inferred from seroprevalence data*, World Health Organization, Oct. 14, 2020, https://web.archive.org/web/20210927174055/https://www.who.int/bulletin/online_first/BLT.20.265892.pdf.

335 John P. A. Ioannidis, *Reconciling estimates of global spread and infection fatality rates of COVID-19: An overview of systematic evaluations*, European J. of Clinical Investigation, Mar. 26, 2021, https://onlinelibrary.wiley.com/doi/10.1111/eci.13554.

336 UK Parliament, *Written questions, answers and statements*, Aug. 27, 2021, http://web.archive.org/web/20210930215017/https://questions-statements.parliament.uk/written-questions/detail/2021-07-12/31381/.

337 Chris Kenny, *'Fear factor' over COVID is 'out of hand'*, Sky News Australia, Jul. 1, 2021, https://www.skynews.com.au/opinion/chris-kenny/fear-factor-over-covid-is-out-of-hand/video/a9464409c0c1747012ac253bb10d0f60.

338 University of Bath, *UK public view COVID-19 as a threat because of lockdowns, new study suggests*, Phys.org, Jul. 7, 2021, https://phys.org/news/2021-07-uk-view-covid-threat-lockdowns.html.

339 Sarah Cook, *Beijing's Global Megaphone*, Freedom House, 2020, https://freedomhouse.org/report/special-report/2020/beijings-global-megaphone.

340 Chrissy Clark, *A Rundown Of Major U.S. Corporate Media's Business Ties To China*, The Federalist, May 4, 2020, https://thefederalist.com/2020/05/04/has-china-compromised-every-major-mainstream-media-entity/; Lee Smith, *The Thirty Tyrants*, Tablet, Feb. 3, 2021, https://www.tabletmag.com/sections/news/articles/the-thirty-tyrants.

341 Liza Lin, *How China Slowed Coronavirus: Lockdowns, Surveillance, Enforcers*, Wall St. J., Mar. 10, 2020, https://www.wsj.com/articles/how-china-slowed-coronavirus-lockdowns-surveillance-enforcers-11583868093.

342 James Griffiths, *China wants to take a victory lap over its handling of the coronavirus outbreak*, CNN, Mar. 10, 2020, https://www.cnn.com/2020/03/10/asia/china-coronavirus-propaganda-intl-hnk/index.html.

343 Anna Fifield, *As coronavirus goes global, China's Xi asserts victory on first trip to Wuhan since outbreak*, Wash. Post, Mar. 10, 2020, https://www.washingtonpost.com/world/asia_pacific/chinas-xi-attempts-a-coronavirus-victory-lap-with-visit-to-wuhan/2020/03/10/ca585ddc-6281-11ea-8a8e-5c5336b32760_story.html.

344 Amy Qin, *China May Be Beating the Coronavirus, at a Painful Cost*, N.Y. Times, Mar. 7, 2020,

https://www.nytimes.com/2020/03/07/world/asia/china-coronavirus-cost.html.

345 Chris Mooney and Gerry Shih, *The U.S. has absolutely no control over the coronavirus. China is on top of the tiniest risks*, Wash. Post, Nov. 10, 2020, https://www.washingtonpost.com/health/2020/11/10/us-has-absolutely-no-control-over-coronavirus-china-is-top-tiniest-risks/.

346 David Wertime, *'Not the World's Number One': Chinese Social Media Piles On the U.S.*, Politico, May 4, 2020, https://www.politico.com/news/magazine/2020/05/04/china-america-struggle-disaster-221741.

347 Javier C. Hernández, *U.S. Says Virus Can't Be Controlled. China Aims to Prove It Wrong*, N.Y. Times, Oct. 30, 2020, https://www.nytimes.com/2020/10/30/world/asia/china-covid-coronavirus.html.

348 Elanah Uretsky, *China beat the coronavirus with science and strong public health measures, not just with authoritarianism*, The Conversation, Nov. 23, 2020, https://theconversation.com/china-beat-the-coronavirus-with-science-and-strong-public-health-measures-not-just-with-authoritarianism-150126.

349 Li Yuan, *In a Topsy-Turvy Pandemic World, China Offers Its Version of Freedom*, N.Y. Times, Jan. 4, 2021, https://www.nytimes.com/2021/01/04/business/china-covid19-freedom.html.

350 Matthew Rozsa, *China eradicated COVID-19 within months. Why won't America learn from them?*, Salon, Feb. 28, 2021, https://www.salon.com/2021/02/28/china-eradicated-covid-19-within-months-why-wont-america-learn-from-them/.

351 Wang Qingxian, *Chinese philosophy of 'Life Comes First' deserves to be taken seriously around the world*, China Daily, Jun. 8, 2020, https://www.chinadaily.com.cn/a/202006/08/WS5ede298ca31083481 72519c0.html.

352 Hu Yuwei, *Prioritizing human rights helps China defeat COVID-19: experts*, Global Times, May 11, 2020, https://www.globaltimes.cn/content/1188066.shtml.

353 @SpokespersonCHN, Twitter, Apr. 11, 2020, https://twitter.com/spokespersonchn/status/1249215532663889923.

354 Lu Xue, *Military lockdown gambit exposes Canberra's double standards*, Global Times, Aug. 1, 2021, https://www.globaltimes.cn/page/202108/1230241.shtml.

355 Yaqiu Wang, *China's Covid Success Story is Also a Human Rights Tragedy*, Human Rights Watch, Jan. 26, 2021, https://www.hrw.org/news/2021/01/26/chinas-covid-success-story-also-human-rights-tragedy.

356 Aidan Powers-Riggs, *Covid-19 is Proving a Boon for Digital Authoritarianism*, CSIS, Aug. 17, 2020, https://www.csis.org/blogs/new-perspectives-asia/covid-19-proving-boon-digital-authoritarianism.

357 Steven Lee Myers *et al.*, *Power, Patriotism and 1.4 Billion People: How China Beat the Virus and Roared Back*, N.Y. Times, Feb. 5, 2021, https://www.nytimes.com/2021/02/05/world/asia/china-covid-economy.html.

358 Peter Hessler, *How China Controlled the Coronavirus*, New Yorker, Aug. 10, 2020, https://www.newyorker.com/magazine/2020/08/17/how-china-controlled-the-coronavirus.

359 Rita Panahi, *One day we'll see the real, deadly damage of lockdowns*, Herald Sun, Jul. 7, 2021, https://www.heraldsun.com.au/news/opinion/rita-panahi/rita-panahi-one-day-well-see-the-real-deadly-damage-of-lockdowns/news-story/4c2f417575a436831d7775c7ff6f6576.

360 Apoorva Mandavilli, *Immunity to the Coronavirus May Persist for Years, Scientists Find*, N.Y. Times, May 26, 2021, https://www.nytimes.com/2021/05/26/health/coronavirus-immunity-vaccines.html.

361 Google Trends, *Variants*, as of Oct. 3, 2021, https://trends.google.com/trends/explore?date=today%205-y&geo=US&q=variants.

362 @rising_serpent, Twitter, Oct. 17, 2021, https://twitter.com/rising_serpent/status/1449809203359592448.

363 Ho-fung Hung, *As U.S. Injustices Rage, China's Condemnation Reeks of Cynicism*, Foreign Policy, Jun. 5, 2020, https://foreignpolicy.com/2020/06/05/us-injustice-protests-china-condemnation-cynical/.

364 Katrin Bennhold, *Germany's Coronavirus Protests: Anti-Vaxxers, Anticapitalists, Neo-Nazis*, N.Y. Times, May 18, 2020, https://www.nytimes.com/2020/05/18/world/europe/coronavirus-germany-far-right.html.

365 Mallory Simon, *Over 1,000 health professionals sign a letter saying, Don't shut down protests using coronavirus concerns as an excuse*, CNN, Jun. 5, 2020, https://www.cnn.com/2020/06/05/health/health-care-open-letter-protests-coronavirus-trnd/index.html.

366 Motoko Rich, *Is the Secret to Japan's Virus Success Right in Front of Its Face?*, N.Y. Times, Jun. 6, 2020, https://www.nytimes.com/2020/06/06/world/asia/japan-coronavirus-masks.html; Simon Denyer, *As infections ebb, Japan hopes it has cracked the covid code on coexisting with the virus*, Wash. Post, Sep. 19, 2020, https://www.washingtonpost.com/world/asia_pacific/as-infections-ebb-japan-hopes-it-has-cracked-the-covid-code-on-coexisting-with-the-virus/2020/09/17/4742e284-eea2-11ea-bd08-

1b10132b458f_story.html; Ferris Jabr, *It's Time to Face Facts, America: Masks Work*, Wired, Mar. 30, 2020, https://www.wired.com/story/its-time-to-face-facts-america-masks-work/; David Ewing Duncan, *If 80% of Americans Wore Masks, COVID-19 Infections Would Plummet, New Study Says*, Vanity Fair, May 8, 2020, https://www.vanityfair.com/news/2020/05/masks-covid-19-infections-would-plummet-new-study-says.

[367] Kyodo News, *Tokyo enters fourth COVID-19 state of emergency as Olympics loom*, Japan Times, Jul. 12, 2021, https://www.japantimes.co.jp/news/2021/07/12/national/fourth-coronavirus-emergency-tokyo/.

[368] Elizabeth Kolbert, *How Iceland Beat the Coronavirus*, New Yorker, Jun. 1, 2020, https://www.newyorker.com/magazine/2020/06/08/how-iceland-beat-the-coronavirus; Megan Scudellari, *How Iceland hammered COVID with science*, Nature, Nov. 25, 2020, https://www.nature.com/articles/d41586-020-03284-3.

[369] Mostafa Rachwani and Elias Visontay, *Victoria achieves Covid 'elimination' and South Australia records no new cases – as it happened*, The Guardian, Nov. 27, 2020, https://www.theguardian.com/australia-news/live/2020/nov/27/victoria-covid-coronavirus-elimination-day-zero-cases-queensland-police-isolate-south-australia-cluster-new-south-wales-live-news; Timothy W. Martin and Dasl Yoon, *How South Korea Successfully Managed Coronavirus*, Wall St. J., Sep. 25, 2020, https://www.wsj.com/articles/lessons-from-south-korea-on-how-to-manage-covid-11601044329; Todd Pollack *et al.*, *Emerging COVID-19 success story: Vietnam's commitment to containment*, Our World in Data, Mar. 5, 2021, https://ourworldindata.org/covid-exemplar-vietnam; Sirachai Arunrugstichai, *A look inside Thailand, which prevented coronavirus from gaining a foothold*, Nat'l Geographic, Jun. 18, 2020, https://www.nationalgeographic.com/history/article/look-inside-thailand-prevented-coronavirus-gaining-foothold.

[370] Libby George and Estelle Shirbon, *Pandemic disruptions push millions of Nigerians into hunger*, Reuters, Jul. 16, 2021, https://www.reuters.com/world/africa/pandemic-disruptions-push-millions-nigerians-into-hunger-2021-07-15/; Francine Du Plessix Gray, *The Journalist and The Dictator*, N.Y. Times, Jun. 24, 1990, https://www.nytimes.com/1990/06/24/books/the-journalist-and-the-dictator.html.

[371] Fiona Harvey, *Coronavirus pandemic 'will cause famine of biblical proportions'*, Guardian, Apr. 21, 2020, https://www.theguardian.com/global-development/2020/apr/21/coronavirus-pandemic-will-cause-famine-of-biblical-proportions.

372 Wall Street Journal, *YouTube's Political Censorship*, Sep. 14, 2020, https://www.wsj.com/articles/youtubes-political-censorship-1160012623o; College of Physicians and Surgeons of Ontario, *Summary of the Decision of the Inquiries, Complaints and Reports Committee: Dr. Kulvinder Kaur Gill*, Feb. 3, 2021, https://doctors.cpso.on.ca/cpso/getdocument.aspx?flash=check&pdfid= itbnEMxT2bg%3d&id=%2084436&doctype=Alert; Rob Merrick, *Boris Johnson urged to sack Tory peer who denied Covid pandemic and said Chinese 'fake videos started this'*, The Independent, Apr. 4, 2021, https://www.independent.co.uk/news/uk/politics/conservatives-covid-china-fake-videos-b1825022.html.

373 Oliver May, *We Cannot Afford to Censor Dissenting Voices During a Pandemic – Prof Martin Kulldorff*, Daily Sceptic, Mar. 31, 2021, https://dailysceptic.org/we-cannot-afford-to-censor-dissenting-voices-during-a-pandemic-prof-martin-kulldorff/.

374 Donald G. McNeil Jr., *How I Learned to Stop Worrying And Love the Lab-Leak Theory*, Medium, May 17, 2021, https://donaldgmcneiljr1954.medium.com/how-i-learned-to-stop-worrying-and-love-the-lab-leak-theory-f4f88446b04d.

375 Paul Schreyer, *How the lockdown came to Germany*, Multipolar, Aug. 4, 2021, https://multipolar-magazin.de/artikel/how-the-lockdown-came-to-germany.

376 Christopher Wray, *The Threat Posed by the Chinese Government and the Chinese Communist Party to the Economic and National Security of the United States*, FBI, Jul. 7, 2020, https://www.fbi.gov/news/speeches/the-threat-posed-by-the-chinese-government-and-the-chinese-communist-party-to-the-economic-and-national-security-of-the-united-states; Mike Pompeo and Miles Yu, *China's Reckless Labs Put the World at Risk*, Wall St. J., Feb. 23, 2021, https://www.wsj.com/articles/chinas-reckless-labs-put-the-world-at-risk-11614102828; Jeffrey Mervis, *Fifty-four scientists have lost their jobs as a result of NIH probe into foreign ties*, Science, Jun. 12, 2020, https://www.sciencemag.org/news/2020/06/fifty-four-scientists-have-lost-their-jobs-result-nih-probe-foreign-ties.

377 David Choi, *Republican senator suggests 'worse than Chernobyl' coronavirus could've come from Chinese 'superlaboratory'*, Bus. Insider, Feb. 3, 2020, https://www.businessinsider.com/tom-cotton-coronavirus-come-from-chinese-super-laboratory-2020-2; Reuters, *Former CDC Chief Redfield Says He Thinks COVID-19 Originated in a Chinese Lab*, U.S. News, Mar. 26, 2021, https://www.usnews.com/news/top-news/articles/2021-03-26/former-cdc-chief-redfield-says-he-thinks-covid-19-originated-in-a-chinese-lab; Olivia Reingold, *Pompeo insists Covid-19 leaked from a Chinese lab*, Politico, Jun. 13, 2021, https://www.politico.com/news/2021/06/13/pompeo-covid-chinese-lab-493986; Mychael Schnell, *Trump-era intelligence chief wants*

Beijing Olympics moved due COVID-19 'cover-up', The Hill, Aug. 3, 2021, https://thehill.com/policy/national-security/566049-trump-era-intelligence-chief-wants-beijing-olympics-moved-due-to.

[378] David Pugliese, *Military leaders saw pandemic as unique opportunity to test propaganda on Canadians: report*, Nat'l Post, Sep. 27, 2021, https://nationalpost.com/news/national/defence-watch/military-leaders-saw-pandemic-as-unique-opportunity-to-test-propaganda-techniques-on-canadians-forces-report-says/wcm/22733c97-39f0-4ba4-8a26-478af5e215f3.

[379] Spencer Mizen, *Genghis Khan: the Mongol warlord who almost conquered the world*, HistoryExtra, Nov. 2018, https://www.historyextra.com/period/medieval/genghis-khan-mongol-warlord-conquered-world-china-medieval/.

[380] Qiao Liang and Wang Xiangsui, Unrestricted Warfare, 1999 (Trans. 2015), ISBN 978-1626543058; Stacey Rudin, *Unrestricted Warfare: "Lockdown" as a New Concept Weapon in the Post-Nuclear Age*, Medium, Nov. 2, 2020, https://staceyrudin.medium.com/unrestricted-warfare-lockdown-as-a-new-concept-weapon-in-the-post-nuclear-age-670086b834a9.

[381] Johns Hopkins Center for Health Security, *Event 201 Pandemic Exercise Underscores Immediate Need For Global Public-Private Cooperation To Mitigate Severe Economic And Societal Impacts Of Pandemics*, Oct. 17, 2019, https://web.archive.org/web/20210823050628/https://www.centerfor healthsecurity.org/event201/191017-press-release.html.

[382] Amesh Adalja and Lane Warmbrod, *CAPS: The Pathogen and Clinical Syndrome*, Event 201, Oct. 18, 2019, http://web.archive.org/web/20210904212649/https://www.centerforhe althsecurity.org/event201/event201-resources/CAPS-fact-sheet-191009.pdf.

[383] Yan-ni Mi *et al.*, *Estimating the instant case fatality rate of COVID-19 in China*, Int'l J. of Infectious Diseases, Apr. 24, 2020, https://www.ijidonline.com/article/S1201-9712(20)30271-X/fulltext. Zhuqing Ding, *et al.*, *Global COVID-19: Warnings and suggestions based on experience of China*, J. of Glob. Health, May 20, 2020, https://www.ncbi.nlm.nih.gov/pmc/articles/PMC7244931/.

[384] Na Zhu, Ph.D., *et. al.*, *A Novel Coronavirus from Patients with Pneumonia in China, 2019*, N Engl J Med, Jan. 24, 2020, https://nejm.org/doi/10.1056/NEJMoa2001017.

[385] Johns Hopkins Center for Health Security, *Event 201 Videos: Segment 4 - Communications Discussion and Epilogue Video*, Oct. 18, 2019, *available at* https://www.youtube.com/watch?v=LBuP40H4Tko.

[386] Kristina Zabirova, *A microbe as a keepsake: Event 201 organizers came up with a "COVID" souvenir a year ago*, May 25, 2020, Novye Izvestia, https://en.newizv.ru/news/world/25-05-2020/a-microbe-as-a-

keepsake-event-201-organizers-came-up-with-a-kovidny-souvenir-a-year-ago.

[387] Revolver, *How Phony Coronavirus "Fear Videos" Were Used as Psychological Weapons to Bring America to Her Knees*, Feb. 4, 2021, https://www.revolver.news/2021/02/how-phony-coronavirus-fear-videos-were-used-as-psychological-weapons-to-bring-america-to-her-knees/.

[388] ZeroHedge, *Is This The Man Behind The Global Coronavirus Pandemic?*, Jan. 29, 2020, https://www.zerohedge.com/health/man-behind-global-coronavirus-pandemic.

[389] Reuters, *Financial market website Zero Hedge knocked off Twitter over coronavirus story*, Feb. 2, 2020, https://www.reuters.com/article/us-china-health-twitter/financial-market-website-zero-hedge-knocked-off-twitter-over-coronavirus-story-idUSKBN1ZW0PZ.

[390] Bloomberg, *Report of Urns Stacked at Wuhan Funeral Homes Raises Questions About the Real Coronavirus Death Toll in China*, Time, Mar. 27, 2020, https://time.com/5811222/wuhan-coronavirus-death-toll/; Arijeta Lajka, *Drop in cellphone users in China wrongly attributed to coronavirus deaths*, Assoc. Press, Mar. 30, 2020, https://apnews.com/article/archive-fact-checking-8717250566.

[391] Nathan Allen and Inti Landauro, *Coronavirus traces found in March 2019 sewage sample, Spanish study shows*, Reuters, Jun. 26, 2020, https://www.reuters.com/article/us-health-coronavirus-spain-science/coronavirus-traces-found-in-march-2019-sewage-sample-spanish-study-shows-idUSKBN23X2HQ.

[392] Masaya Kato, *China PCR test orders soared before first confirmed COVID case*, Nikkei, Oct. 5, 2021, https://asia.nikkei.com/Spotlight/Coronavirus/China-PCR-test-orders-soared-before-first-confirmed-COVID-case.

[393] Vladimir Shkolnikov *et al.*, *Short-term Mortality Fluctuations*, Human Mortality Database, as of Oct. 4, 2021, https://mpidr.shinyapps.io/stmortality/.

[394] John P.A. Ioannidis, *A fiasco in the making? As the coronavirus pandemic takes hold, we are making decisions without reliable data*, STAT, Mar. 17, 2020, https://www.statnews.com/2020/03/17/a-fiasco-in-the-making-as-the-coronavirus-pandemic-takes-hold-we-are-making-decisions-without-reliable-data/.

[395] Zach Dorfman, *Botched CIA Communications System Helped Blow Cover of Chinese Agents*, Foreign Policy, Aug. 15, 2018, https://foreignpolicy.com/2018/08/15/botched-cia-communications-system-helped-blow-cover-chinese-agents-intelligence/.

[396] Steve Bannon, *War Room: Pandemic*, https://warroom.org/; Jordan Schachtel, *COVID-19 'whistleblower' published 'COVID bioweapon' report with fake co-authors & misleading credentials*, The Dossier, Sep.

23, 2020, https://dossier.substack.com/p/covid-19-whistleblower-published.

397 Aruna Viswanatha and Kate O'Keeffe, *Chinese Tycoon Holed Up in Manhattan Hotel Is Accused of Spying for Beijing*, Wall St. J., Jul. 22, 2019, https://www.wsj.com/articles/chinese-tycoon-holed-up-in-manhattan-hotel-is-accused-of-spying-for-beijing-11563810726. Michael Thau, *The 'Whistleblower' Who Told Tucker Carlson COVID-19 Is a Chinese Bioweapon May Be Playing a Very Devious Game*, RedState, Sep. 17, 2020, https://redstate.com/michael_thau/2020/09/17/920958-n254575; Jordan Schachtel, *COVID-19 'whistleblower' published 'COVID bioweapon' report with fake co-authors & misleading credentials*, The Dossier, Sep. 23, 2020, https://dossier.substack.com/p/covid-19-whistleblower-published.

399 Agence France-Presse, *Chinese Citizen Journalist Jailed For 4 Years For Wuhan Virus Reports*, NDTV, Dec. 28, 2020, https://www.ndtv.com/world-news/chinese-citizen-journalist-zhang-zhan-jailed-for-4-years-for-wuhan-coronavirus-reports-2344421.

400 *E.g.*, Josie Ensor, *Meet the man China is desperate to silence*, The Telegraph, May 3, 2021, https://www.telegraph.co.uk/news/2021/05/03/meet-man-china-taking-desperate-measures-silence/; Ashlee Vance, *The Undergrad Who Found China's Nuclear Arsenal*, Substack, Jul. 16, 2021, https://ashleevance.substack.com/p/the-undergrad-who-found-chinas-nuclear.

401 C. S. Lewis, *The Humanitarian Theory of Punishment*, 20th Century: An Australian Philosophy Quarterly 3, 1949.

402 Fujun Peng *et al.*, *Management and Treatment of COVID-19: The Chinese Experience*, Can J Cardiol Vol. 36(6), Apt. 17, 2020, https://www.ncbi.nlm.nih.gov/pmc/articles/PMC7162773/.

403 Travis Fain, *Raleigh PD calls protesting "non-essential activity"*, WRAL, Apr. 15, 2020, https://www.wral.com/coronavirus/raleigh-pd-calls-protesting-non-essential-activity/19057352/.

404 Susan Wood, *Northern California citizens call tip lines on mask, social distancing offenders*, North Bay Bus. J., Aug. 24, 2020, https://www.northbaybusinessjournal.com/article/industrynews/northern-california-citizens-call-out-mask-social-distancing-offenders/.

405 Wall Street Journal, *YouTube's Political Censorship*, Sep. 14, 2020, https://www.wsj.com/articles/youtubes-political-censorship-1600126230.

406 Xinhua, *Xi Jinping talks charity with Bill Gates*, China Times, May 29, 2012, http://web.archive.org/web/20210506151017/https://thechinatimes.com/online/2012/05/3634.html.

[407] Xinhua, *Xi praises co-op with Bill & Melinda Gates Foundation*, China Daily, Apr. 9, 2013, https://www.chinadaily.com.cn/business/boao2013/2013-04/09/content_16385960.htm; Xinhua, *Chinese President meets Bill Gates*, People.cn, Mar. 29, 2015, http://en.people.cn/n/2015/0329/c90883-8870566.html.

[408] Zhang Niansheng, *Bill Gates: "I am impressed of how hard President Xi works"*, Peope.cn, Apr. 6, 2017, http://en.people.cn/n3/2017/0406/c90000-9199651.html.

[409] Jane Perlez, *Xi Jinping's U.S. Visit*, N.Y. Times, Sep. 22, 2015, https://www.nytimes.com/interactive/projects/cp/reporters-notebook/xi-jinping-visit/president-xi-of-china-arrives-in-seattle.

[410] Ashley Stewart, *Bill Gates invited the Chinese President to dinner but Xi never replied*, Puget Sound Bus. J., Sep. 30, 2015, https://www.bizjournals.com/seattle/blog/2015/09/bill-gates-invited-the-chinese-president-to-dinner.html.

[411] Xinhua, *Full text of Chinese President Xi's letter to Bill Gates*, Feb. 22, 2020, http://www.xinhuanet.com/english/2020-02/22/c_138807641.htm.

[412] Jackie Salo, *Bill Gates says China 'did a lot of things right' with coronavirus response*, N.Y. Post, Apr. 27, 2020, https://nypost.com/2020/04/27/bill-gates-defends-chinas-response-to-coronavirus/.

[413] Shawn Langlois, *Bill Gates: Millions more will die in this pandemic, and 'freedom' hinders the disappointing U.S. response*, MarketWatch, Aug. 22, 2020, https://www.marketwatch.com/story/bill-gates-the-worst-of-the-pandemic-is-yet-to-come-and-freedom-played-a-part-in-the-disappointing-us-response-2020-08-20.

[414] CNN, *Transcripts: Anderson Cooper 360 Degrees*, Aug. 4, 2021, https://transcripts.cnn.com/show/acd/date/2021-08-04/segment/01; Sky News Australia, *Police powers to be strengthened in NSW*, Aug. 12, 2021, https://www.skynews.com.au/australia-news/crime/police-powers-to-be-strengthened-in-nsw/video/e95f77313894ee6e37278ec53bd61674.

[415] CNN, *Transcripts: Anderson Cooper 360 Degrees*, Aug. 4, 2021, https://transcripts.cnn.com/show/acd/date/2021-08-04/segment/01.

[416] Emily Flitter and Matthew Goldstein, *Long Before Divorce, Bill Gates Had Reputation for Questionable Behavior*, N.Y. Times, May 16, 2021, https://www.nytimes.com/2021/05/16/business/bill-melinda-gates-divorce-epstein.html.

[417] Nate Day, *Zhe 'Shelly' Wang: Who is Bill Gates' interpreter?*, Fox Bus., May 4, 2021, https://www.foxbusiness.com/lifestyle/zhe-shelly-wang-who-is-bill-gates-interpreter; Li Donglei, *Gates divorced, a ghost spread rumors to slander an innocent Chinese girl*, WeChat, May 5, 2021,

http://web.archive.org/web/20210506000956/https://mp.weixin.qq.co
m/s/fDSXmhF6zZGKmJro--kRhA.
[418] Global Times, *China shows world the right way for pandemic
response: The Lancet chief editor,* May 2, 2020,
https://www.globaltimes.cn/content/1187265.shtml.
[419] Richard Horton, *This wave of anti-China feeling masks the west's
own Covid-19 failures,* The Guardian, Aug. 3, 2020,
https://www.theguardian.com/commentisfree/2020/aug/03/covid-19-
cold-war-china-western-governments-international-peace.
[420] Charles Calisher *et al., Statement in support of the scientists, public
health professionals, and medical professionals of China combatting
COVID-19,* The Lancet Vol. 395(10226), Mar. 7, 2020,
https://www.thelancet.com/journals/lancet/article/PIIS0140-
6736(20)30418-9/fulltext.
[421] Talha Burki, *China's successful control of COVID-19,* The Lancet Vol.
20(11), Oct. 8, 2020,
https://www.thelancet.com/journals/laninf/article/PIIS1473-
3099(20)30800-8/fulltext.
[422] @chenweihua, Twitter, Oct. 16, 2020,
https://twitter.com/chenweihua/status/1317014216532963330.
[423] Denis Campbell, *Who's Matt Hancock? The health secretary's only
legacy will be how quickly he's forgotten,* The Guardian, Jul. 24, 2019,
https://www.theguardian.com/society/commentisfree/2019/jul/24/mat
t-hancock-health-secretary-legacy-quickly-forgotten-nhs.
[424] @MattHancock, Twitter, Sep. 17, 2018,
https://twitter.com/MattHancock/status/1041692833994993665.
[425] National Health Commission of the People's Republic of China, *NHC
minister speaks on phone with UK health secretary,* Apr. 23, 2020,
http://en.nhc.gov.cn/2020-04/23/c_79551.htm?bsh_bid=5572099213.
[426] CGTN, *Public health experts from China and UK move to develop
greater cooperation,* May 16, 2020,
https://newseu.cgtn.com/news/2020-05-16/Public-health-experts-
from-China-and-UK-move-to-strengthen-ties-
QwmBNLjJp6/share_amp.html
[427] George Grylls, *Boris Johnson backs Matt Hancock over 'affair with
aide Gina Coladangelo',* Times of London, Jun. 25, 2021,
https://www.thetimes.co.uk/article/matt-hancock-accused-of-affair-
with-aide-gina-coladangelo-qsbmzsjnr.
[428] Joan Bryden, *Nothing prepared Patty Hajdu for this,* Canada's Nat'l
Observer, Apr. 6 2020,
https://www.nationalobserver.com/2020/04/06/features/nothing-
prepared-patty-hajdu.; Christy Somos, *China praises Canada, slams
U.S. over coronavirus response,* CTV News, Feb. 3, 2020,
https://www.ctvnews.ca/world/china-praises-canada-slams-u-s-over-
coronavirus-response-1.4795270.

429 Graeme Wood, *Questioning WHO and China virus data feeds conspiracy theories: Health Minister*, Richmond News, Apr. 2, 2020, https://web.archive.org/web/20200409133450/https://www.richmond -news.com/questioning-who-and-china-virus-data-feeds-conspiracy-theories-health-minister-1.24111603.

430 *Id.*

431 Robyn Urback, *Canadians have been gaslit on China*, The Globe and Mail, Apr. 30, 2020, https://www.theglobeandmail.com/opinion/article-canadians-have-been-gaslit-on-china/.

432 True North, *Hajdu stands by praise for Chinese government and wanting to keep borders open*, Apr. 30, 2020, https://tnc.news/2020/04/30/hajdu-stands-by-praise-for-chinese-government-and-wanting-to-keep-borders-open/.

433 Spencer Fernando, *Propaganda Patty Defends Communist China Yet Again*, Sept. 13, 2020, https://spencerfernando.com/2020/09/13/propaganda-patty-defends-communist-china-yet-again/.

434 @chenweihua, Twitter, Apr. 3, 2020, https://twitter.com/chenweihua/status/1245987548717035520.

435 Ministry of Foreign Affairs of the People's Republic of China, *Foreign Ministry Spokesperson Wang Wenbin's Regular Press Conference on September 18, 2020*, Sep. 18, 2020, https://www.fmprc.gov.cn/mfa_eng/xwfw_665399/s2510_665401/t181 6244.shtml.

436 Kaeli Conforti, *Melbourne Begins Strict Stage 4 Lockdown This Week After Another Covid-19 Spike*, Forbes, Aug. 3, 2020, https://www.forbes.com/sites/kaeliconforti/2020/08/03/melbourne-begins-strict-level-4-lockdown-this-week-after-another-covid-19-spike/?sh=4ae9aa3150f9; Victoria Department of Health and Human Services, *Victoria's restriction levels*, https://web.archive.org/web/20200804100544/https://www.dhhs.vic. gov.au/victorias-restriction-levels-covid-19.

437 ABC News, *Prime Minister Scott Morrison, Victorian Premier Daniel Andrews clash over China deal*, Nov. 6, 2018, https://www.abc.net.au/news/2018-11-07/scott-morrison-daniel-andrews-clash-over-china-deal/10472026.

438 Richard Baker, *'China's gateway': Daniel Andrews' Belt and Road pitch to Beijing*, The Age, Oct. 3, 2020, https://www.theage.com.au/politics/victoria/china-s-gateway-daniel-andrews-belt-and-road-pitch-to-beijing-20201002-p561b9.html.

439 Damon Johnston, *Daniel Andrews's BRI broker praises China on virus*, The Australian, Jun. 12, 2020, https://www.theaustralian.com.au/nation/politics/daniel-andrewss-bri-broker-praises-china-on-virus/news-story/eb8f6f79682e859331eb4393215ba31d.

440 Rachel Baxendale, *Daniel Andrews staffer Nancy Yang did Chinese Communist propaganda course*, The Australian, Jun. 29, 2020, https://www.theaustralian.com.au/nation/politics/daniel-andrews-staffer-nancy-yang-did-chinese-communist-propaganda-course/news-story/eb49801365855bda4904c1a25a85650d; Alison Bevege, *Labor staffer with Chinese Communist Party links pushes bizarre conspiracy theory coronavirus was created by the U.S. and spread around the globe by its army*, Daily Mail Australia, Jun. 1, 2020, https://www.dailymail.co.uk/news/article-8376701/Labor-staffer-Chinese-Communist-Party-links-pushes-bizarre-coronavirus-conspiracy-theory.html.

441 Advance Australia, *How CCP Influence Runs Deep in Oz*, Jun. 12, 2020, https://www.advanceaustralia.org.au/how_ccp_influence_runs_deep_in_oz.

442 Tom Minear, *'Community ambassadors' linked to Chinese Community Party*, Herald Sun, Dec. 1, 2020, https://www.heraldsun.com.au/news/victoria/community-ambassadors-linked-to-chinese-community-party/news-story/d5ce8fc1f27465f74a25e3ceaa3f4980.

443 Xinhua, *China, US eye cooperation in fighting global epidemic diseases*, Global Times, May 13, 2015, https://www.globaltimes.cn/content/921533.shtml.

444 Helen Branswell, *WHO elects Ethiopia's Tedros Adhanom Ghebreyesus as its new director general*, STAT, May 23, 2017, https://www.statnews.com/2017/05/23/who-director-general-tedros/.

445 Donald G. McNeil Jr., *Candidate to Lead the W.H.O. Accused of Covering Up Epidemics*, N.Y. Times, May 13, 2017, https://www.nytimes.com/2017/05/13/health/candidate-who-director-general-ethiopia-cholera-outbreaks.html.

446 Jonathan Ames, *Tedros Adhanom: WHO chief may face genocide charges*, Times of London, Dec. 14, 2020, https://www.thetimes.co.uk/article/who-chief-tedros-adhanom-ghebreyesus-may-face-genocide-charges-2fbfz7sff; Frank Report, *The Ethiopian Terrorist in Charge of the World Health Organization — Dr. Tedros Adhanom*, Apr. 14, 2020, https://frankreport.com/2020/04/14/the-ethiopian-terrorist-in-charge-of-the-world-health-organization-dr-tedros-adhanom/.

447 @SusanMichie, Twitter, Mar. 3, 2020, https://twitter.com/SusanMichie/status/1234854069392625664.

448 The Spectator, *Sage scientist claims social distancing should remain 'forever'*, Jun. 10, 2021, https://www.spectator.co.uk/article/covid-professor-claims-social-distancing-should-remain-forever-.

449 Jordan Lancaster, *COVID Lockdown Zealot Gets Into Testy Exchange When Host Asks About Her Membership In Communist*

Party, Daily Caller, Jul. 7, 2021,
https://dailycaller.com/2021/07/07/covid-lockdown-susan-michie-
host-richard-madeley-membership-communist-party/.

450 Clarín, *The lie that a whole country believed: he said he was an
epidemiologist and that he works on the coronavirus vaccine*, Jul. 24,
2020, https://www.clarin.com/internacional/mentira-creyo-pais-dijo-
epidemiologo-trabaja-vacuna-coronavirus_0_g7LF611T7.html.

451 Cortney O'Brien, *CNN medical analyst suggests life 'needs to be hard'
for unvaccinated Americans*, Fox News, Jul. 10, 2021,
https://www.foxnews.com/media/cnn-medical-analyst-life-hard-
unvaccinated.

452 University of Maryland School of Medicine, *Leana Wen, Baltimore
City Health Commissioner, to Deliver Graduation Address to
University of Maryland School of Medicine's 207th Graduating Class*,
Apr. 13, 2016,
https://web.archive.org/web/20160421033456/http://somvweb.som.u
maryland.edu/absolutenm/templates/?a=3315&z=41.

453 Tom Bartlett, *This Harvard Epidemiologist Is Very Popular on
Twitter. But Does He Know What He's Talking About?*, The Chronicle of
Higher Educ., Apr. 17, 2020, https://www.chronicle.com/article/this-
harvard-epidemiologist-is-very-popular-on-twitter-but-does-he-know-
what-hes-talking-about/.

454 @DrEricDing, Twitter, Sep. 12, 2021,
https://twitter.com/DrEricDing/status/1437031231217184774.

455 @yaneerbaryam, Twitter, Apr. 26, 2020,
https://twitter.com/yaneerbaryam/status/1254455465200816134.

456 @yaneerbaryam, Twitter, Mar. 8, 2020,
https://twitter.com/yaneerbaryam/status/1236803093561520131.

457 @yaneerbaryam, Twitter, Mar. 14, 2020,
https://twitter.com/yaneerbaryam/status/1238828417187012610.

458 @yaneerbaryam, Twitter, Jul. 18, 2020,
https://twitter.com/yaneerbaryam/status/1284585257761734656.

459 Freddie Sayers, *Inside the Zero Covid campaign*, UnHerd, Feb. 4,
2021, https://unherd.com/2021/02/inside-the-zero-covid-campaign/.

460 *Id.*

461 Sam Cooper, *Chinese vaccine company executives worked in
program now targeted by Western intelligence agencies*, Global News,
Dec. 2, 2020, https://globalnews.ca/news/7483970/cansino-nrc-covid-
vaccine/.

462 Guillermo S. Hava, *The Other Chan: Donation Sanitization at the
School of Public Health*, The Harvard Crimson, Oct. 19, 2020,
https://www.thecrimson.com/column/for-
sale/article/2020/10/19/hava-the-other-chan/.

463 Jeffrey Mervis, *Fifty-four scientists have lost their jobs as a result of
NIH probe into foreign ties*, Science, Jun. 12, 2020,

https://www.sciencemag.org/news/2020/06/fifty-four-scientists-have-lost-their-jobs-result-nih-probe-foreign-ties; Office of Public Affairs, *Harvard University Professor and Two Chinese Nationals Charged in Three Separate China Related Cases*, U.S. Dep't of Justice Press Release No. 20-99, Jan. 28, 2020, https://www.justice.gov/opa/pr/harvard-university-professor-and-two-chinese-nationals-charged-three-separate-china-related.

[464] Ryan Lovelace, *U.S. scientists feared compromised by China*, Wash. Times, Apr. 22, 2021, https://www.washingtontimes.com/news/2021/apr/22/us-scientists-feared-compromised-china/.

[465] U.S. National Institutes of Health, *Emails from Anthony Fauci*, 2020, *available at* https://www.documentcloud.org/documents/20793561-leopold-nih-foia-anthony-fauci-emails.

[466] Jeffrey Tucker, *The Fauci Email Dump Proves the Trifecta's Lockdown Plot*, Gilder's Daily Prophecy, Jun. 3, 2021, https://gildersdailyprophecy.com/posts/the-fauci-email-dump-proves-the-trifectas-lockdown-plot.

[467] Michael Barbaro *et al.*, *The Coronavirus goes global* (Podcast), N.Y. Times, Feb. 27, 2020, https://www.nytimes.com/2020/02/27/podcasts/the-daily/coronavirus.html.

[468] Donald G. McNeil Jr., *To Take On the Coronavirus, Go Medieval on It*, N.Y. Times, Feb. 28, 2020, https://www.nytimes.com/2020/02/28/sunday-review/coronavirus-quarantine.html.

[469] U.S. National Institutes of Health, *Emails from Anthony Fauci*, 2020, *available at* https://www.documentcloud.org/documents/20793561-leopold-nih-foia-anthony-fauci-emails.

[470] *Id.*

[471] *Id.*

[472] Anthony S. Fauci, M.D., H. Clifford Lane, M.D., and Robert R. Redfield, M.D., *Covid-19 — Navigating the Uncharted*, N Engl J Med 382, Mar. 26, 2020, https://www.nejm.org/doi/full/10.1056/nejme2002387.

[473] Doug Gollan, *COVID-19 Travel Update: Fauci Says Cruising Is OK If You Are Healthy*, Forbes, Mar. 9, 2020, https://www.forbes.com/sites/douggollan/2020/03/09/fauci-says-cruising-is-ok-if-you-are-healthy/?sh=75c6572f2d4d; MSNBC, *Dr. Fauci: I Expect More Cases And I Expect An Acceleration Of Testing | Morning Joe, available at* https://www.youtube.com/watch?v=a3C05T7F16E.

[474] Associated Press, *Fauci open to a 14-day national shutdown to stem coronavirus*, L.A. Times, https://www.latimes.com/world-

nation/story/2020-03-15/fauci-open-to-a-14-day-national-shutdown-to-stem-virus.

475 Eric Lipton and Jennifer Steinhauer, *The Untold Story of the Birth of Social Distancing*, N.Y. Times, Apr. 22, 2020, https://www.nytimes.com/2020/04/22/us/politics/social-distancing-coronavirus.html; Michael Lewis, The Premonition, 2021, ISBN 978-0393881554.

476 Noreen Quails *et al.*, United States, 2017.

477 Cnty. of Butler v. Wolf, 486 F. Supp. 3d 883 (W.D. Pa. 2020), https://casetext.com/case/cnty-of-butler-v-wolf-1.

478 Tom Grundy, *Video: Top WHO doctor Bruce Aylward ends video call after journalist asks about Taiwan's status*, Hong Kong Free Press, Mar. 29, 2020, https://hongkongfp.com/2020/03/29/video-top-doctor-bruce-aylward-pretends-not-hear-journalists-taiwan-questions-ends-video-call/.

479 CNN, *Transcripts: Anthony Fauci on Capitol Hill*, Mar. 18, 2021, http://transcripts.cnn.com/TRANSCRIPTS/2103/18/cnr.09.html.

480 Louis Jacobson, *Why did the federal guidance on mask-wearing change so quickly?*, Tampa Bay Times, https://www.tampabay.com/news/health/2021/05/25/why-did-the-federal-guidance-on-mask-wearing-change-so-quickly/.

481 @SpokespersonCHN, Twitter, Aug. 13, 2020, https://twitter.com/SpokespersonCHN/status/1293822438988320769.

482 Jordan Schachtel, *Fauci and the Communists*, Am. Inst. for Econ. Rsch., Mar. 10, 2021, https://www.aier.org/article/fauci-and-the-communists/.

483 Eva Fu, *Beijing Seizes Upon Fauci's Calls for Solidarity to Push COVID-19 Propaganda*, Epoch Times, Mar. 12, 2021, https://www.theepochtimes.com/mkt_app/beijing-seizes-upon-faucis-call-for-solidarity-to-push-covid-19-propaganda_3731620.html.

484 Simone McCarthy, *India can learn from China's experience fighting Covid-19, says top US adviser Anthony Fauci*, S. China Morning Post, May 1, 2021, https://www.scmp.com/news/china/diplomacy/article/3131906/india-can-learn-chinas-experience-fighting-covid-19-says-top; Press Trust of India, *Anthony Fauci suggests few weeks' lockdown in India to break the chain*, Bus. Standard, May 1, 2021, https://www.business-standard.com/article/current-affairs/anthony-fauci-suggests-few-weeks-lockdown-in-ndia-to-break-the-chain-121050100266_1.html.

485 BBC, *Covid-19 disruptions killed 228,000 children in South Asia, says UN report*, Mar. 17, 2021, https://www.bbc.com/news/world-asia-56425115.

486 Ed Dean, *People Are Moving To Florida Thanks, In Part, to the Coronavirus Pandemic*, Florida Daily, Feb. 2, 2021, https://www.floridadaily.com/people-are-moving-to-florida-thanks-in-part-to-the-coronavirus-pandemic/.

[487] Scott Sutton, *Florida Gov. Ron DeSantis: 'We will never do any of these lockdowns again'*, WPTV, Aug. 31, 2020, https://www.wptv.com/news/state/florida-gov-ron-desantis-we-will-never-do-any-of-these-lockdowns-again.

[488] Allysia Finley, *Vindication for Ron DeSantis*, Wall St. J., Mar. 5, 2021, https://www.wsj.com/articles/vindication-for-ron-desantis-11614986751.

[489] David Frum, *The Rise of Ron DeSantis*, The Atlantic, Apr. 23, 2021, https://www.theatlantic.com/ideas/archive/2021/04/what-ron-desantis-knows/618673/.

[490] Ivan Pentchoukov and Jan Jekielek, *Gov. DeSantis Says CCP Should Be Held Accountable for Abetting Pandemic*, Epoch Times, Apr. 19, 2021, https://www.theepochtimes.com/mkt_app/desantis-ccp-should-be-held-accountable-for-abetting-pandemic_3780641.html.

[491] Katherine Fung, *Florida Gov. Ron DeSantis Blames COVID on Chinese Communist Party, Signs Bills Thwarting Chinese Influence in Schools*, Newsweek, Jun. 7, 2021, https://www.newsweek.com/florida-gov-ron-desantis-blames-covid-chinese-communist-party-signs-bills-thwarting-chinese-1598214.

[492] Fox News, *Transcripts: 'Sunday Morning Futures' on Big Tech censorship, Biden's handing of immigration crisis*, Jun. 13, 2021, https://www.foxnews.com/transcript/sunday-morning-futures-on-big-tech-censorship-bidens-handing-of-immigration-crisis.

[493] Jonathan Sumption, *Zero Covid is a mirage*, Daily Mail, Feb. 6, 2021, https://www.dailymail.co.uk/debate/article-9231807/Zero-Covid-mirage-says-JONATHAN-SUMPTION-virus-stay.html.

[494] Jonathan Sumption, *Liberal democracy will be the biggest casualty of this pandemic*, The Telegraph, Feb. 15, 2021, https://www.telegraph.co.uk/news/2021/02/15/liberal-democracy-will-biggest-casualty-pandemic/.

[495] Jayanta Bhattacharya, *A Conversation with Lord Sumption*, Brownstone Institute, Sep. 22, 2021, https://brownstone.org/articles/a-conversation-with-lord-sumption/.

[496] Jacobson v. Massachusetts, 197 U.S. 11 (1905).

[497] South Bay United Pentecostal Church v. Newsom, 590 U. S. ____ (2020), *available at* https://www.supremecourt.gov/opinions/19pdf/19a1044_pok0.pdf; Kimberly Strawbridge Robinson, *Roberts Holds Line on Judicial Second-Guessing of Covid Orders*, Bloomberg, Aug. 3, 2020, https://news.bloomberglaw.com/us-law-week/roberts-holds-line-on-judicial-second-guessing-of-covid-orders; Jess Bravin, *Supreme Court Chief Justice John Roberts Is Pivot in Coronavirus Cases*, Wall St. J., Aug. 19, 2020, https://www.wsj.com/articles/supreme-court-chief-justice-john-roberts-is-pivot-in-coronavirus-cases-11597846463.

[498] Buck v. Bell, 274 U.S. 200 (1927); Alex Gutentag, *The Plague of the Poor*, Tablet, Sep. 29, 2021, https://www.tabletmag.com/sections/news/articles/plague-poor-gutentag.

[499] Daniel Horowitz, *Why Dershowitz is wrong to apply Jacobson decision in support of vaccine passports*, The Blaze, Aug. 2, 2021, https://www.theblaze.com/blaze-news/horowitz-why-dershowitz-is-wrong-to-apply-jacobson-decision-in-support-of-vaccine-passports; Jamal Greene, *The Anticanon*, 125 Harv. L. Rev. 379, Dec. 20, 2011, https://harvardlawreview.org/2011/12/the-anticanon/.

[500] Union Pac. Ry. Co. v. Botsford, 141 U.S. 250, 251 (1891).

[501] Andreas Kluth, *We Must Start Planning For a Permanent Pandemic*, Bloomberg, Mar. 23, 2021, https://www.bloomberg.com/opinion/articles/2021-03-24/when-will-covid-end-we-must-start-planning-for-a-permanent-pandemic.

[502] Alvin Powell, *What might COVID cost the U.S.? Try $16 trillion*, Harvard Gazette, Nov. 10, 2020, https://news.harvard.edu/gazette/story/2020/11/what-might-covid-cost-the-u-s-experts-eye-16-trillion/.

[503] Josh Blackman, *Comparing CJ Roberts's South Bay "Superprecedent" and Justice Kavanaugh's Alabama Non-Precedent*, Reason, Aug. 8, 2021, https://reason.com/volokh/2021/08/08/comparing-cj-robertss-south-bay-supreprecedent-and-justice-kavanuaghs-alabama-non-precedent/.

[504] Wisconsin Legislature v. Palm, 2020 WI 42, 942 N.W.2d 900 (2020), https://www.wicourts.gov/sc/opinion/DisplayDocument.pdf?content=pdf&seqNo=260868.

[505] Cnty. of Butler v. Wolf, 486 F. Supp. 3d 883 (W.D. Pa. 2020), https://casetext.com/case/cnty-of-butler-v-wolf-1.

[506] WKYT, *Boone County judge orders permanent injunction against Gov. Beshear's COVID-19 orders*, Jun. 8, 2021, https://www.wkyt.com/2021/06/09/boone-county-judge-orders-permanent-injunction-against-gov-beshears-covid-19-orders/; Daniel Horowitz, *KY judge rules Gov. Beshear's COVID, mask orders unconstitutional in breakthrough lawsuit*, The Blaze, Jun. 9, 2021, https://www.theblaze.com/op-ed/horowitz-ky-judge-rules-gov-beshears-covid-mask-orders-unconstitutional-in-breakthrough-lawsuit.

[507] 2020 News, *District judge in Weimar: Corona-VO unconstitutional*, Jan. 21, 2020, https://2020news.de/amtsrichter-in-weimar-corona-vo-verfassungswidrig/.

[508] 2020 News, *Sensational judgment from Weimar: no masks, no distance, no more tests for students*, Apr. 14, 2021, https://2020news.de/sensationsurteil-aus-weimar-keine-masken-kein-abstand-keine-tests-mehr-fuer-schueler/.

[509] Natasha Donn, *Judges in Portugal highlight "more than debatable" reliability of Covid tests*, Portugal Resident, Nov. 20, 2020,

https://www.portugalresident.com/judges-in-portugal-highlight-more-than-debatable-reliability-of-covid-tests/.

[510] Natasha Donn, *Portuguese judges "won't be disciplined" over controversial ruling highlighting doubts over Covid test reliability*, Portugal Resident, Dec. 3, 2020, https://www.portugalresident.com/portuguese-judges-wont-be-disciplined-over-controversial-ruling-highlighting-doubts-over-covid-test-reliability/.

[511] Human Rights Watch, *El Salvador: President Defies Supreme Court*, Apr. 17, 2020, https://www.hrw.org/news/2020/04/17/el-salvador-president-defies-supreme-court.

[512] Amy Jones, *Leading businessman launches legal challenge against Government's lockdown measures*, The Telegraph, May 1, 2020, https://www.telegraph.co.uk/politics/2020/05/01/leading-businessman-launches-legal-challenge-against-governments/.

[513] Dolan. v. Secretary of State for Health and Social Care, [2020] EWCA Civ 1605 (2020), judiciary.uk/wp-content/uploads/2020/12/Dolan-v-SSHSC-judgment-011220-.pdf.

[514] Lisa M Brosseau, ScD, and Margaret Sietsema, PhD, *Masks-for-all for COVID-19 not based on sound data*, Univ. of Minn., Apr. 1, 2020, https://www.cidrap.umn.edu/news-perspective/2020/04/commentary-masks-all-covid-19-not-based-sound-data.

[515] Sarah Fitzpatrick *et al.*, *Coronavirus testing must double or triple before U.S. can safely reopen, experts say*, NBC News, Apr. 17, 2020, https://www.nbcnews.com/news/us-news/coronavirus-testing-must-double-or-triple-u-s-can-safely-n1185881.

[516] Xinhua, *Xi urges G20 cooperation to contain COVID-19, stabilize world economy*, Global Times, Mar. 27, 2020, https://www.globaltimes.cn/content/1183981.shtml.

[517] The Economist, *The pandemic has eroded democracy and respect for human rights*, Oct. 17, 2020, https://www.economist.com/international/2020/10/17/the-pandemic-has-eroded-democracy-and-respect-for-human-rights.

[518] Zachary Evans, Chinese Company Suspected of Spying on U.S. Citizens Donates Police Drones to 22 States, Nat'l Review, Apr. 20, 2020, https://www.nationalreview.com/news/chinese-company-suspected-of-spying-on-u-s-citizens-donates-police-drones-to-22-states/.

[519] Bureau of Industry and Security, *Addition of Entities to the Entity List, Revision of Entry on the Entity List, and Removal of Entities from the Entity List*, U.S. Dep't of Commerce, 15 CFR 744 Docket №201215–0347, Dec. 22, 2020, https://public-inspection.federalregister.gov/2020-28031.pdf.

[520] Wall Street Journal, *YouTube's Political Censorship*, Sep. 14, 2020, https://www.wsj.com/articles/youtubes-political-censorship-11600126230.

[521] Michael Collins, *The WHO and China: Dereliction of Duty*, CFR, Feb. 27, 2020, https://www.cfr.org/blog/who-and-china-dereliction-duty.
[522] @SwedenTeam, Twitter, May 14, 2021, https://twitter.com/SwedenTeam/status/1393383874063970315.
[523] Wall Street Journal, *YouTube's Assault on Covid Accountability*, Apr. 8, 2021, https://www.wsj.com/articles/youtubes-assault-on-covid-accountability-11617921149.
[524] The Independent, Apr. 4, 2021, https://www.independent.co.uk/news/uk/politics/conservatives-covid-china-fake-videos-b1825022.html.
[525] College of Physicians and Surgeons of Ontario, *Summary of the Decision of the Inquiries, Complaints and Reports Committee: Dr. Kulvinder Kaur Gill*, Feb. 3, 2021, https://doctors.cpso.on.ca/cpso/getdocument.aspx?flash=check&pdfid=itbnEMxT2bg%3d&id=%2084436&doctype=Alert.
[526] Julius Ruechel, *Who's in Charge? The Rule Makers, Power Brokers, and Influencers of Lockdown Wonderland*, Apr. 12, 2021, https://www.juliusruechel.com/2021/04/whos-in-charge-rule-makers-power.html.
[527] Xinhua, *Xi urges Germany, EU to cooperate with China to bring more certainty, stability to world*, Global Times, Apr. 7, 2021, https://www.globaltimes.cn/page/202104/1220475.shtml; Reuters, *Merkel Backs Tougher COVID Lockdown in Germany*, U.S. News, Apr. 7, 2021, https://www.usnews.com/news/world/articles/2021-04-07/merkel-backs-tougher-covid-lockdown-in-germany.
[528] Cordula Klaus, *et al.*, *Study on the Future of Human Value Appropriations in Our Country*, Fed. Ministry of Educ. and Rsch., Aug. 2020, https://web.archive.org/web/20210629200609/https://www.voraussch au.de/SharedDocs/Downloads/vorausschau/de/BMBF_Foresight_Wert estudie_Langfassung.pdf?__blob=publicationFile&v=1; Welt 25, *German Ministry of Research toying with China's social credit system*, Jun. 28, 2021, http://web.archive.org/web/20210629185322/https://welt25.com/2021 /06/28/deutsches-forschungsministerium-liebaeugelt-mit-chinas-social-credit-system/.
[529] Berkeley Lovelace Jr., *WHO warns coronavirus vaccine alone won't end pandemic: 'We cannot go back to the way things were'*, Aug. 21, 2020, https://www.cnbc.com/2020/08/21/who-warns-a-coronavirus-vaccine-alone-will-not-end-pandemic.html.
[530] Lucia Binding, *COVID-19: Social distancing and masks here to stay as new variants 'inevitable', expert says*, Sky News, Jun. 23, 2021, https://news.sky.com/story/covid-19-social-distancing-and-masks-here-to-stay-as-new-variants-inevitable-expert-says-12339775.

[531] NotiUlti, *"The masks are here to stay, at least while we have the flu virus"*, Oct. 13, 2021, https://notiulti.com/las-mascaras-llegaron-para-quedarse-al-menos-mientras-tengamos-el-virus-de-la-gripe/.

[532] @ElonBachman, Twitter, Dec. 22, 2020, https://threadreaderapp.com/thread/1341465108736827394.html.

[533] Andrew Restuccia and Max Colchester, *G-7 Summit Precautions for Covid-19 Include Elbow Bumps*, Wall St. J., Jun. 11, 2021, https://www.wsj.com/articles/g-7-summit-precautions-for-covid-19-include-daily-tests-elbow-bumps-11623438166; Lokmat, G7 Leaders Kick Off Summit in Cornwall, Jun. 12, 2021, https://english.lokmat.com/international/g7-leaders-kick-off-summit-in-cornwall/.

[534] Michael Holden, *Are you supposed to be enjoying yourselves? Queen Elizabeth asks G7*, Reuters, Jun. 12, 2021, https://www.reuters.com/world/uk/britains-queen-elizabeth-hosts-biden-g7-reception-2021-06-11/.

[535] Amy Mek, *Mind Control: Germany Models COVID Restrictions After Chinese Torture Methods*, RAIR Found., Mar. 20, 2021, https://rairfoundation.com/mind-control-germany-models-covid-restrictions-after-chinese-torture-methods-video/.

[536] Joe Mcdonald and Huizhong Wu, *Top Chinese official admits vaccines have low effectiveness*, Assoc. Press, Apr. 10, 2021, https://apnews.com/article/china-gao-fu-vaccines-offer-low-protection-coronavirus-675bcb6b5710c7329823148ffbff6ef9.

[537] World Health Organization, *COVID-19 Virtual Press conference transcript*, Apr. 12, 2021, https://www.who.int/publications/m/item/covid-19-virtual-press-conference-transcript---12-april-2021; Joe Concha, *Fauci fatigue sets in as top doc sows doubt in vaccine effectiveness*, The Hill, Apr. 13, 2021, https://thehill.com/opinion/healthcare/547826-fauci-fatigue-sets-in-as-top-doc-sows-doubt-in-vaccine-effectiveness; Sarah Young and Alistair Smout, *UK's Johnson warns lockdown, not vaccines, behind drop in COVID deaths*, Reuters, Apr. 13, 2021, https://www.reuters.com/world/uk/uks-johnson-warns-lockdown-not-vaccines-behind-drop-covid-deaths-2021-04-13/.

[538] Dan Diamond, Lena H. Sun and Isaac Stanley-Becker, *'Vaccine passports' are on the way, but developing them won't be easy*, Wash. Post, Mar. 28, 2021, https://www.washingtonpost.com/health/2021/03/28/vaccine-passports-for-work/.

[539] Paul Mozur, Raymond Zhong and Aaron Krolik, *In Coronavirus Fight, China Gives Citizens a Color Code, With Red Flags*, N.Y. Times, Mar. 1, 2020, https://www.nytimes.com/2020/03/01/business/china-coronavirus-surveillance.html; Aaron Sibarium, *COVID Tracking Apps Have Eerie Echoes of Chinese Surveillance System*, Wash. Free Beacon,

Mar. 30, 2021, https://freebeacon.com/coronavirus/covid-tracking-apps-have-eerie-echoes-of-chinese-surveillance-system/.
540 VOA News, *EU Parliament Approves Digital COVID-19 Travel Certificate*, Jun. 9, 2021, https://www.voanews.com/a/covid-19-pandemic_eu-parliament-approves-digital-covid-19-travel-certificate/6206819.html.
541 @gluboco, Twitter, Oct. 23, 2021, https://threadreaderapp.com/thread/1451714806721957891.html.
542 @MichaelPSenger, Twitter, Oct. 25, 2021, http://web.archive.org/web/20211026031556/https://twitter.com/MichaelPSenger/status/1452754517070516229.
543 Francesco Zecchini, *Italy's mandatory health pass not boosting jabs as hoped, data shows*, Reuters, Oct. 11, 2021, https://www.reuters.com/world/europe/italys-mandatory-health-pass-not-boosting-jabs-hoped-data-shows-2021-10-11/.
544 France 24, *Anti-lockdown protests erupt across Europe as tempers fray over tightening restrictions*, Mar. 21, 2021, https://www.france24.com/en/europe/20210321-anti-lockdown-protests-erupt-across-europe-as-tempers-fray-over-tightening-restrictions.
545 Pilatus Today, *Criminal charges filed against the National Task Force*, May 14, 2021, https://www.pilatustoday.ch/coronavirus/strafanzeige-gegen-die-nationale-task-force-eingereicht-141907839.
546 Filipp Piatov, *Our fear must not be abused*, Bild, Jun. 10, 2021, https://www.bild.de/politik/kolumnen/kolumne/kommentar-zum-intensivbetten-betrug-unsere-angst-darf-nicht-missbraucht-werden-76698320.bild.html.
547 Sarah Anne Hughes, *Voters back curtailing Wolf's emergency powers in win for GOP lawmakers*, Spotlight PA, May 19, 2021, https://www.spotlightpa.org/news/2021/05/pa-primary-2021-ballot-question-disaster-declaration-results/.
548 Oli Smith, *Emmanuel Macron shamed into embarrassing U-turn after violence erupts on French streets*, Daily Express, Jul. 20, 2021, https://www.express.co.uk/news/world/1464334/Emmanuel-Macron-France-protests-Paris-Covid-health-pass-latest-news-vn.
549 Michael McGowan, *Sydney anti-lockdown protest organiser sentenced to eight months' jail*, The Guardian, Aug. 20, 2021, https://www.theguardian.com/australia-news/2021/aug/20/sydney-anti-lockdown-protest-organiser-sentenced-to-eight-months-jail.
550 Conor Friedersdorf, *Australia Traded Away Too Much Liberty*, The Atlantic, Sep. 2, 2021, https://www.theatlantic.com/ideas/archive/2021/09/pandemic-australia-still-liberal-democracy/619940/.
551 ABC News, *Police clear protestors at Melbourne's Shrine of Remembrance* (Video), Sep. 22, 2021,

https://www.abc.net.au/news/2021-09-22/police-clear-protestors-at-melbournes-shrine-of/13553706; Reuters, *Amnesty says Greek police using pandemic to crush protests*, Jul. 14, 2021, https://www.reuters.com/article/greece-police-amnesty/amnesty-says-greek-police-using-pandemic-to-crush-protests-idUSL8N2OQ37X.

552 Anjali Sundaram, *Yelp data shows 60% of business closures due to the coronavirus pandemic are now permanent*, CNBC, Sep. 16 2020, https://www.cnbc.com/2020/09/16/yelp-data-shows-60percent-of-business-closures-due-to-the-coronavirus-pandemic-are-now-permanent.html.

553 Pedro Nicolaci da Costa, *The Covid-19 Crisis Has Wiped Out Nearly Half Of Black Small Businesses*, Forbes, Aug. 10, 2020, https://www.forbes.com/sites/pedrodacosta/2020/08/10/the-covid-19-crisis-has-wiped-out-nearly-half-of-black-small-businesses/#2fc8c8334310.

554
Bethan Staton and Judith Evans, *Three million go hungry in UK because of lockdown*, Fin. Times, Apr. 10, 2020, https://www.ft.com/content/e5061be6-2978-4c0b-aa68-f372a2526826.

555 Colin Perkel, *Long-term care residents beg to go outside after year-long COVID-19 confinement*, CBC, Mar. 30, 2021, https://www.cbc.ca/news/canada/toronto/long-term-care-covid-confinement-1.5969825.

556 Morganne Campbell, *Canadians reporting higher levels of anxiety, depression amid the pandemic*, Global News, Oct. 10, 2020, https://globalnews.ca/news/7391217/world-mental-health-day-canada/.

557 American Medical Association, *Issue brief: Reports of increases in opioid- and other drug-related overdose and other concerns during COVID pandemic*, Dec. 9, 2020, https://www.ama-assn.org/system/files/2020-12/issue-brief-increases-in-opioid-related-overdose.pdf; Betsy McKay, *U.S. Drug-Overdose Deaths Soared Nearly 30% in 2020, Driven by Synthetic Opioids*, Wall St. J., Jul. 14, 2021, https://www.wsj.com/articles/u-s-drug-overdose-deaths-soared-nearly-30-in-2020-11626271200.

558 Cory Stieg, *More than 7 in 10 Gen-Zers report symptoms of depression during pandemic, survey finds*, CNBC, Oct. 21 2020, https://www.cnbc.com/2020/10/21/survey-more-than-7-in-10-gen-zers-report-depression-during-pandemic.html.

559 Amanda Prestigiacomo, *New CDC Numbers Show Lockdown's Deadly Toll On Young People*, The Daily Wire, Oct. 22, 2020, https://www.dailywire.com/news/new-cdc-numbers-show-lockdowns-deadly-toll-on-young-people.

560 *Id.*

561 Lauren M. Rossen, PhD *et al.*, *Excess Deaths Associated with COVID-19, by Age and Race and Ethnicity — United States, January 26–October 3, 2020*, U.S. CDC MMWR Morb Mortal Wkly Rep Vol. 69(42), Oct. 23, 2020, https://www.cdc.gov/mmwr/volumes/69/wr/pdfs/mm6942e2-H.pdf.

562 Nazrul Islam *et al.*, *Excess deaths associated with covid-19 pandemic in 2020: age and sex disaggregated time series analysis in 29 high income countries*, Supplementary Appendix, BMJ 2021(373), May 19, 2021, https://www.bmj.com/content/bmj/suppl/2021/05/19/bmj.n1137.DC1/isln065519.ww1.pdf; Aaron O'Neill, *Age distribution in the United States from 2010 to 2020*, Statista, Jul. 21, 2020, https://www.statista.com/statistics/270000/age-distribution-in-the-united-states/; Statista, *Resident population of the United States by sex and age as of July 1, 2020*, Sep. 10, 2021, https://www.statista.com/statistics/241488/population-of-the-us-by-sex-and-age/; Aaron O'Neill, *Sweden: Age structure from 2010 to 2020*, Statista, Jul. 20, 2021, https://www.statista.com/statistics/375493/age-structure-in-sweden/; Statista, *Population in Sweden from 2010 to 2020, by age group*, Feb. 22, 2021, https://www.statista.com/statistics/521717/sweden-population-by-age/.

563 Tyler Sonnemaker and Andy Kiersz, *80% of US coronavirus deaths have been among people 65 and older, a new CDC report says — here's what it reveals about the US cases*, Bus. Insider, Mar. 18, 2020, https://www.businessinsider.com/most-us-coronavirus-deaths-ages-65-older-cdc-report-2020-3.

564 Nazrul Islam *et al.*, *Excess deaths associated with covid-19 pandemic in 2020: age and sex disaggregated time series analysis in 29 high income countries*, Supplementary Appendix, BMJ 2021(373), May 19, 2021, https://www.bmj.com/content/bmj/suppl/2021/05/19/bmj.n1137.DC1/isln065519.ww1.pdf.

565 Save the Children, *'Children at risk of lasting psychological distress from coronavirus lockdown': Save the Children*, UN OCHA Reliefweb, May 8, 2020, https://reliefweb.int/report/world/children-risk-lasting-psychological-distress-coronavirus-lockdown-save-children.

566 Save the Children, *'Children at Risk of Lasting Psychological Distress from Coronavirus Lockdown': Save the Children*, May 8, 2020, https://www.savethechildren.net/news/%E2%80%98children-risk-lasting-psychological-distress-coronavirus-lockdown%E2%80%99-save-children.

567 The Economist, *Lockdowns could have long-term effects on children's health*, Jul. 19 2020, https://www.economist.com/international/2020/07/19/lockdowns-could-have-long-term-effects-on-childrens-health.

[568] Rebecca T. Leeb, PhD *et al.*, *Mental Health–Related Emergency Department Visits Among Children Aged <18 Years During the COVID-19 Pandemic — United States, January 1–October 17, 2020*, U.S. CDC MMWR Morb Mortal Wkly Rep Vol. 69(45), Nov. 13, 2020, https://www.cdc.gov/mmwr/volumes/69/wr/mm6945a3.htm.

[569] Perry Stein, *In D.C., achievement gap widens, early literacy progress declines during pandemic, data show*, Wash. Post, Oct. 30, 2020, https://www.msn.com/en-us/news/us/data-indicate-worsening-early-literacy-progress-and-widening-achievement-gap-among-district-students/ar-BB1ay8vc.

[570] Sally Weale, *Children regressing and struggling mentally in lockdown, says Ofsted*, The Guardian, Nov. 9, 2020, https://www.theguardian.com/education/2020/nov/10/children-regressing-and-struggling-mentally-in-lockdown-says-ofsted.

[571] Arielle Mitropoulos, *Thousands of students reported 'missing' from school systems nationwide amid COVID-19 pandemic*, ABC News, Mar. 2, 2021, https://abcnews.go.com/US/thousands-students-reported-missing-school-systems-nationwide-amid/story?id=76063922.

[572] Tess McClure, *New Zealand children falling ill in high numbers due to Covid 'immunity debt'*, The Guardian, Jul. 8, 2021, https://www.theguardian.com/world/2021/jul/08/new-zealand-children-falling-ill-in-high-numbers-due-to-covid-immunity-debt.

[573] Jai Sidpra *et al.*, *Rise in the incidence of abusive head trauma during the COVID-19 pandemic*, Archives of Disease in Childhood, Jul. 2, 2020, http://dx.doi.org/10.1136/archdischild-2020-319872.

[574] Isabel van Brugen and Jan Jekielek, *Scott Atlas: Lockdowns Not Only a 'Heinous Abuse' of Power, They Also Failed to Protect the Elderly*, Epoch Times, May 20, 2021, https://www.theepochtimes.com/scott-atlas-lockdowns-not-only-a-heinous-abuse-of-power-they-also-failed-to-protect-the-elderly_3823487.html.

[575] Phoebe Southworth, *Lockdowns are 'the single biggest public health mistake in history', says top scientist*, The Telegraph, Jun. 10, 2021, https://www.telegraph.co.uk/news/2021/06/10/lockdowns-single-biggest-public-health-mistake-history-says/.

[576] Rajesh Roy, *India Tries to Stem Migrant Worker Exodus Amid Coronavirus Lockdown*, Wall St. J., Mar. 29, 2020, https://www.wsj.com/articles/india-tries-to-stem-migrant-worker-exodus-amid-coronavirus-lockdown-11585499312.

[577] Channel News Asia, *Hunger stalks India's poor in COVID-19 pandemic double blow*, May 30, 2021, https://web.archive.org/web/20210530050633/https://channelnewsasia.com/news/asia/india-covid-19-pandemic-hunger-poverty-economic-crisis-14914348.

[578] Toby Green and Jay Bhattacharya, *Lockdowns are killers in the global south*, UnHerd, Jul. 22, 2021,

https://unherd.com/thepost/lockdowns-are-killers-in-the-global-south/.

579 *Id.*

580 *Id.*

581 *Id.*

582 Jennifer Rigby, *'Back to square one': pandemic has led to one million missing TB patients*, The Telegraph, Mar. 18, 2021, https://www.telegraph.co.uk/global-health/science-and-disease/back-square-one-pandemic-has-led-one-million-missing-tb-patients/.

583 Toby Green and Jay Bhattacharya, *Lockdowns are killers in the global south*, UnHerd, Jul. 22, 2021, https://unherd.com/thepost/lockdowns-are-killers-in-the-global-south/.

584 Reuters, *Miles-long lines for food in South Africa* (Video), YouTube, Apr. 30, 2020, https://www.youtube.com/watch?v=pl-R7KeUm5o; Joseph Cotterill, *South Africa counts the cost of its worst unrest since apartheid*, Fin. Times, Jul. 24, 2021, https://www.ft.com/content/1b0badcd-2f81-42c8-ae09-796475540ccc.

585 UNICEF, *COVID pushes millions more children deeper into poverty, new study finds*, UN News, Sep. 17, 2020, https://news.un.org/en/story/2020/09/1072602.

586 Tom Moran, *Lockdown was a choice*, The Critic, May 13, 2021, https://thecritic.co.uk/lockdown-was-a-choice/.

587 CNBC, *WHO says 10% of global population may have been infected with virus*, Oct. 5, 2020, https://www.cnbc.com/2020/10/05/who-10percent-of-worlds-people-may-have-been-infected-with-virus-.html.

588 International Monetary Fund, *World Economic Outlook, October 2020: A Long and Difficult Ascent*, Oct. 2020, https://www.imf.org/en/Publications/WEO/Issues/2020/09/30/world-economic-outlook-october-2020.

589 Simon Leys, *The Art of Interpreting Nonexistent Inscriptions Written in Invisible Ink on a Blank Page*, ChinaFile, Oct. 11, 1990, https://www.chinafile.com/library/nyrb-china-archive/art-interpreting-nonexistent-inscriptions-written-invisible-ink-blank.

590 Lily Kuo, *'Fake, Fake': senior Chinese leader heckled by residents on visit to coronavirus city*, The Guardian, Mar. 6, 2020, https://www.theguardian.com/world/2020/mar/06/fake-fake-senior-chinese-leader-heckled-by-residents-on-visit-to-coronavirus-epicentre.

Printed in Great Britain
by Amazon

77634782R00130